ARTWORK AS SOCIAL MODEL

STEPHEN WILLATS

ARTWORK AS SOCIAL MODEL

A MANUAL OF QUESTIONS AND PROPOSITIONS

RGAP 2012

INTRODUCTION

This manual is intended as a tool for any artist looking to find a meaningful relationship with contemporary society, and intervening to transform norms and conventions, to provide a new vision of a possible future.

The structure of the manual has been designed so that the reader can freely choose to explore any of the areas of attention, denoted by a progression of subject headings. Individual texts and images that make up the content of the subject headings are drawn from existing material, but are represented here in a new context and format.

The thirty-two subject headings each have four sub-headings, A, B, C and D which present sometimes tangential fragments of information to stimulate lateral connections for the reader, and are included here to represent the perceptual position of the artist. The headings pinpoint the polemics, procedures and questions likely to concern the artist seeking a coherent model of how practice can interact with society.

1

FORMING MODELS ABOUT ART

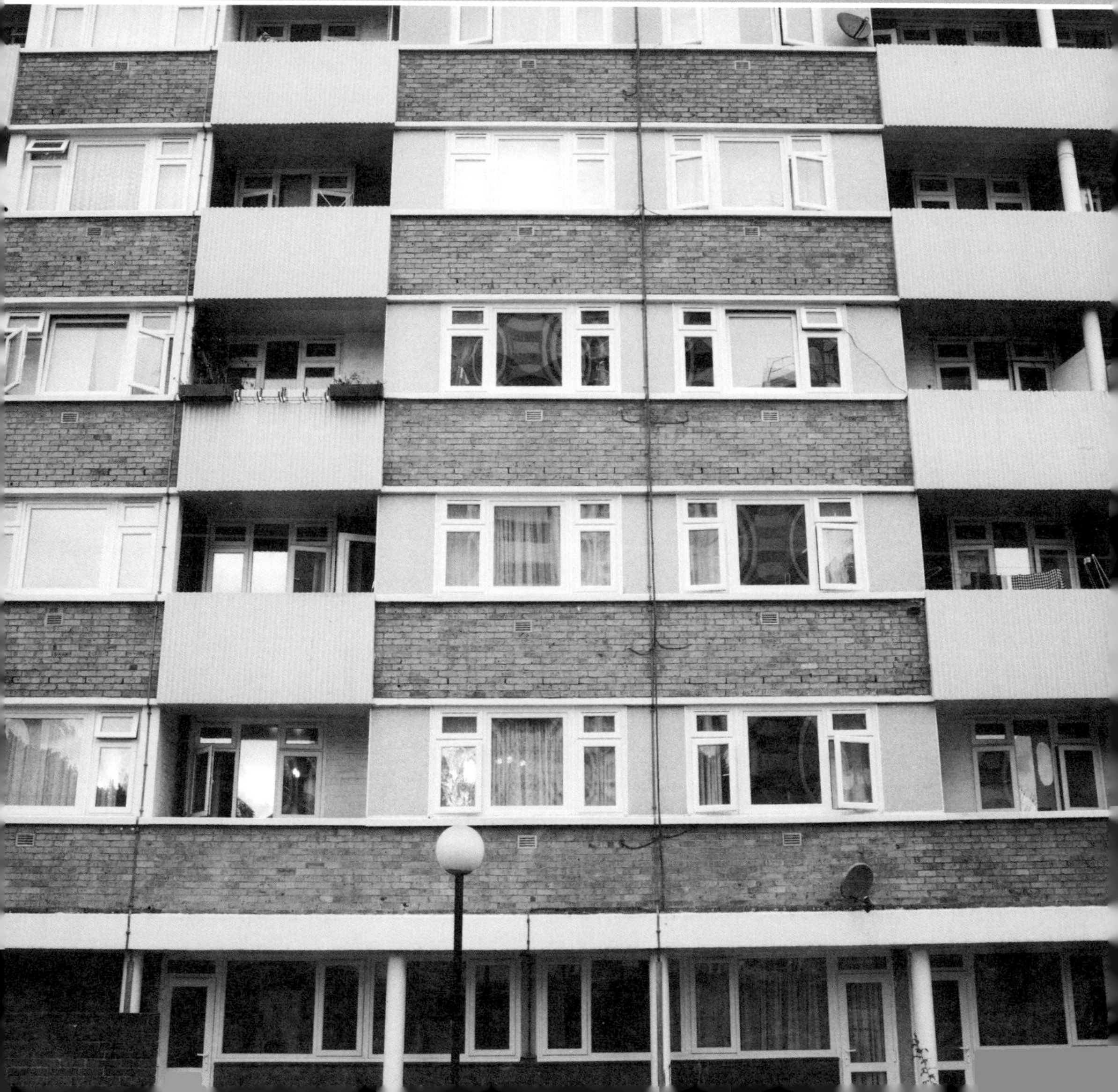

INTIMATE AND DISTANCE MODELS OF PERCEPTION

There are numerous ways in which a person acquires their perception of an event or phenomenon, though generally they can be considered to fall into two categories:

1. An external source transmits information to them which subsequently affects their perception, e.g. A tells B about X.
2. They experience the event or phenomenon directly, e.g. A sees X.

Although, inevitably, a person acquires information by a combination of both means. Similarly, in looking at perceptions of art practice as an activity within society two different viewpoints can be defined:

1. Perceptions that are formed through a person directly experiencing art practice, either as an artist, audience or some other role.
2. Perceptions that are formed on art practice via some intermediary body, newspapers, television etc.

Perceptions derived from direct experience result in what I have termed Intimate Models, and indirectly formed perceptions result in Distance Models, the term 'Model' referring to the mental orderings a person has made about art practice. If art is seen as fulfilling some direct function for a person they are likely to form an Intimate Model. These functions can be diverse, but in each case direct experience plays an important part for fulfilment. If a high priority for attending to art is a dependent condition for an Intimate Model, on the other hand a low priority might be equated with a Distance Model. While it certainly might be generally true that a dividing line can be seen between people involved in the development of art, i.e. the so-called avant-garde, and the general public in terms of Intimate and Distance Models, the situation becomes more complex in practice.

For example, art might be engaged in to meet like-minded persons, so a person joins an evening institute and within their class room they develop Intimate Models of a particular mode of operation, but as far as the avant-garde is concerned, they retain a Distance Model. In this case a further definition is required for Intimate Models, and that is that a person is able to bring to bear on a work the world of references used by the artist. Distance models have a function to the communities and individuals that hold them; for example, though a person might not have met a millionaire, their Distance Models of their life style might play an important part in determining their aspirations and motivations. In a similar way, though a person holds a Distance Model of art, has not been to an Art Gallery, or met an artist, it still has some function for them.

THE TRANSMITTED PICTURE SEEKING CONSISTENCY

The two modes of communication have been discussed by myself elsewhere, but suffice it to say here that the transmissional relationship, as depicted in Fig. 1, is the mode of communication associated with dominant culture. By our being placed unwittingly in the position of receiver, the way we process communicated information, and our expectations from it have been conditioned. The essential flow of information within the relationship is from Transmitter to Receiver, there being no permissible way for the latter to directly influence the former. Nearly all media, newspapers, books, television etc., give the person decoding content a passive role. The pressure is to accept the distant authority of the message, and in this legislative way reality is presented as a *fait accompli*, already constructed for us to accommodate within the world we know. This passivity has developed an expectation to be fed an easily assimilated authoritative message or model. The nature of much contemporary art practice has been founded on such expectations, leading to the common view that it embodied a universality that was somehow independent of context. Such assumptions ultimately inhibit the development of new forms of practice that seek to question and free themselves from the determinism inherent in our culture.

A conflict in artworks that forward a social consciousness of interaction (Fig. 2), but employ a transmissional mode of communication, has undermined attempts to externalise such a consciousness as a cultural force. In trying to find a consistency between what is forwarded and the means of operation the artist needs to consider how both could exist within the everyday reality, as perceived by the audience. It is quite clear that self-realisation is more meaningful than someone legislating to you their more distant and removed experience. A consciousness founded on an ideological belief of social interaction needs to manifest that belief in its methodology so that there is no separation between a work's form and its content. The point here is that such work will assign the audience a different role than they have traditionally occupied, and will require them to approach the work in a fundamentally different way. Instead of presenting 'the' view, a work is used by the audience to construct themselves the forwarded consciousness as part of their own reality.

Fig. 1.

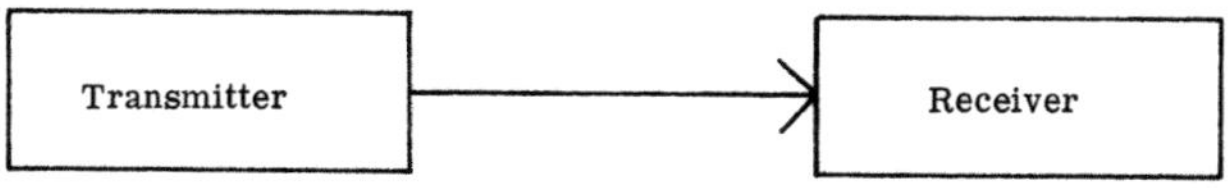

The basic relationship between two nodes within the autoritative network.

Fig. 2.

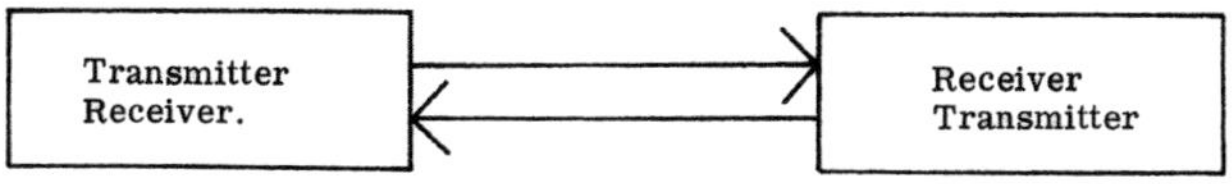

The basic relationship of two nodes within the interactive network.

DISTANCE MODELS OF THE ARTIST FROM THE CENTRE FOR BEHAVIOURAL ART SURVEY CARRIED OUT IN LONDON AND COVENTRY IN 1973

	GROUP ONE	GROUP TWO
1. Can you name someone you consider to be an artist		
Possible responses	34	38
Actual responses	27	28
2. What does he do?		
Paints	21	6
Makes sculpture	0	3
Writes songs or music	0	6
Architect	1	2
Plays a musical instrument	0	6
Sings	0	10
Acts	0	6
Graphic designer	1	1
Writes plays or novels	1	2
Writes poetry	1	3
Produces films	0	3
Fashion designer	0	0
Other	Teaches art	Photography, a wit
3. If the artist that you have mentioned is not a painter or sculptor can you name a painter or sculptor.		
Possible responses	11	10
Actual responses	6	3
4. What sort of painting or sculpture does the artist named in Question 1 or 3 do?		
Still life	5	5
Landscape	8	9
Seascapes	2	0
Portraits	9	8
Abstracts	8	9
Pop Art	2	1
Others	Dramatic painting, Wild life, Collages	Animals, Human Sculpture
4b. In your own words, can you describe a painting or sculpture that the artist has done?		
Acknowledge existence of a work	6	7
Acknowledge existence of a work and described its composition	10	12
Acknowledged existence of a work, described its composition and their response to it	2	5
5. How do you know of this artist?		
Television	3	8
Gallery	5	10
Newspapers	4	5
Books	13	17
Films	1	3
Radio	1	1
You know him personally	2	3
Other	General knowledge 2	Exhibition, postcards, Birds Eye Frozen Foods, shops
6. Which of the following do you consider most typical of the artist? What is the artist's attitude towards his art?		
A means of earning a living	8	6
A means of achieving fame	3	4
Needs to express himself	17	20
An excuse to live in a peculiar way	1	4
As a form of self-satisfaction	9	13
None in particular	2	0
How do people in general value his art?		
As a means of communication	4	9
As a comment on society	4	9
As an investment	8	7
As decoration	7	16
As a means of educating people	4	3
People in general don't value art	5	5
None in particular	3	2

DISTANCE MODELS OF THE ARTIST'S ARTWORK FROM THE CENTRE FOR BEHAVIOURAL ART SURVEY CARRIED OUT IN LONDON AND COVENTRY IN 1973

GROUP ONE

(Scores per unit)

	Entertaining	*Boring*	*Useful to society*	*Useless to society*	*A significant effect on your life*	*Difficult to understand*	*Not a form of art*
Painting	15	1	13	0	5	5	0
Sculpture	9	1	9	0	4	14	0
Films	21	3	15	2	6	2	3
Theatre	23	3	12	1	3	2	1
Ballet	11	11	5	2	1	8	0
Opera	9	10	5	2	0	9	1
Pop music	18	6	5	3	2	0	7
Classical music	19	4	8	0	6	2	0
Poetry	10	10	8	3	5	5	1
Novels	20	2	11	1	7	1	6
Dancing	24	2	10	1	4	0	6

No response 2

GROUP TWO

(Scores per unit)

	Entertaining	*Boring*	*Useful to society*	*Useless to society*	*A significant effect on your life*	*Difficult to understand*	*Not a form of art*
Painting	14	3	4	1	7	11	0
Sculpture	13	6	7	3	8	10	0
Films	29	2	16	1	9	1	7
Theatre	27	5	12	2	1	1	0
Ballet	19	11	9	2	2	2	0
Opera	15	14	6	4	2	4	0
Pop music	17	9	6	4	4	2	7
Classical music	23	4	6	0	6	6	0
Poetry	16	6	7	1	10	9	1
Novels	23	4	14	1	7	2	2
Dancing	20	3	9	1	2	1	6

2
THE ARTWORK AS A PRODUCT OF SOCIETY

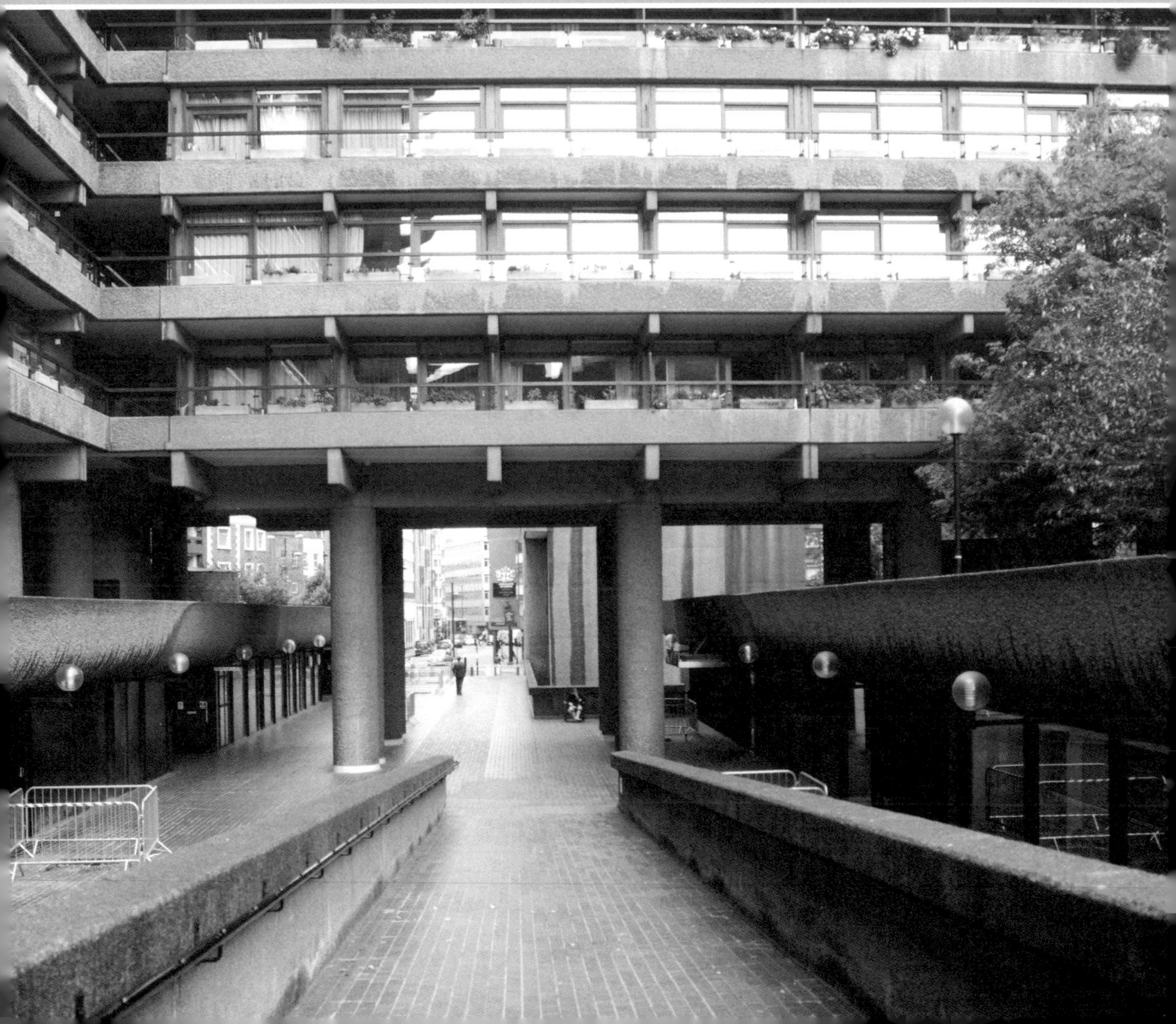

EXTENDING THE SOCIAL MEANING OF ART

In examining how art relates to society two fundamental modes of operation can be observed.

1. Art that reinforces perceptual stereotypes of society, while not necessarily originating them.
2. Art that instigates changes in the way we view perceptual stereotypes of society.

The first mode of operation is the most prevalent one within society as it is bound up with the process of maintaining its status quo of values and beliefs, however it is the second relationship that concerns the work of this text.

Various mechanisms within society exert pressure on the community for perceptual conformity as part of the process of stabilising social behaviour. In the absence of a counter pressure directed at initiating changes in social perception, cultural rigidity and stagnation follow. The second cited mode of operation relating art to society functions as an important agent in countering the pressure for perceptual conformity. Stereotypes are projected in society as embodying ideal representations of that society, and stem from such interconnected ideological constructs as its beliefs, aspirations, projections etc. The social need to be seen to be correct, alone, is enough to ensure that the emulation of projected stereotypes in society is a major pre-occupation in a person's life. In attempting to emulate projectional stereotypes a person contextualises them into their own group's structure of behaviour norms and conventions.

ART AND ITS DEPENDENCY ON RELATIONSHIPS BETWEEN PEOPLE

The realisation that all 'art' is dependent on society, dependent on the relationships between people, and not the sole product of any one person, is becoming increasingly important to the shaping of future culture. This divestment of authorship is seen as more relevant to an emerging culture founded on networks of exchange, fluidity, transience, and mutuality, as it ultimately offers us the prospect of self-organisation in person and interpersonal society.

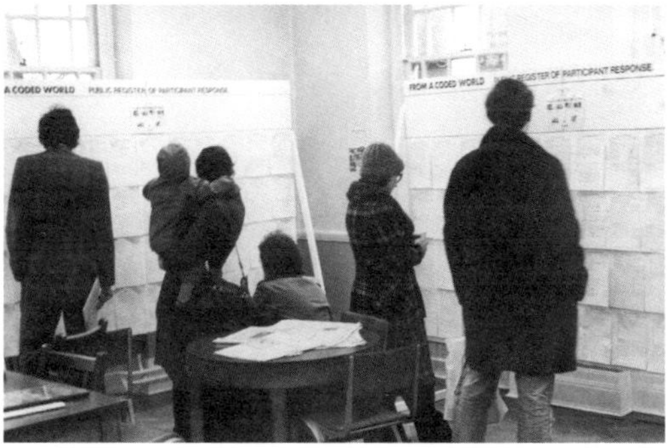

Viewing participants' responses on the Public Register Boards, 'From A Coded World'. Perivale Library.

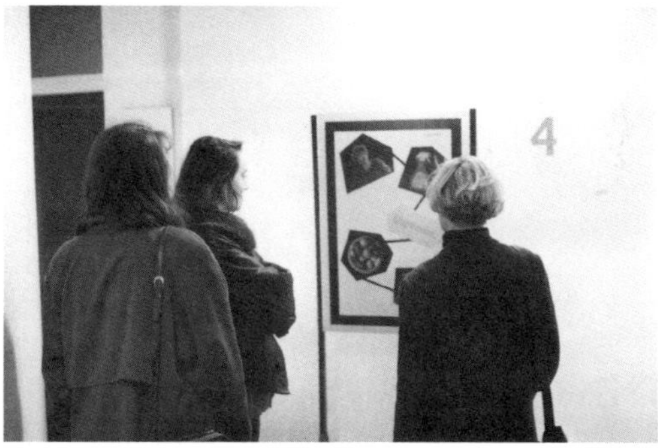

Residents of Linacre Court viewing Display Board as part of the work 'Living Tower'.

ONE LAYER NETWORKS

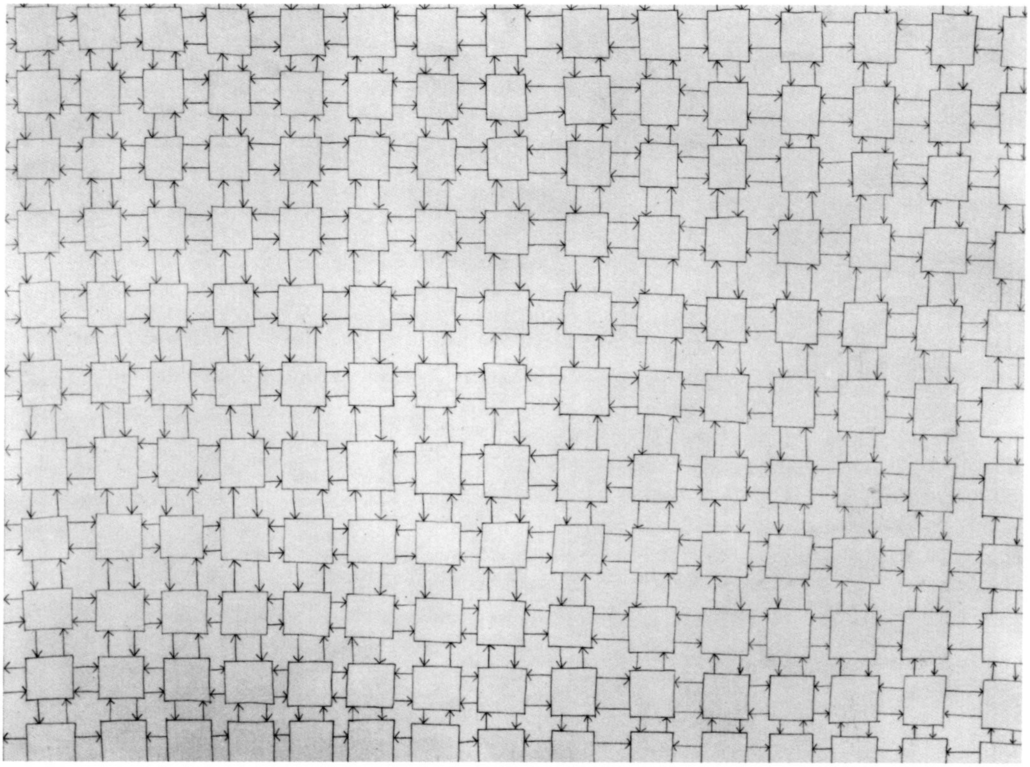

Homeostat Drawing No.1, 1969.

INFORMAL NETWORKS

Informal networks between people are usually spontaneous, transient, casual affairs arising through exchanges that are defined by some need for society, by the participants.

Almost by definition, informal networks are not designed as a part of any 'plan', or predetermined as a consequence of a dictate given by a higher authority, but grow out of the associations and behaviours generated between participants themselves made in relation to some priority or need. While most informal networks entwine with the cultural fabric of normality and are virtually invisible from the symbols of normality when viewed from outside the grouping, other networks have formed specifically around an alienation, even opposition, to that normality and even want to express their separation, to the extent that the separation appears highly visible. This separation from normality is visibly expressed by participants in the network even though the reality is that they are still dependent upon it. Thus there is usually an *ad hoc* coexistence between the values and beliefs held in the fabric of relationships self-created by the informal grouping and the deterministic formal fabric of society, that effectively leads to these networks operating as a parallel 'counter culture', which has transformed the language of the dominant society, giving it new meanings specific to their own special grouping.

3

PLURALISM IN THE FUNCTION OF ART

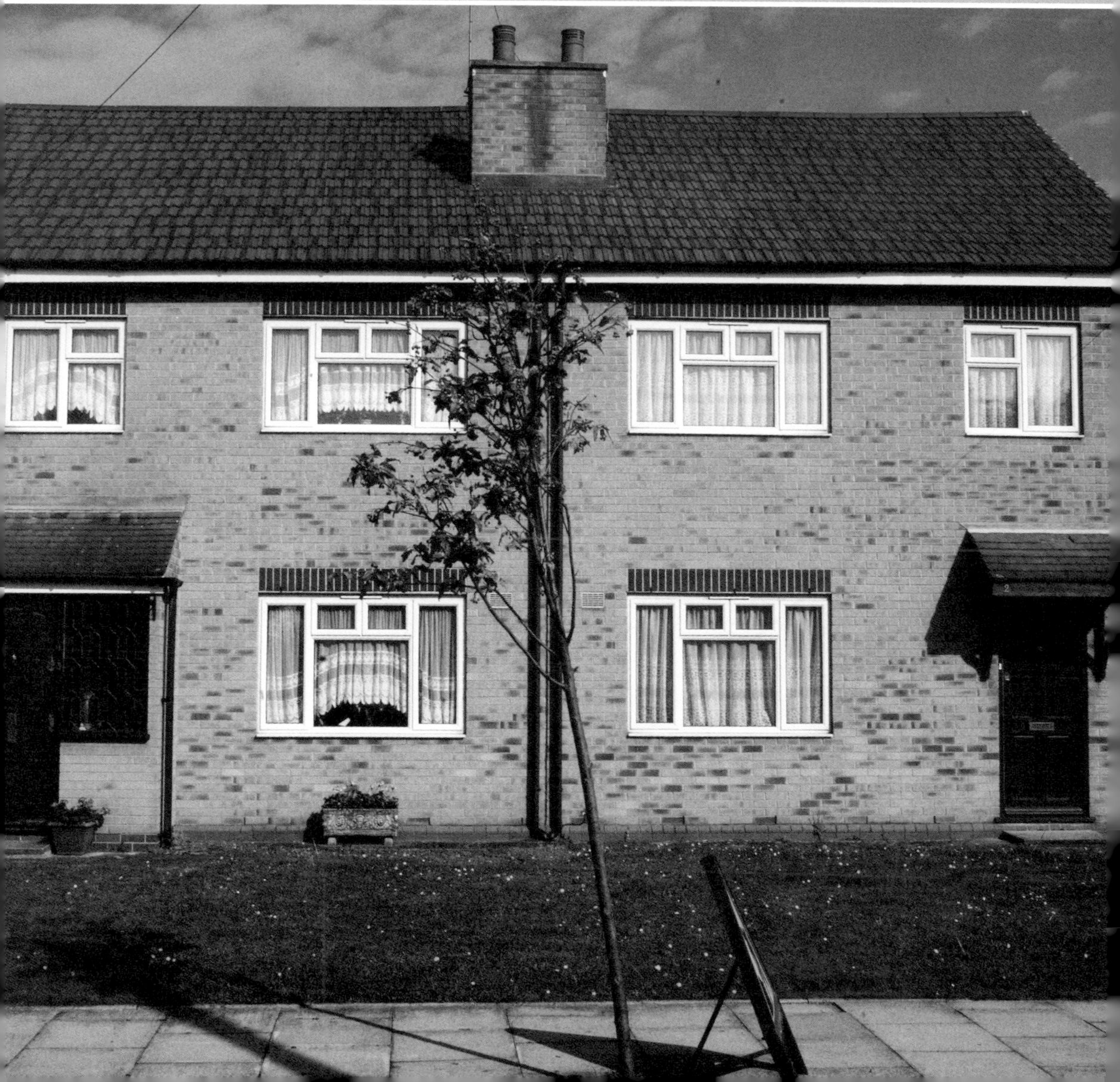

CULTURAL INFLUENCE THROUGH THE ARTWORK

Artists have long been considered essential to the process by which society generates new cultural sensibilities. Whether the artist has participation in this process as a coherently stated objective is another matter, as such intentions are rarely explicitly specified. For the influence of the artist has historically been accepted as implicit, hidden, or confused with the other functions which society projects onto the artwork. Yet still the means, and it is the means that are fundamentally important, by which the artist seeks cultural influence is through the 'artwork' and hence its central position between the artist's conception and society. In this way there is a tacit understanding that the intention of the artwork is ultimately mediational, that it does, in some unspecified way, interrupt to change perceptions and understandings of an audience. But in reality this is denied by an artwork's plurality, for what is projected onto the artwork by different vested interests is a multiplicity of functions all of which, while diverse, are simultaneously significant.

There are, undoubtedly, many individual, sometimes personally defined functions for art, all of which are equally valued by society, however, they are all the ones that reinforce what society wants from its art. For example: art is a means of denoting social status, but is also a means of psychological therapy; art is a means of financial investment and is also used in education as a means of learning, and so the list goes on. But all these existing functions directly neutralise the idea of an artwork intervening to instigate change in social and cultural perception. In all these functions an intimate passivity is implied, if not directly stated, for the artist, whereby he either reinforces the existing and dominant ideological foundations of the culture, or relieves the personal and social stress and conflict that stem from their ramifications.

This neutralisation of the artist is despite the fact that most artists, without questioning the social model of their practice, will still claim that they want to, and do, influence the social consciousness of society. But in general their unquestioning acceptance of what has been defined through art history and current social norms as a legitimate procedure for art practice, has entrapped them into reiterating existing precedence.

And this is the crux of the matter, that there is a clear historical and social division in art's function within contemporary Western society between that which reinforces and projects existing cultural idealisations, and an art that instigates changes in cultural and ultimately social perception. It must be self evident that an art which reinforces existing cultural idealisations is going to be by far the most prevalent and visible, for clearly society promotes an art that will fulfil its vested interests. This reinforcement of existing idealisations does not deny the artist the fulfilment of self-expression, providing that the meaning and form of this self-expression is held within what society has legitimised, designated through its institutions as acceptable art practice.

So I see that one outcome of my developing workshop practice for the Art Museum is that I am demonstrating the perceptual relativity inherent in institutional space, by giving it a new social parameter, one that will represent something of the complexities of external realities and societies, and conjoins the inner space of the art museum directly to those outside worlds.

RECOLLECTIONS OF THE MEANING IN 'VERTICAL LIVING'

Project Operator

We introduced it, in fact, as an art work and there was never any questioning that fact that it was. I don't know whether that's because they accepted that it was, or because the concept of an art work in a Tower Block was so completely alien to them that they didn't actually think about it at all. When it actually came to the more conceptual ideas that wasn't really enlarged upon until a bit later. But it wasn't till fairly near the end of the introduction that we actually asked people if they wanted to participate. Some people seemed to say yes it's a good idea because when we mentioned the problems of living in a flat, they had one specific problem most in their mind which they wanted to get out straightaway. And others seemed to be interested in the idea of the piece and interested in the way it was going to evolve. When we first introduced the work obviously as I said there were quite a number of differing reactions to it, a number of different receptions and there were obviously, sort of quizzical, sceptical looks. Are you from the Council? How much do we have to pay? How do I know that you are telling me the truth? What do you want me to do? and so on, and people were obviously waiting to see whether we were actually going to do what we said we were going to do. Once we actually put up the first display and had come back the next time, people seemed more ready to accept what we were doing at face value because they could actually see that we were doing what we said we were going to do and there was a display and we were coming to collect their responses and we were going to put up another display that evening.

Participant

I missed the displays when they went—the photographs on the floor—I really did because I felt I don't know I can't explain—I really thought there's someone living here you know. I knew there was someone living here because there was that board up there with those responses from people that lived here and they went and it was absolutely blank by the lift, and you know my heart dropped I thought well that's it finished-should be pictures like that every day of the week. But the point is you have got to get people to take part in it haven't you—agree to do these things—but I don't know I think we should have some pictures on the wall or a notice board—one certain spot in the building where we can pass the time of day or get talking, something like that. I think someone's put those there, there is somebody else here. Well I don't know about art, but I suppose it was. It was a different form of art to what you were brought up to or educated to understand. It was something we hadn't done before, and it was the first time anyone's ever approached us to do anything like this.

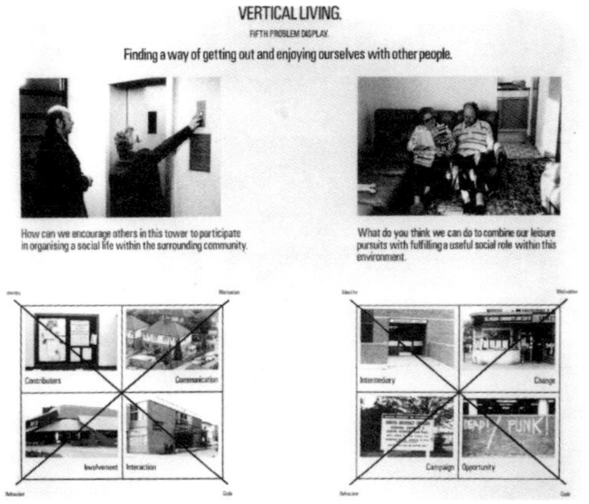

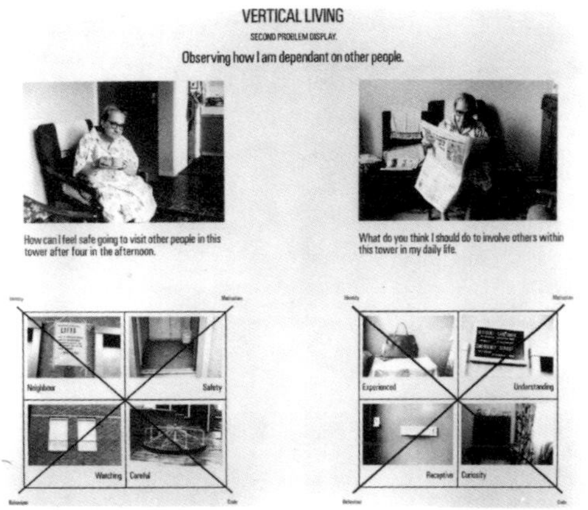

Photographs of Display Boards in 'Vertical Living'.

INSTITUTIONAL SUB-CULTURES

Curator

I've been criticised in the press for referring to the art world, and the particular groupings of the art world as subculture, which people take to be a pejorative, people take the term 'sub-culture' to be a pejorative term, to me it is not a pejorative term, it is simply a description of what is a fact and quite certainly the art world is made up of a number of subcultures, some of them comprising one person only, or even one person at a certain time only and there are subcultures within cultures, families, groups of artists, artists who are associated with a kind of work, artists who are associated with a certain gallery, artists who are just friends, artists who went to a certain school together or have been combining for whatever reason and certainly, if you go to private views at all you find at different private views a different balance of, or selection of this larger sub-culture. I manifestly belong to the Tate sub-culture, unmistakeably.

PARALLEL MODELS OF ART

Well, I think that's how people perceive it, I mean some years ago I did a piece of research with Kevin Lole and we went around to various housing estates and made a questionnaire about peoples' distance perceptions of art and artists, these were people that didn't go to art galleries and museums very much, and we found that even in the most kind of remote kind of location almost, that people still have a model of artists that were very important to them, even if it was sort of a very, I don't know, a model of art that was quite clearly different from how most artists would see themselves working, you know, then have this idea that even though maybe they were in some boring job or heavily sort of regimented life, there was someone out there who was outside the system engaged in kind of intervening in it to change it or something, I don't know how they thought, but it was sort of interesting that they did have a, there was a model of art that was important to them.

4

THE SOCIAL CONTAINMENT OF ART PRACTICE

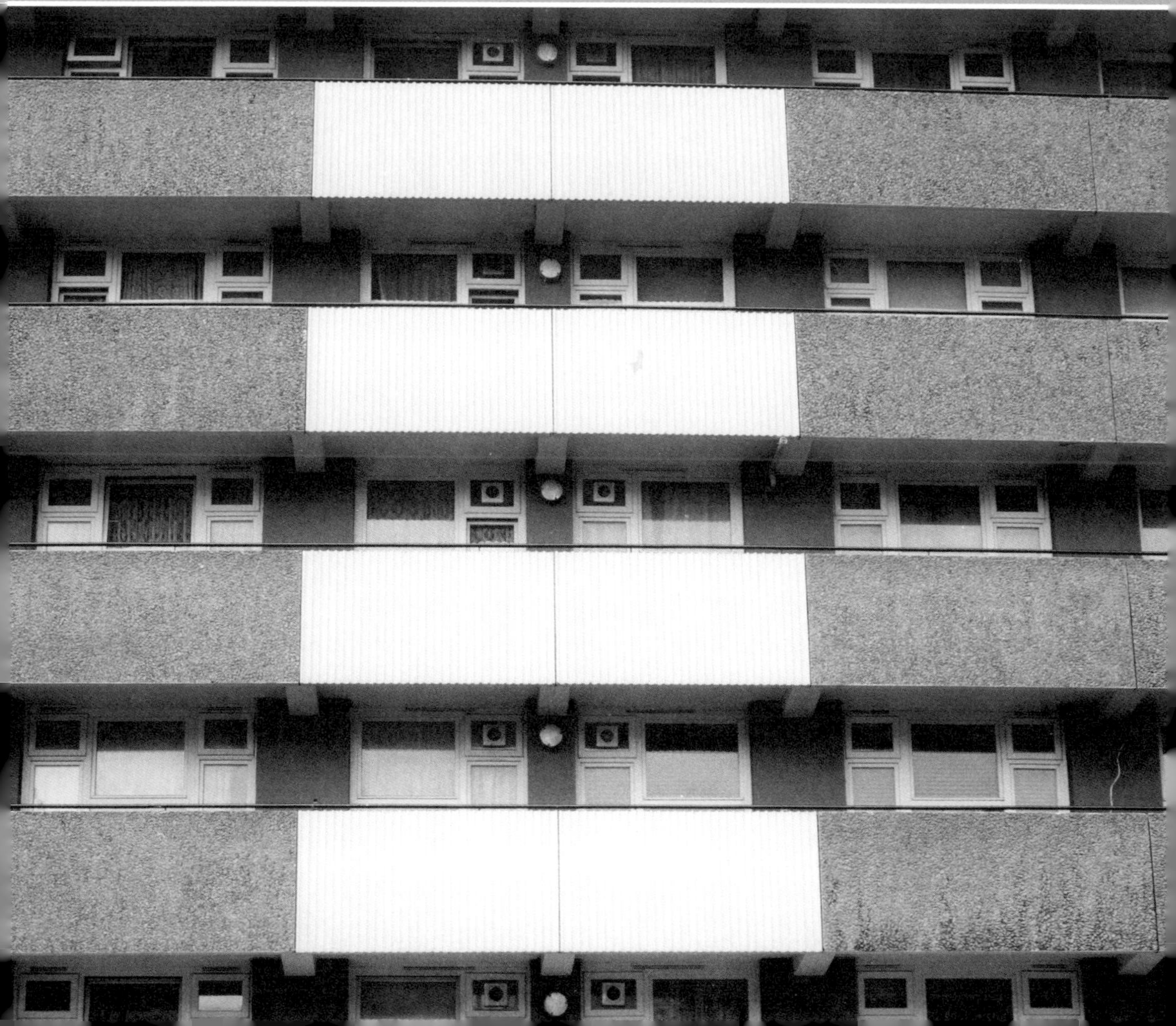

THE POWER OF THE MUSEUM

It is an implicit and seemingly unquestioned fact of contemporary culture that art practice is dependent upon, and contained within, 'art institutions' and, in particular, the 'Art Museum'. Yet, this is despite the almost continual debate amongst artists, theoreticians, the public, and museum curators, for an art beyond the walls of the Museum. Notwithstanding this periodic call for an art practice that exists within the fabric of everyday life, art in general is still confined to the rarefied interior of the art museum and, perhaps, therefore it is not surprising that it has evolved as a form that fits the physical and social conditions prevailing within the gallery.

The power of the art museum has grown considerably in the last few decades and, recently, the concept has become fashionable among curators that the art museum is a kind of 'mausoleum'. In this state the art museum separates itself, and the art objects that it contains, from the world outside, reflecting a higher order; a purity that is timeless, untouchable and unchallengeable. The internal referencing of the art museum is reflected in the internal referencing of its artworks, both are abstract, and this reflects the modernist movement in art since the 1960s. The obscurity of 'conceptual art' and the blankness of 'minimal art' meant that they could well exist within a club like atmosphere of pre-knowledge, that their hidden codes for audience behaviour, the specialisation of the visual language used by the artist, elevated the possessor of that special knowledge: the museum curator.

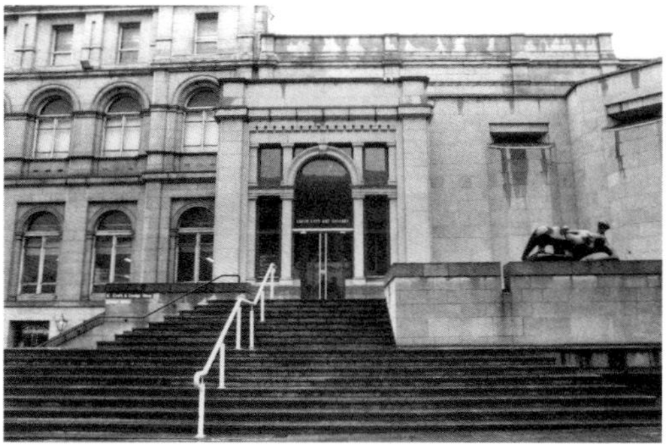

Leeds City Art Gallery.

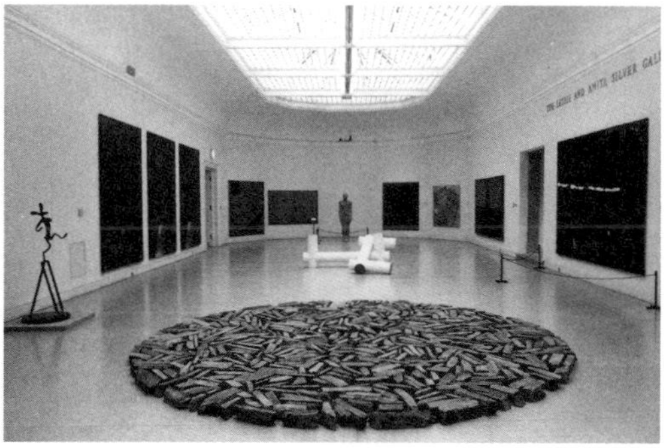

'From Different Worlds'.

ART PRACTICE OUTSIDE THE INSTITUTIONAL BOX

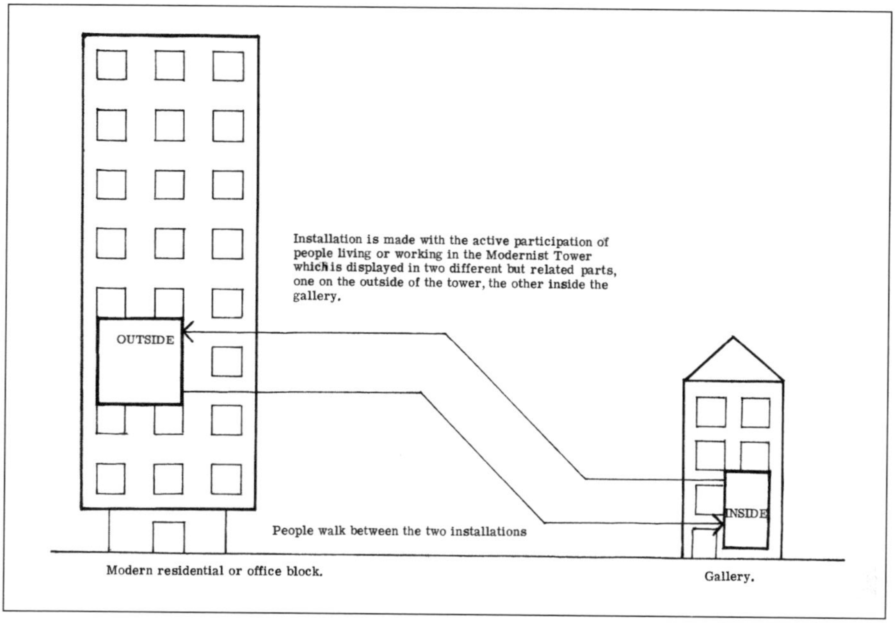

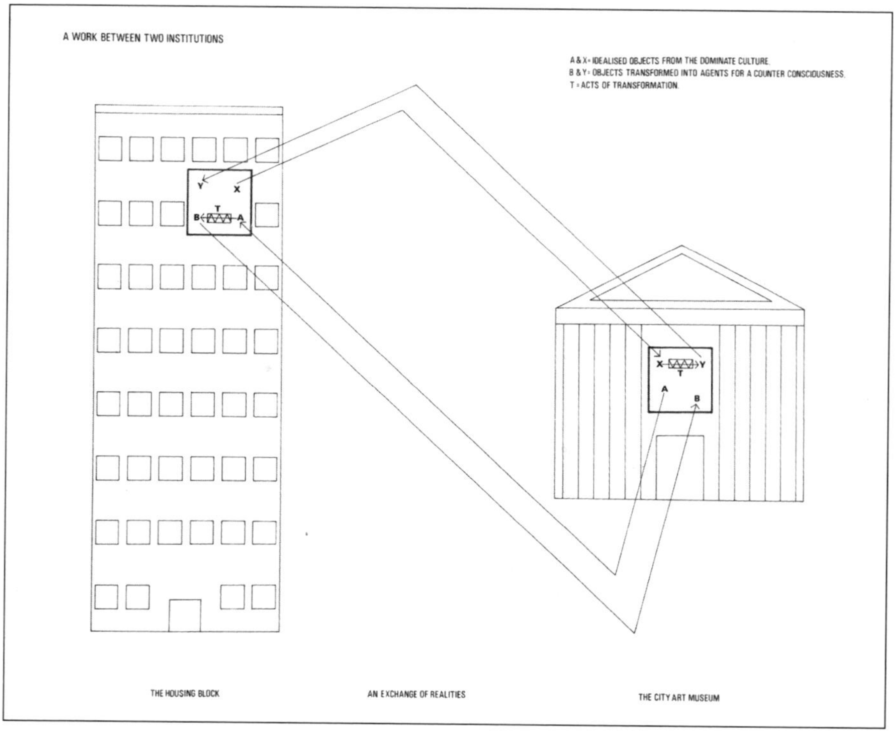

MULTI-CHANNEL WORKSHOP PRACTICE IN THE ART MUSEUM

Within the institutional realm in which contemporary art predominately currently exists, a realm of art museums, art journals, art schools, art collectors etc., there is still an innate aversion to the agencying of practices in art that are founded on the complexities of social exchange. Thus the 'art museum' is represented as a context that defines a social environment that is to be looked up to as a symbol of a transmissional authority, a *modus operandi* for society's institutions that is increasingly at odds with the social processes of exchange that are actually shaping modern daily life. It is in other areas of art activity, in other social environments in which art exists, such as in educational art, community art, psychiatric art, that models of exchange in communication between people and the rich complexity that they generate are seen as valued practice. But with the realm of the institutional art world these more mutualistic social practices in art are at best marginalised, if not excluded altogether as they are deemed to undermine the authoritative criteria of authorship and of ownership based on possession. And this is the crux of the problem for within these social practices there is an implicit divestment of authorship, and the emphasis on art practice being a process based experience, a process in time, not contained in an immortalised object. But the point I wish to emphasise that the way in which we approach an institutionalised space is all dependent on our starting point. i.e. the physical environment may beyond out capabilities to rebuild as we desire, but what we represent within it, how we use that space, can enable our psychological approach to change and embrace quit divergent ideologies and perceptions. For the space in reality is relative to how we enter it, what perceptual framework we bring to bear on the experience.

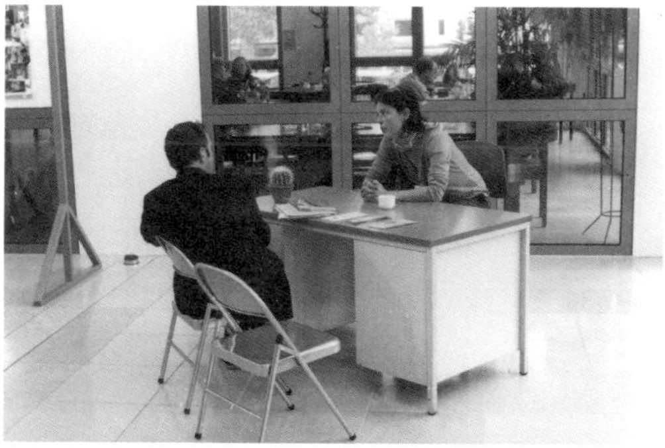

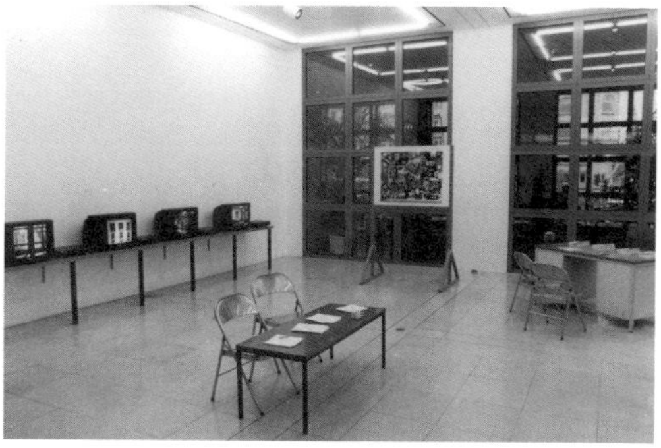

Multi-channel workshop inside the Kunsthalle, Hamburg.

BETWEEN OBJECTS AND PEOPLE

Leeds City Art Gallery
"I have directed my work to the here and now of life today, intervening in issues that affect us all. I consider that the prominence and power of objects in our culture, the importance they have come to assume in our daily life, gives me an available and accessible language that I can employ strategically in my artwork to engage a wider public audience. I am constantly seeking out and isolating those symbolic objects that are relevant to contemporary life. These objects can be readily recognised and understood as representing basic ideological and polemical statements about our culture."

'From Different Worlds'
The dependency of works of art on 'art institutions' and their containment within is an inescapable feature of art practice within the present culture. Reinforcing this locating of art has been the rise in prominence of the 'modernist' movement within the art museum, a phenomenon that has taken place as a mirror of society's investment in a similar increase in the social power of the 'object'. The relationship between the 'modern art museum' and 'modernist' art objects has become inextricably bound to the point where the 'museum' and 'object' have created a self-referencing that has effectively sealed off the availability and meaning of what is contained inside the museum from the experience of reality beyond its walls. Thus at the start of planning my exhibition of new works, 'Between Objects and People' at Leeds City Art Gallery (21st September–15th November 1987), an installation was commissioned that would create a direct connection between those works (which centred on people's different relationships with objects from modern life) and the actual everyday experiences of people living in Leeds. 'From Different Worlds' was the resulting new work, and it was conceived to open up the possibilities of a model of art practice that would involve the 'art museum' in a social interaction with the surrounding community. For my work embodied the City Art Gallery as an integral part of its structure and created an exchange of realities with two other symbolic institutions—the nearby tower blocks of Marlborough Towers and Lovell Park Towers.

5 THE MYTHOLOGY OF CREATIVITY

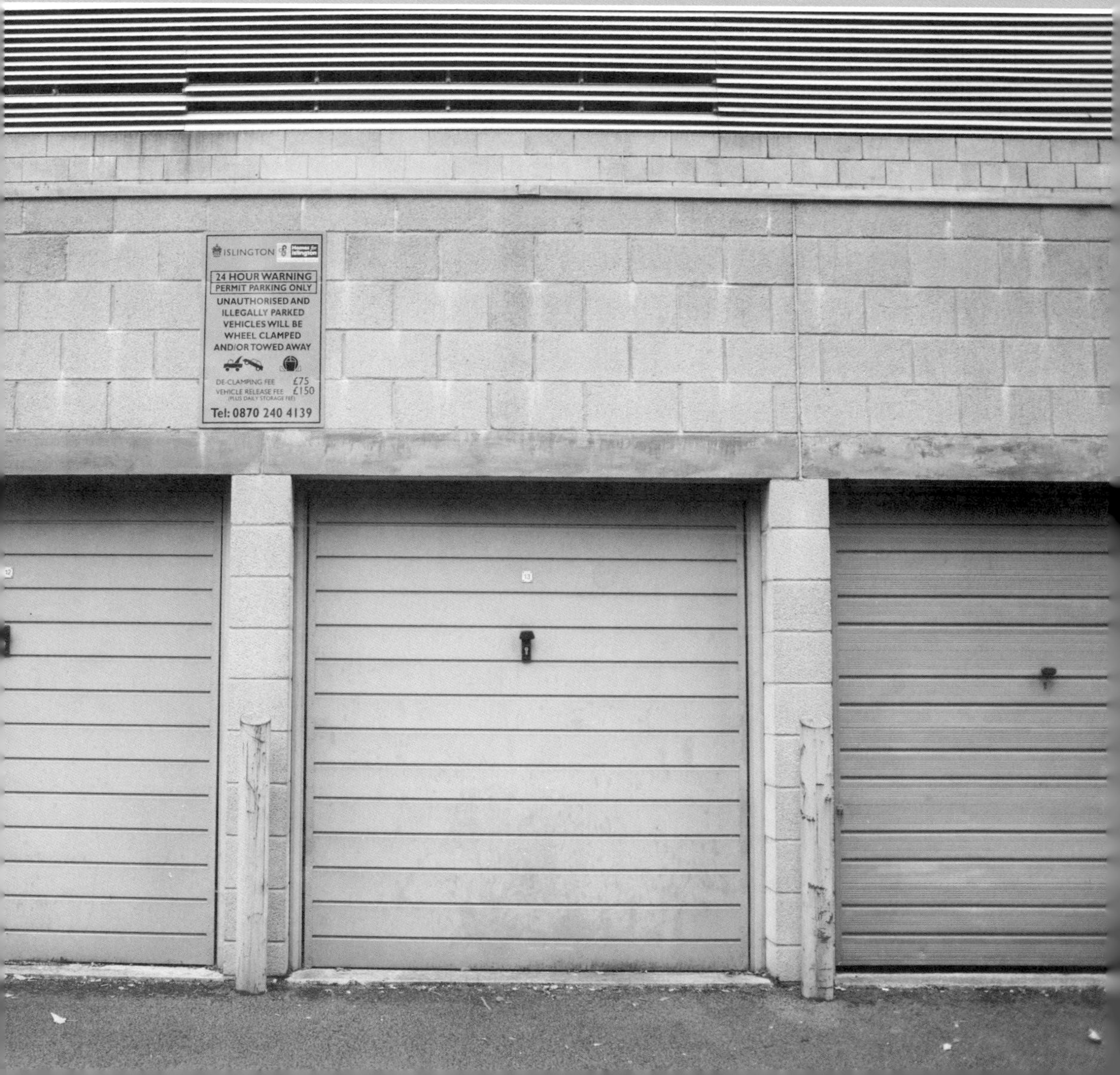

THE COMPETITIVE FREE WILL ENVIRONMENT

An important part of the mythical ethos surrounding the practice of artists has been that the artwork is in a competitive free will environment, in which 'good art' will somehow magically win out, but at the same time at the core of this competitive environment there is an institutionalised career path that will verify, legitimise, competition into what it can hold up as 'good art'. The resulting hegemony strived for in competition has been accompanied by a psychology that has reduced the complexity of the artwork's social interface. Closely linked to this reduction has been a tendency towards object-based perception, the containment inherent in objects detaches the self from the complexity of that interface. Coupled with this is an expression of the values of exclusivity, the holding of special knowledge, being a prerogative within an authoritative cultural setup, elevating the status of the holder. Relationships between individuals caught up in this competitive and exclusive realm are highly demarcated, different territories of information being associated with a variety of specific identities, such as curator and critic, each with their own specialised languages, behaviours and values.

CREATING CULTURE

'What Is The Difference Between The Inside And The Outside' is one of a series of my works that have centred on different positions individuals occupy in the creation of cultural stereotypes of Western society today. In making this work, as a co-operation with another artist, I wanted to acknowledge the central role that the artist occupies in embodying and manifesting the mythological idealisations of Western Culture. The daily reality of the artist locked into a now traditional, or institutionally accepted, studio-bound mode of practice is at root the same as any other person confined to a single space in that they feel distanced, even isolated from the world and other people around them, and ineffectual in having any real influence upon it. This distancing from the actuality of surrounding reality is almost a parallel experience to people entrapped in the tower block or behind an office desk, but in contrast if the powerful inference of this creativity is to have an effect on that world outside the studio. The conflict between mythology and reality, between expectation and actuality (the circumstance) creates its own innate alienation in the psychology of the artist from the dominant culture. I see this alienation as a result of containment that mirrors everyone's inhibition of individual creativity within the framework of the dominant culture.

FROM INSIDE THE STUDIO

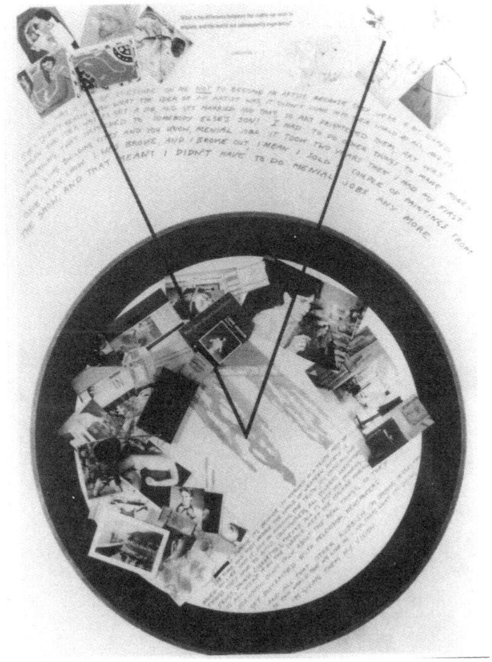

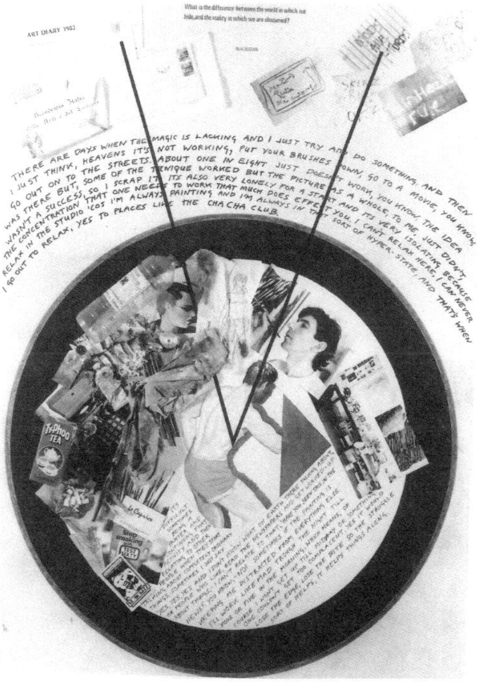

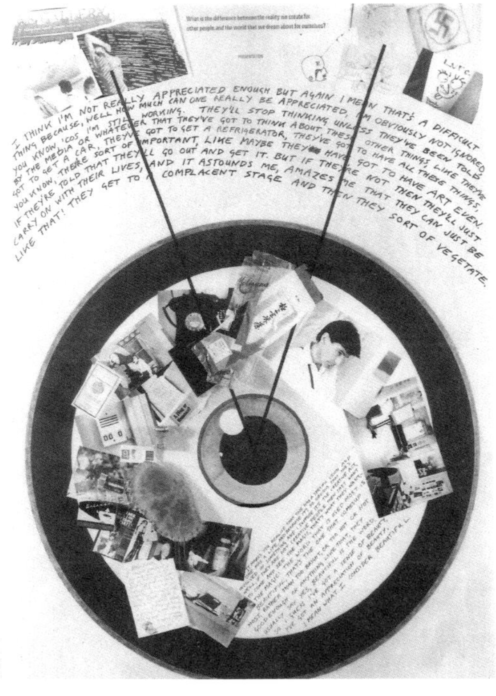

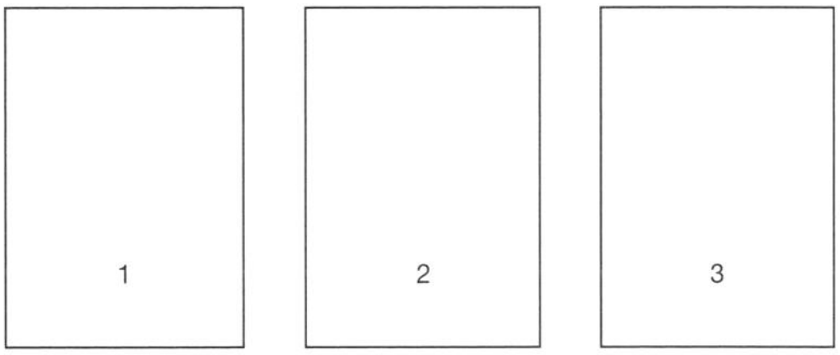

'What Is The Difference Between The Inside And The Outside'.
Three panels in a row, 1–3: left to right, top to bottom.

THE TESTIMONY OF THE ARTIST

From an interview with a painter

It's very lonely for a start, and it's very isolating because the concentration that one needs to work that much does affect you when one is with other people and quite often I get distracted to the point that people can be talking to me and I'm not even listening to them 'cos I'm thinking about what I'm painting and why aren't I back in the studio doing it rather than sitting in this silly party or whatever, then other times I get where my mind is blanked out completely and I can sit in the launderette and talk to the lady in the launderette about the weather and you know, her husband, and she's got kids and all this sort of thing and I get totally fascinated by that I mean like really the mundane.

I can remember being in America and I was sitting on a beach and like these people they'd come up and they'd say "What are you doing, what are you doing" and I'd say, "Well, I'm painting that", and I'd just sort of like throw my arm up in a broad sweep and they said, "what", you know, and I said, "Well, that, can't you see it", and they'd said, "What, what are you looking at and what can you see", and then you'd realise that you see things that people don't see, that you are different, one is different, so in fact one's got the key I suppose and one's opening the door.

6

THE STYLISM OF THE CONTEMPORARY AVANT GARDE

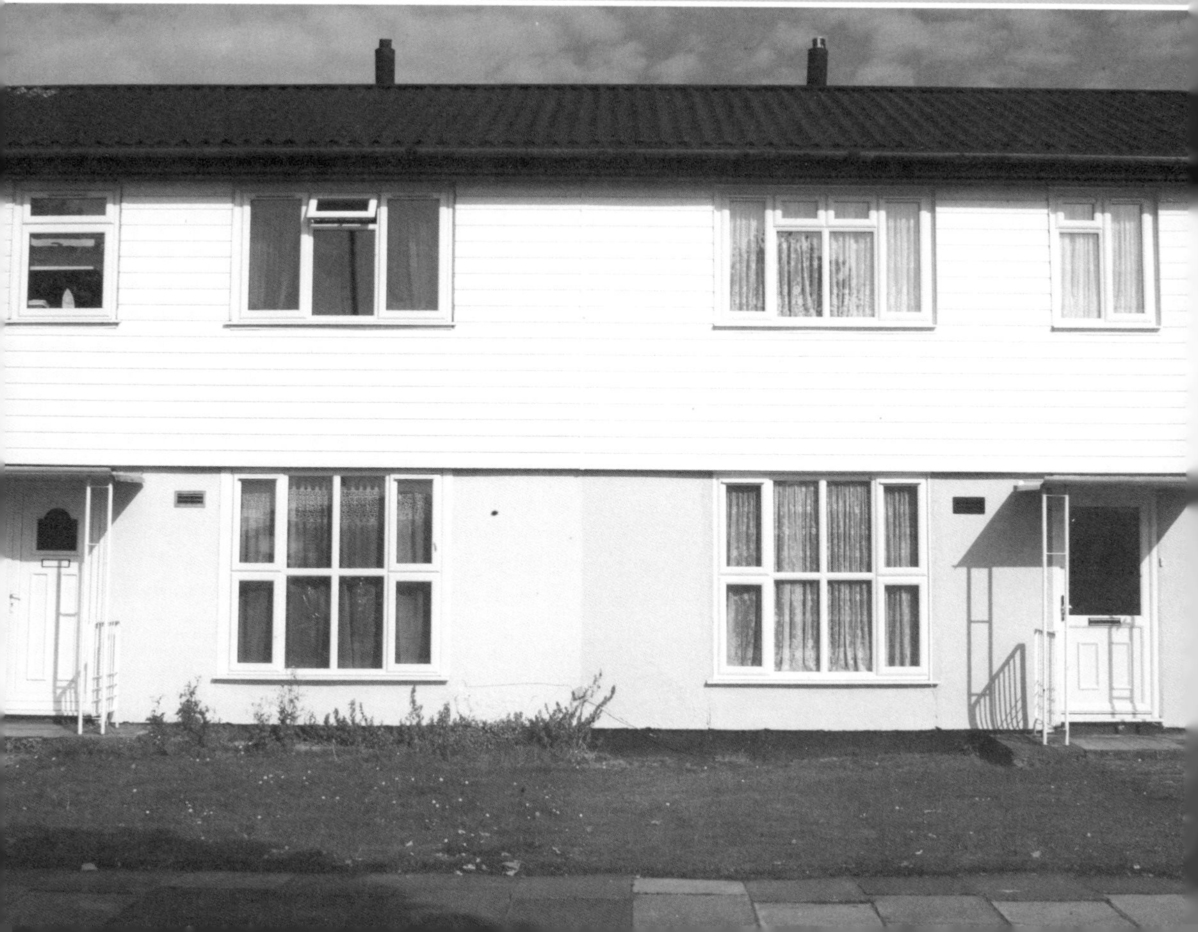

THE CHARISMA OF UNIQUENESS AND STYLE

The value which uniqueness has in the elevation of possessive power has given the combination of the object within stylism an overwhelming dominance, creating enormous pressures on the artist to go into production of stylistically dexterous objects. By production I mean that from one original conception a succession of works are produced, each a variation on the first original concept.

The artist has been caught between two directly conflicting pressures, one unavoidable, emitting from the effects of changes in society on the street, the other from an aloof institutional art world, to produce unique objects resulting in no more than a further dexterous twist in stylism.

'Newness' has a definite currency within a market that is directed at the private collector, also the link between the act of discovery and newness becomes an attribute seized on by the art professional to give status. Something new is in itself attention grabbing and, while the pressure of the art world's vested interests to do something new is enormous, so is the pressure from the artist's personal drive to give fulfilment to the ego. However, should the audience try to penetrate beyond the new stylisms and search for a deeper social meaning it becomes quickly apparent that what is being made is just a manipulation of language for its own sake.

THE POSSESSIVE OBJECT

Epitomising art produced in the '80s has been the well-crafted, self-referenced, modernistic, possessible object. 'Style' in the art object has come to reflect the outface of culture's other 'objects', the conception of these objects increasingly, it seems, being dislocated, separated from their polemical, ideological precedence and the means of their production. The proliferation of objects as design fetishisms has paralleled the rising dominance of the '80's ideology of the innovative market as the determining force in culture, conditioning all its norms and conventions... Thus, while art objects have come to mirror other cultural objects, they have also been thrown into competition with them for attention, and consequently there has been a general, and perceived as acceptable, development of them not expressing any serious or critical ideologies and polemical meaning.

THE PERPETUATION OF THE AVANT GARDE

The perpetuation and celebration of the avant garde notion has alone been enough to ensure that there is a continual evolution of the visual language made by artists. For as long as there are vested interests working to further the social and property functions of the art object then innovation in language has a validity, it injects new life into the system and gives it a facade of being up to date. However, this generation of new languages is not coupled with any real change in the parameters governing the form, context and social meaning of the artwork. Innovation in language is supposed to be made by the artist to show individual identity, to state uniqueness and separation from other artists, thus the onus is on the artist to stamp a recognisable mark onto the artwork through innovating an original style in language, and it is this pursuit that I call stylism. It is a fact that the pursuit of stylism goes on quite independently of the priorities, preoccupations, of the world outside the 'art professional' and attendant institutions. This self-centred, academic closing off is culturally celebrated, and even signals separateness to the public through the self-referenced, abstract languages that have been especially created by the artist. In the art history of the dominant culture, stylism is equated with progression in the evolution of art; the creation of precedence that gives further creative twists to self-referenced languages which are rarefied, sanctified by the art institutions to which they are bound.

THE KISS OF DEATH

Curator

It's one thing to plan a Francis Bacon exhibition five years ahead for example—I should say in relation to the art not perhaps in relation to the artist but it's quite another when the artist is in his or her thirties shall we say or early forties because the artist is very likely to be doing different kind of work and certainly the climate of opinion, you know, the likelihood of the show being well received and so on may be affected by this change of, you know by changes that have been going on in the arts generally and I thought certainly in the period when we used to do big retrospective exhibitions of so called middle generation artists for example you will remember Turnbull or Denny and so on—Dick Smith—Paolozzi—I began to feel that these were very often damaging to the artists rather than helpful to them. In some way they were the sort of, 'kiss of death' you know—one had gone too far in trying to encapsulate, trying to historicise their work.

7

THE FORMATION OF BELIEFS AND ATTITUDES ABOUT ART

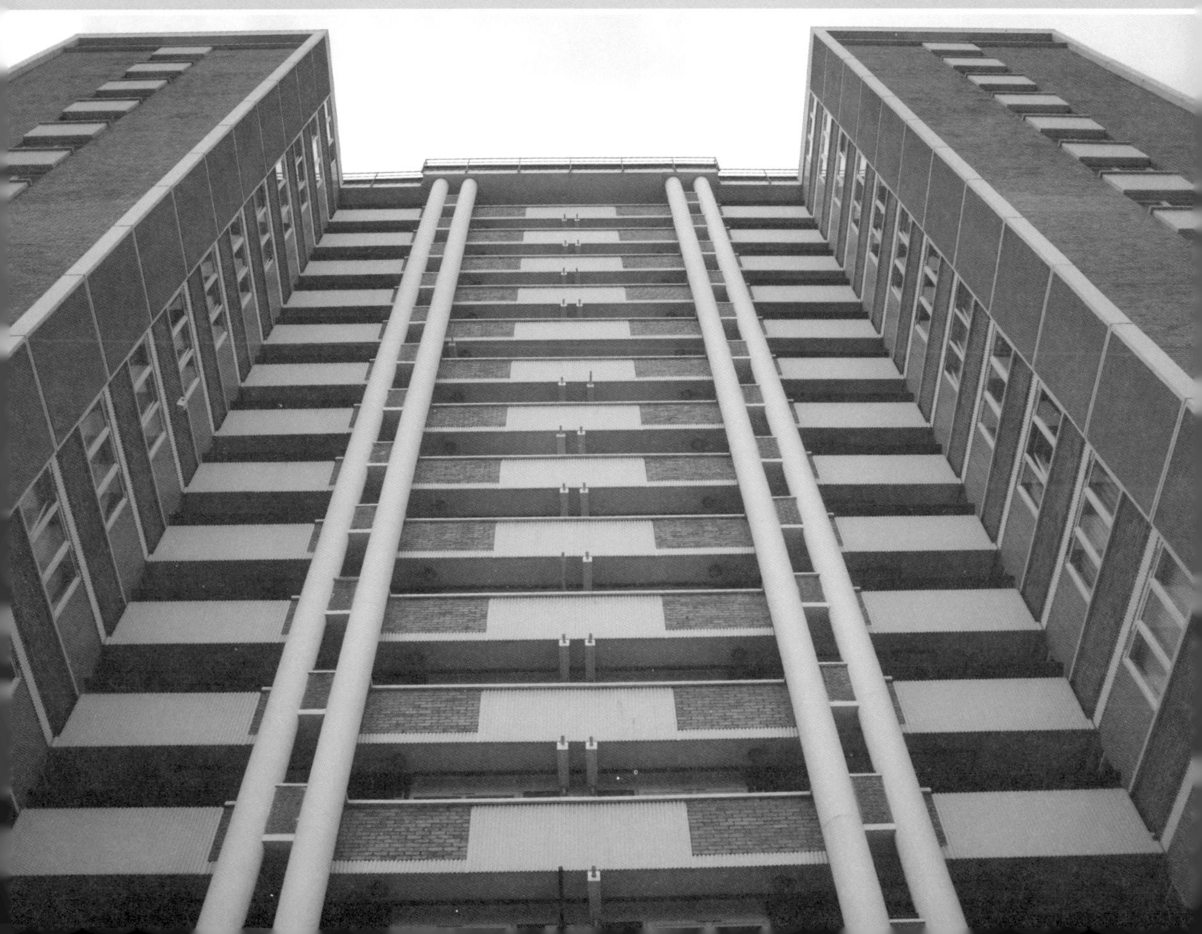

REINFORCING THE CULTURE OF THE COLLECTOR

What has happened is that most artists' activities, especially those made within the private gallery have, instead of exerting a polemical intervention, come to reinforce and reflect the culture of the collector. Generated in an atmosphere of priorities based on the economics of shopping, which has, and still is, projected as an important, very acceptable pastime, art has been equated with the notion of desirable object, that is an object that will reflect in its material outface and fabrication, the social charisma and power of the possessor.

AN ENVIRONMENT FOR EMULATIVE CONFORMITY

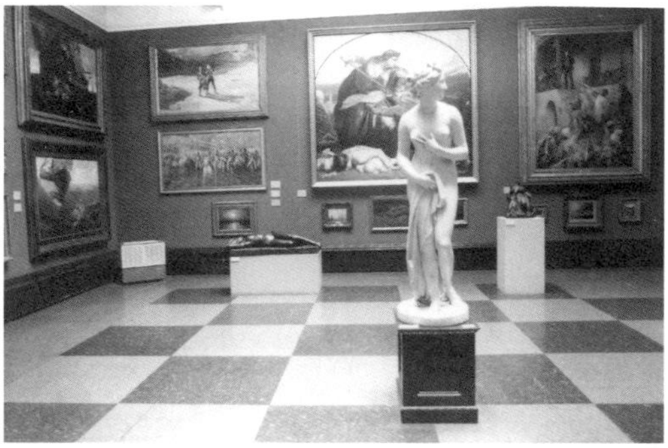

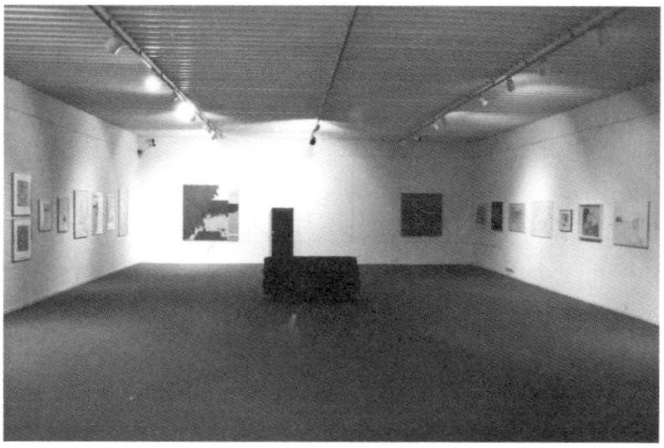

Inside Leeds City Art Gallery.

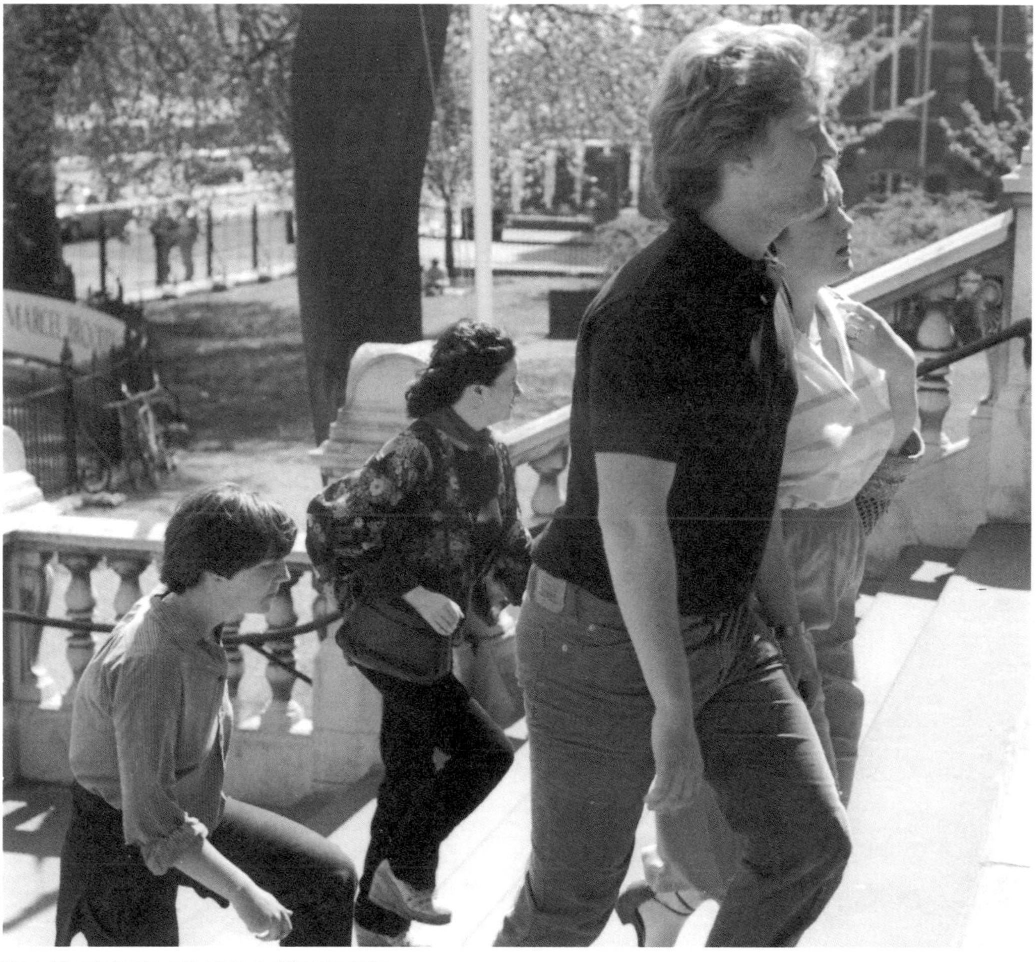

The public entering the main entrance of the Tate Gallery.

AGENTS IN THE AUTHORITATIVE FORMATION OF ATTITUDES

Tate Gallery curator

It is almost inconceivable that people could respond suitably, that is to say with some richness to contemporary works of art without having some considerable experience of art, it's not quite the same as saying that you couldn't understand, you couldn't respond properly to a poem in Latin if you knew no Latin and knew nothing about rhythm or metre and so on, but there is an element of the same although it operates in a different way.

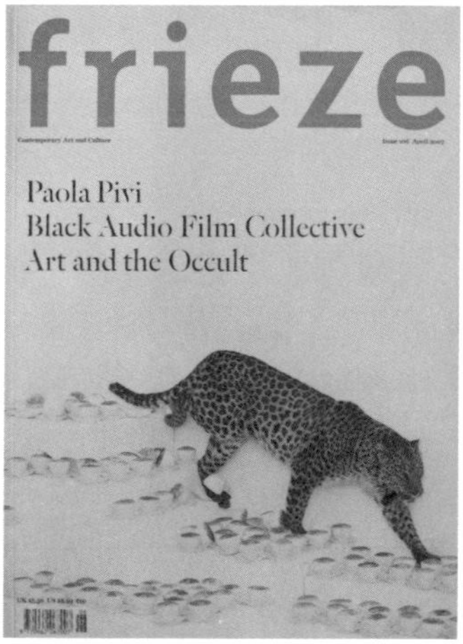

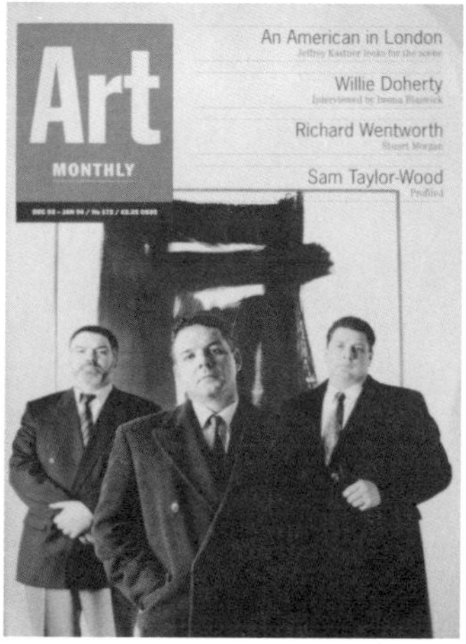

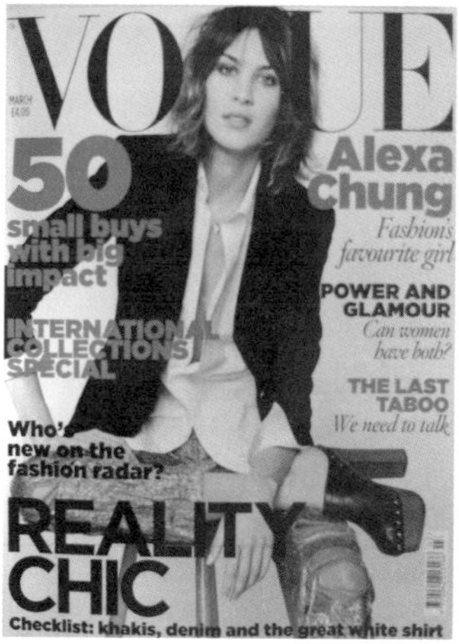

THE CAMERA AS AN OBJECT OF DETERMINISM

There's no denying the important role as an object that the camera assumes in modern consumer culture—valued not so much as a means of self-expression or a practical tool for framing records of reality but as a possession and adornment denoting to others the owner's social power, attainments and aspirations. The physicality and styling of the camera, its architecture, has become increasingly monumental, radiating a confidence in the object that has been carefully culturally propagated and conferring on it an authoritative presence for possessor and witness alike. Thus even the camera's physical form has been influenced by norms for its use that reflect a dominant culture founded on an authoritative determinism, the fabric of which is transmissional and exclusive. While the scientific mechanics of photography may well be more or less unalterable, it is the way in which those mechanics are used to frame and encode reality that is so biased towards the possession-based ideology of the dominant culture that is closest to owning the means of the camera's production.

Within the dominant culture's conventions there is an accepted way to use the camera, in which the possessor imposes authority through the camera lens onto reality by being solely responsible for deciding what will be included in the frame, and thus ultimately encoding those elements of reality onto the photographic negative, acquiring them as forms of possession.

This activity is undertaken without the subject of the photographer's attention being able to feed back directly any decisions into the framing process, which corresponds closely to the transmitter-receiver network of information and command that underpins the interpersonal fabric of present culture. The encoding process of photography made in this manner is inherently reductive: in this transmitter-receiver mode, the photographer and the photographic print cannot acknowledge the full dynamic complexity surrounding the subject but rather reduce it all to the level of static objects.

The cultural elevation of the camera to icon and its projection of a transmissional mode of making photography is further reinforced by the creation of an authoritative mythology of professionalism. This linkage between an image of professionalism and authority is increased by the similarity of the camera's finish, now usually matt black, to other professional and middle-class desirable equipment, such as hi-fi systems, executive cars, kitchen installations, etc. Also the sexual projection of the professional photographer's lifestyle through advertising and other media forms, with the camera portrayed as an essential adornment, puts it in the same bundle of carefully orchestrated mythologies that underlie the essential stimulation of consumer wish fulfilment. Now, as an inhibitor to free creativity and the self-organization of meaning, professionalism has a major effect, as it presents the camera owner with already formed ideal types that are there to be emulated, which can only be achieved through the acquisition of difficult to obtain special knowledge and equipment. These projected ideal types invade everyone's consciousness; there is simply no escape from what become stereotypes, giving a desirable (right) and undesirable (wrong) way to frame reality, leading to such simplistic notions as good and bad photographs. Such rigidity exerts a pressure on the photographer that neutralizes any acknowledgement, let alone acceptance, of the relative meaning the photograph might have in the context/situation in which it was made.

Thus there has grown up a strong distinction between what is professional and what is amateur—centring on judgements such as where the subject should be placed in the frame, what to include or what not, colour or black and white, in focus or out of focus—that perhaps is really only overcome in the tolerated innocence of holiday and home snaps. Unlike the professional photograph, the holiday snap is firmly rooted in the knowledge of the context in which it was taken, and is usually not only made socially, but is subsequently, as one in a packet of prints, or as a framed picture, etc., used socially as a vehicle for interaction. Here quality as a criterion determined by professionalism is subsumed by what the content means to those related to the situation in which the photograph was taken. Though even here, the simple apparatus and unassuming look of the traditional home camera has given way to increasingly more complex, sophisticated but user-proof cameras (again usually now matt black) that enable anyone to feel they can emulate the idealized framings of the professional. So within the most spontaneous social occasions it is still a social norm to be seen displaying the right equipment, as well as being seen to follow a correct and stereotyped way of organizing the subject—just think of how people are herded together to fill the frame in a wedding photograph. The effect of these imposed norms results in the camera owner, the photographer, being made to feel self-conscious as to its legitimate use, and inevitably that must result in an inhibition to creative free expression.

Thus in our daily experience of culture as it is projected to us through the institutional fabric of society we cannot help being bombarded with a multiplicity of idealized images of objects, amongst which the camera is built up into a super object, an icon, for us to desire, possess and display. At the same time we are also immersed in a mediarised environment of images that confront us with perfect framings of an idealized reality. So that, within our seeming random experience of the mosaic of perceptual reality, there are in fact precisely laid out attractors for us to focus our attention upon, and then to emulate, which of course leads to our conformity.

8
THE APPROPRIATION OF ART PRACTICE

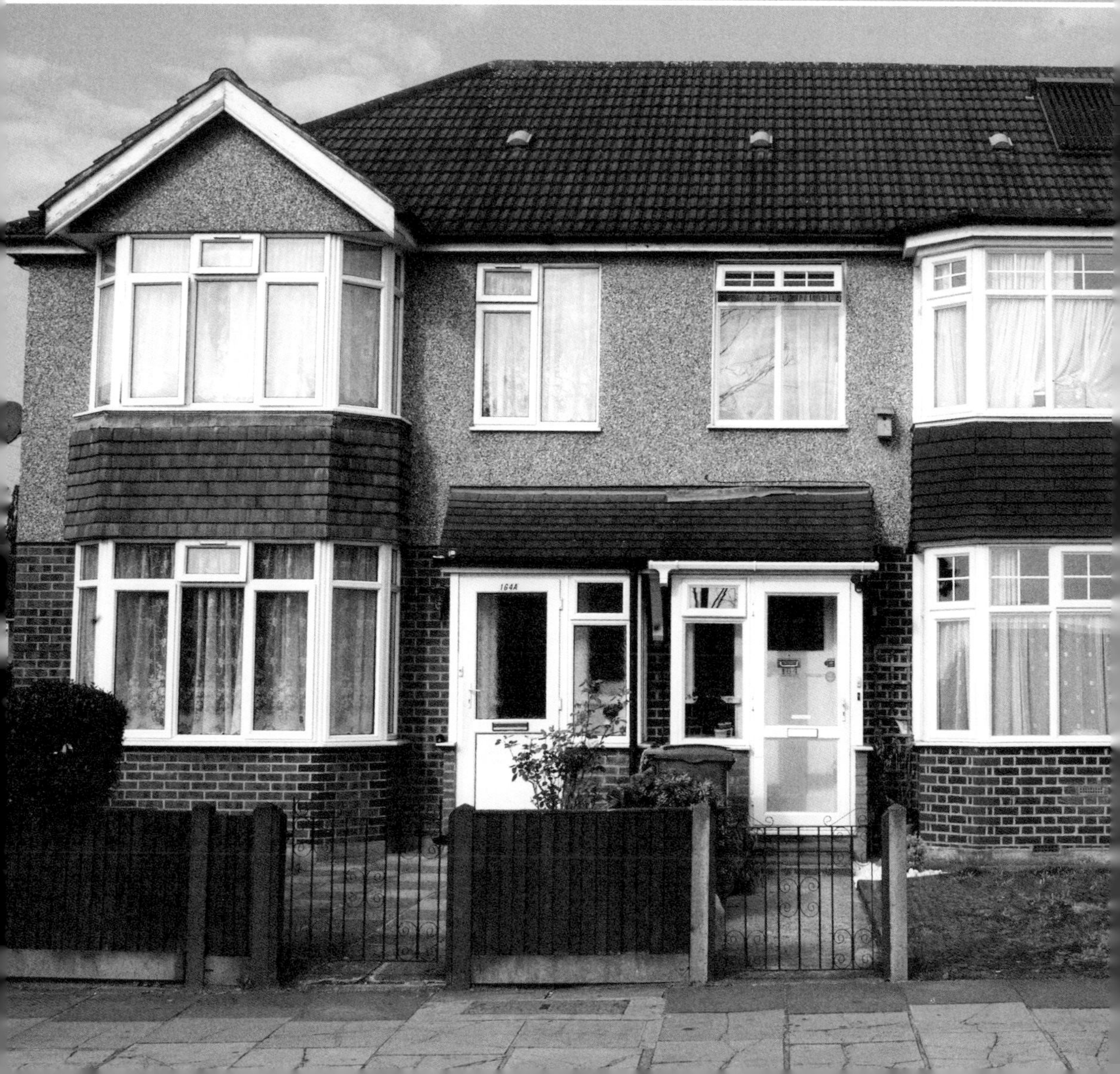

PASSIVE METHODOLOGIES

The adherence by artists to a method of operation in which the 'art work' is seen as a passive manifestation and confirmation of their theoretical notions, mental models, which are addressed to themselves and to other members of art's social environment, has imposed limitations on the social effectiveness of contemporary art practice. The existence of this method of operation can be attributed to the absence of control or concern by the artist over the function of an 'art work' within the present social setting. In this respect the artist is in compliance with the social attitudes prevalent within a monolithic social structure, where the presumption of non-responsibility is prescribed to its membership as a functioning criterion. It is within these social conditions that the precedence for contemporary art practice can be considered to have been formed, having considerably limited its social effect, and relevance, through the prescription of social functions that the artist did not determine, or for which he was not held responsible. This lack of concern by the artist over social function has enabled society to misuse, or to develop its own use of 'art works', with respect to their functioning in accordance with the artist's intention. In practice, an 'art work' being taken out of context inherent within its intention, through the absence of any constraining specifications made by the artist, and prescribed functions by society which result in the 'art work' being integrated into another criteria. For instance, in the case of an 'art work' being collected as an investment, this results in the criteria for assessing its performance changing from the artist's intentions to its market performance, i.e. percentage increase over x years.

An important feature in the adoption of the cited model of operation by the artist, has been its development with regard to functioning and operating within contained social conditions, the boundaries of which have been demarcated by the extent of art's social environment.

CONFLICT BETWEEN INTENTION AND RESPONSE

It was made quite clear from the results of The Centre For Behavioural Art Survey, that a large majority of people regarded a 'work of art' existing in a domestic space as a decoration, and then lower down the scale as an investment. The work of art was seen as reflecting, or reinforcing what was already the intended function or sensibility for that domestic space, not as a means of communicating something in its own right, and certainly it was not valued as a means of communicating the artist's intentions.

ARTWORK AS OBJECT

From a conversation with an art curator

What I think has happened in recent history is that the artwork has become 'object' in the sense that the artwork has become concerned with its own mediarisation and its own consumability and this has totally divorced the artist away from the concerns of ideology, social ideology and concepts of reality other than the reality of the possessional-object and I think that this kind of divorcement which has certainly accelerated in the last five or six years has created such a gulf between the potential... almost the historical direction that art seemed to be going in and where it has ended up now.

I think that the classical struggle to find aesthetic personal language (which is to my way of thinking totally meaningless) which most artists would say they are concerned with in some way was an idea that always happened in a difficult coexistence with the culture. But in the last five years you have had a different idea that the artist becomes part of the culture, part of a monetarist culture, and it celebrates the monetarism in the culture and this sort of development does happen... I mean it happens from time to time that artists get into this position, but the end result is that the artist becomes a kind of plaything, a kind of craftsman, and becomes some sort of puppet of the culture.

EXPECTATIONS AND DISAPPOINTMENT

In conceptual art quite often artists would proclaim various Socialist or Marxist meanings and messages for their works but they would actually operate well within the bandwidth of Capitalism and such a huge gulf; well it was ignored… As soon as the artist varies his audience outside the art-social environment (in other words an environment of people made up of art critics, collectors, people who are directly engaged and who would have some prior knowledge of the language that the artist employs, some prior knowledge of how to behave in relationship to an artwork) as soon as he moves outside this and engages directly with the world where people have other priorities and these other priorities are bigger priorities than engaging with art and the work itself has to communicate, has to have a connection, the audience has to see within it some function, some meaning, something to engage with. And therefore the work must be articulate and such a conflict between ideology and practice cannot exist because it will be seen—detected immediately—and people will become inhibited and just not deal with it. I mean, I remember hearing about Barry Flanagan bemoaning the fact that he left some sandbags—some sculptures—on the streets of Bristol I think it was, years ago, it was an idea to engage with people on the streets and he'd got these bags, sort of hessian bags, and he had filled them with sand and he left them around the street and the next day they were all gone… people just thought that they were bags of sand… They'd taken them away, and he was outraged: "How could this happen to my work!"

9

UNIVERSAL MEANING AND TRANSMISSIONAL NETWORKS

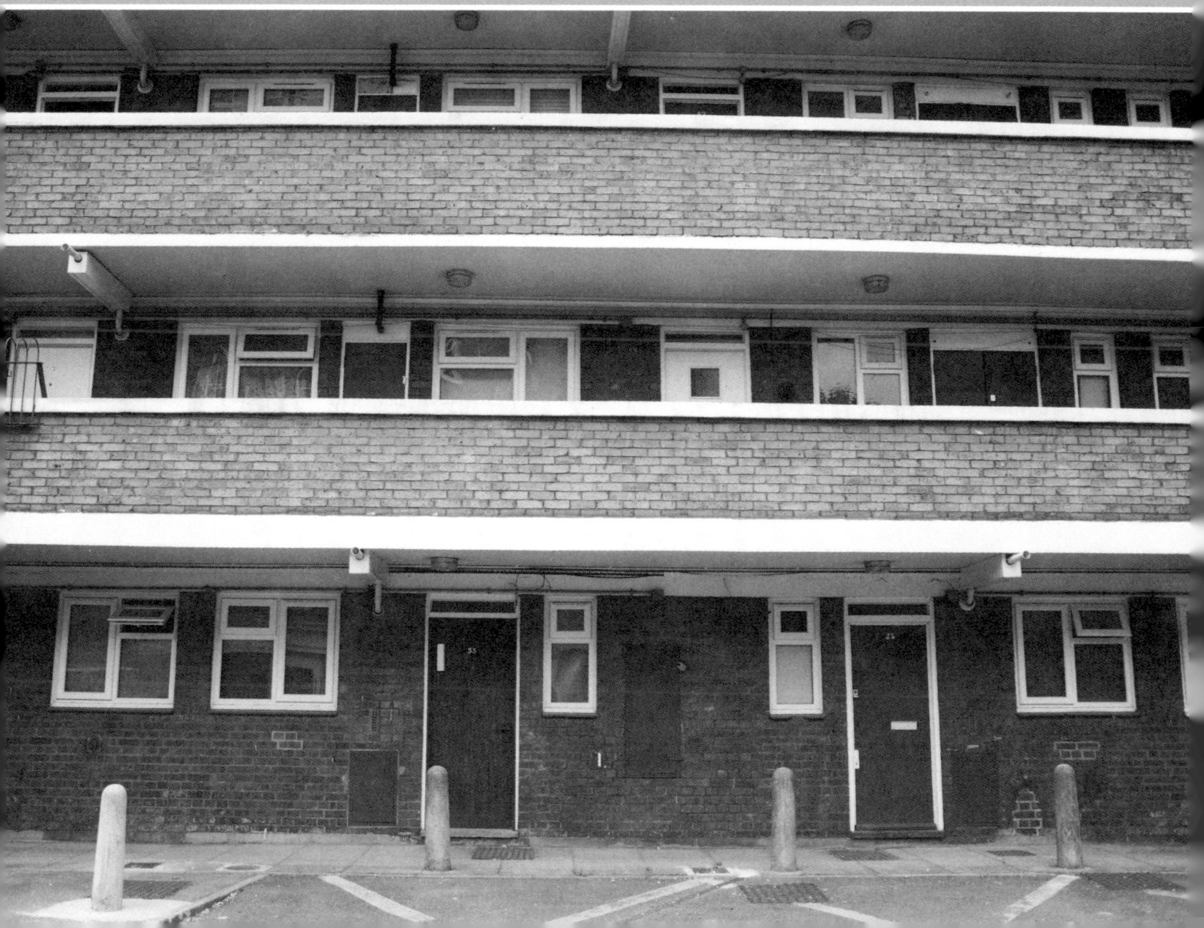

THE SEPARATION OF ART PRACTICE FROM MOST PEOPLE'S SOCIAL REALITY

The divorcing of art practice from a root in social reality has been a developing cultural process. A loss of a direct link with everyday experience has fostered notions that an artwork can acquire an independent reality and be perceived as a discreet object. Vested with an assumed independence from time and context the artwork is also free from any ideological base. Such a freedom is illusory, for the artwork can still be appropriated within the dominant value structure of our commodity centred culture. In fact the lack of a tie with social reality must considerably help ease the artwork's enmeshment into a structure of values that work against any manifestation of ideology. Reinforcement is provided by the artwork being locked into a transmissional relationship with the audience that physically distances them. In this relationship the audience is given the role of passive receiver, there being no provided means by which they can influence the transmitter. Transmissional communication is a major expression of an authoritative consciousness within our culture, dominating interpersonal perception and values. The distancing of self when in a position of transmitter, from others as receiver, is a tendency that stems from a consciousness founded on relative positions of authority, a more extreme manifestation being to perceive those in the role of receiver as objects. This has effectively been the result of recent practices. The artist has denied his audience a social reality, instead they have become unwilling appendages to the internal referencing of the transmitting object.

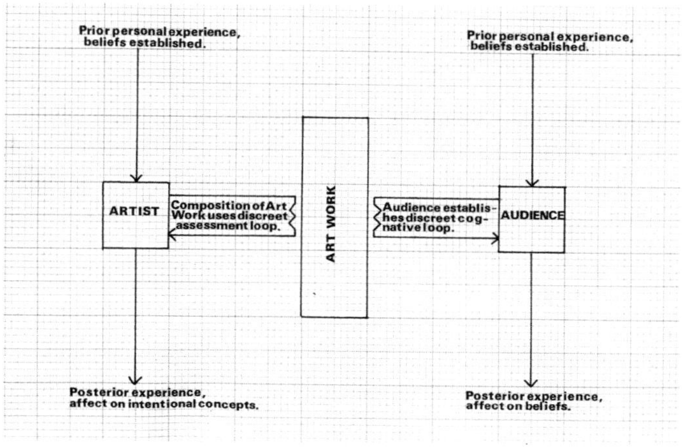

Relationship of artist to audience. Traditional model.

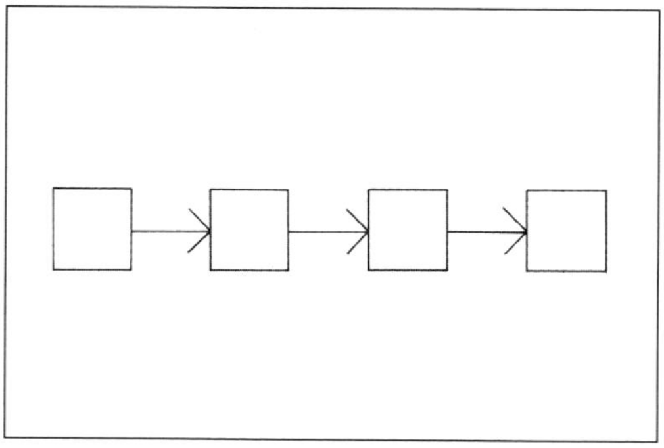

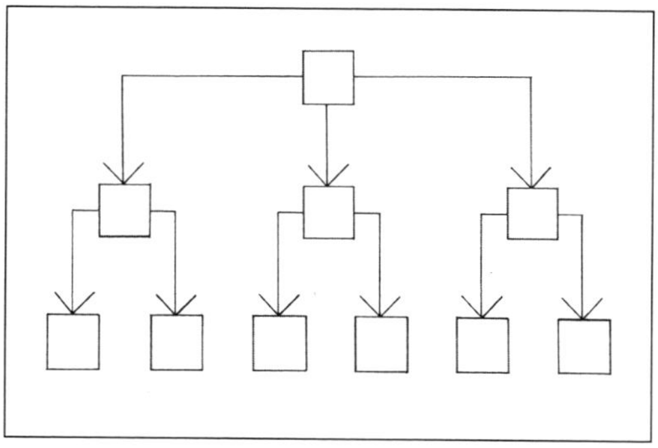

Two forms of transmissional network.

PERMANENCE AND IMMORTALITY

Another inhibitory consequence of this desire for permanence is that nearly all art we look at through art institutions is old, belonging to some past moment in culture, from which we appropriate what we can reinterpret as relevant to the present. It is my opinion that, rather than address the polemical issues of today in the community surrounding the museum, they have become disproportionately loaded up with objects, as monuments from the past, creating a psychological distance from those entering, from the here and now. But this is where most people encounter art, 'art objects', so that the potential relevance of art activity to the present is denied them. The idea of an ordered permanence, be it an institutionally arranged one, is undoubtedly attractive in defining a predictive world, but its almost complete dominance in the pre-occupations of the museum environment has further entrapped us into a culture preoccupied with its own heritage. Projecting the iconography of the past on to what is represented as a virtual present, and the attendant monumentality that it has been given, has led to the promotion of these objects as immortal, that radiate universal object-based truths to be emulated. But in reality, art is not universal, but contextual and dependent on social complexities, although the message from the mythology of art is otherwise.

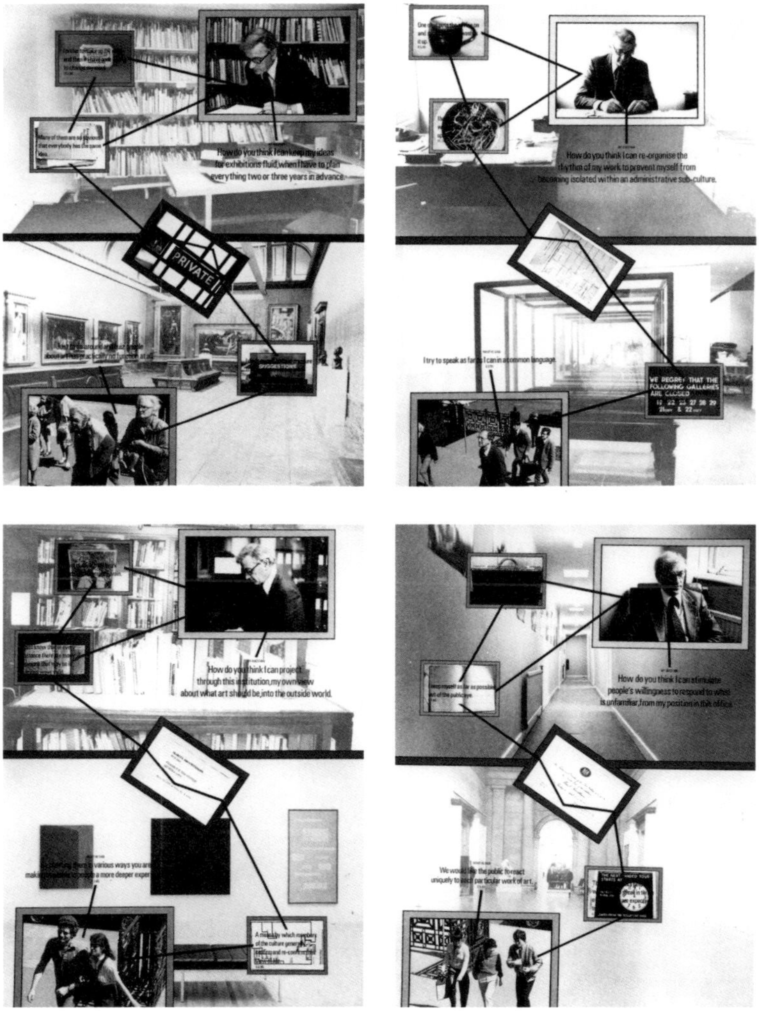

'From Inside This Institution'. Four panels in a row, 1–4: top to bottom, left to right.

ENVIRONMENTAL MESSAGE TRANSMISSION

Going home at the end of the working day is a fundamental journey, a routine between different realities that are associated with quite separated psychologies and behaviours, and it is a journey undertaken by more or less anyone and everyone at some point. Going home is usually an established behaviour routine undertaken on 'automatic,' as you go through a process of being in transit. The journey is undertaken in a channel, both psychological and physical, in which movement through a fluid and entropic world is made to feel certain. By centering the work 'Going Home' on Bond Street Station, Oxford Street, in London's West End in the rush hour at 5pm during the week, it focusses on a fundamental parameter of social behaviour where an individual is thrown into a situation which at first sight might seem chaotic and complex, but where there can also be seen to be an implicit society made up of a throng of others also in movement. For in the seeming chaos there is an underlying code of behaviour that maintains a structure, an order in the way people move in relation to each other as they all progress in a steady momentum, which is hard for an individual to resist or counter. Viewing this progression as an event that has both symbolical and psychological ramifications that lead from the conscious reality symbolised by the chaotic world of Oxford Street at this time of day, through the specially encoded, engineered channel that becomes a tunnel and a funnel into the unconscious underworld below, where the individual is then whisked off by train to the secure environment of home.

The configuration of people in transit at any one time is not entirely unpredictable in that individuals do have routines, but a person entering into this channel is likely to encounter a diverse, fast moving, potentially unstable situation that is ultimately unmemorable. But here the paradox is that configurations of people are both informal in their fleeting composition, but also formal in that a person understands the conventions surrounding their personal space and their relationships with others while in transit. The sequence of physical environments that enable order in the process of transition, the steps leading down from the street into the booking hall, the ticket barriers, escalators, etc, all create a time line to the process of transition that is quite difficult to reverse once engaged. However, the language of the environment you pass through on your way, while perhaps on the periphery of your consciousness, is still registering messages that reflect the values and beliefs of the society that has moulded the very fabric you are encountering, and as a stream of multichannel information bombarding your sensory system is also providing a psychological framework of security. So behind the creation of this physical environment there are beliefs and aspirations somewhere, that are hidden, but still omnipresent in the physical fabric of the place. Behind these beliefs and aspirations there are ideologies, philosophical outlooks and visions, that influence the direction of cultural endeavour and expression and, importantly, validation.

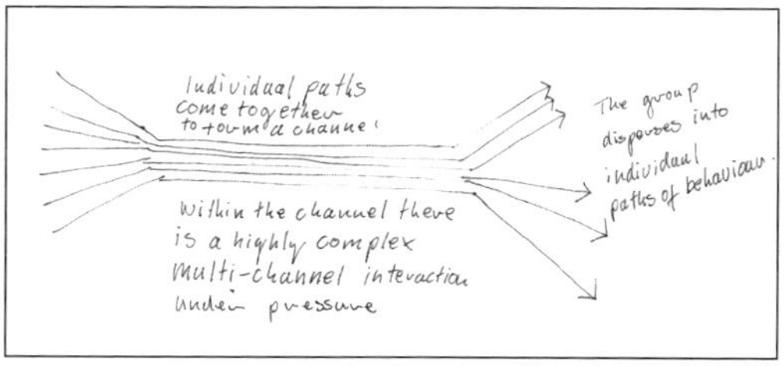

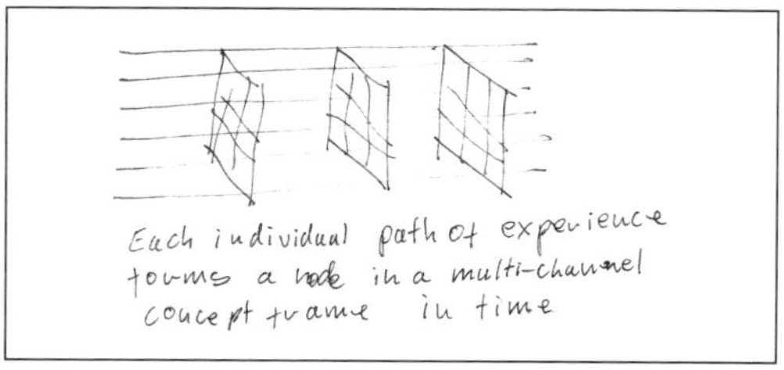

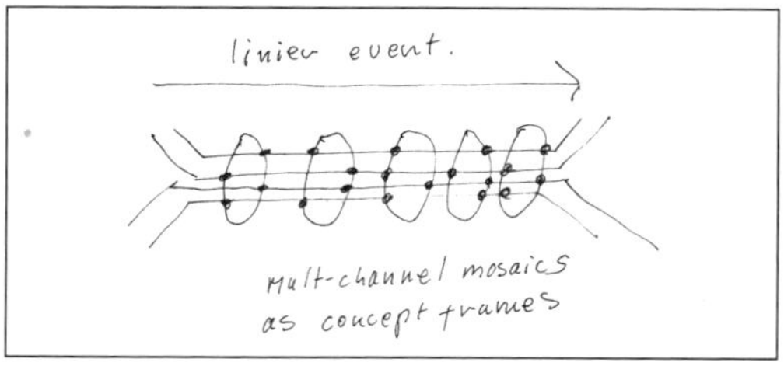

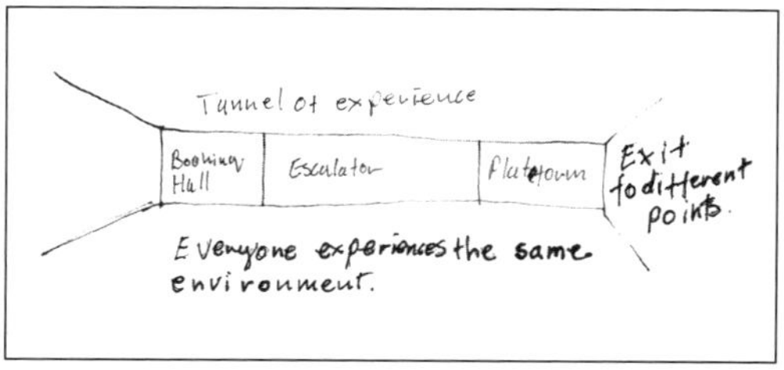

RANDOM NETWORKS

I consider that the relevance of 'networks' to art practice is that in communication and interpersonal relationships, networks are the very parameters to society, for they not only mould our consciousness but also denote to us how we experience secondary as well as primary sources of information. Our position within or in relation to a communication network, and the nature of the channels by which information flows through to us has a major influence of how we are going to perceive reality, in that it will determine what, when and how we receive information. While the idea of networks, especially social ones, is abstract, in that networks don't have solid forms, that we still all have a relationship with many at the same time is implicitly understood by us, and this relationship will be a major preoccupation in our daily lives. The importance of networks for us, is that how we receive and impart information affects how we relate to other people, and consequently fashions our interpersonal realm. Thus there are networks that are experienced directly as primary social realms, and networks that are indirectly experienced as secondary information via another medium, that is referential to a remote experience from ourselves. While art practice involves both primary and secondary experience it usually falls within the realm of what I call secondary communication networks where in all cases there is a process of encoding and decoding of a symbolic language that will be fundamental to the form the message takes. The three basic elements to a secondary network are encoding of message, transmission of message and decoding of message, with a desired optimum of parity between the cognition of what is encoded with what is decoded at the other end. A fundamental distinction can be made between those networks where the message/information is unidirected as in a transmission between A and B, where B has no influence on the encoding process of A as optimised in the radio broadcast, and where A and B are in an exchange as in a conversation on a phone, where both can have a mediating influence on each other, i.e. there is a two way flow. I see an important influence between the forms different networks take, and the state of interpersonal consciousness being formed by an individual who is connected in a receptive mode in some way. So that on one hand in a purely transmissional network, the encoder is quite separate from the decoder, to the point that recognition of the latter is usually nominal or abstracted, giving rise to an object based perception of the receiver, where it is seen as reductive and passive. In complete contrast a network of exchange is built upon the dynamic principal that each individual is both encoder and decoder, and that as such there is the basic recognition of another as a dynamic entity. Moreover in a mode of exchange, reductive perceptions can be replaced by perceptions that acknowledge the complexity of the other person. i.e. person centred perception. In the transmissional network the resulting reductive perceptual mode is linked to an ideological stance of determinism as expressed in a hierarchical network of people as statistics and objects. However a network in the mode of exchange can lead to an ideology of mutuality and agreement. Of course, I acknowledge that there is also the possibility of those within a network changing it, so as to create another cognitive framework, in which the *modus operandi* of the fabric of the network can be altered. In daily life the all-embracing totality of the social and communication networks into which people find themselves locked, means that an individual's psychology is largely set or given by the network and therefore the ideological transformation of a network by those caught up within it is a rare event. On an everyday basis the experience of the interpersonal networks we find ourselves encountering consists of constantly fluid, and random information that bombards us from all sides. In our decoding mode we make sense of this bombardment in our attempts to create a predictive order from the information we have come across, and also how that information is to be stored so as to be acted upon later. While actual experience of an event is ultimately likely to be more meaningful than referential experience, an experience that has been relayed to you by someone or something else, it is the latter that will exert the major influence on our formation of attitudes, beliefs, and consequently actions. This is because relayed referential transmissions are important to stability and meaning in our perception of ourselves and of our future, and thus an all embracing environment of symbols is provided that maintains the referential transmissions and signs which can exist peripherally in relation to our focus of priorities. These peripheral signs nevertheless provide us with constant messages about attitudes and behaviour. The physical world, the landscape in which we operate, its composition and fabrication are essential elements in the perception of constants; whether its fabrication is in wood or concrete, straw or brick, gives us different messages. But rarely is the construction of the physical world made to be dynamically responsive to the fluidity in people's behaviour, the onus being on individual groups to adapt, alter, change in relation to a perceived immovable constant. So while the focus of priorities and behaviours can evolve as behaviours of exchange, the fabric of the environment in which those behaviours take place remains as an unchanging, continual transmission. As a passive constant it provides the psychological framework upon which other immediate, fluid psychologies are founded and grow. The physical world as a product of culture, consists of layers of signs which are in competition for our attention creating an encoded jungle. This jungle is transmitting messages that are both in focus and unfocussed existing on the periphery, these transmissions are filtered by us in degrees from passive to active according to how they figure in relation to central priorities. My point here is that different networks can exist, even co-exist in the same psychological realm of the individual, and indeed our relationship to them can change as we move through the landscape of reality.

So in one sense nothing is fixed, we are all in a network, that is a potential jungle, a tangled fabric of different transmitting channels. In our search for certainty, in projecting probability onto what we encounter, complexity is reduced in the information we are receiving; the result especially from already encoded, authoritatively projected information is to accept the stability inherent in what is presented. In this sense there is an innate tendency to want to believe, for the other option of disbelief is ultimately leading to far more complex ramifications.

Random networks are, I consider, of particular philosophical interest in speculating about possible states of being in the society between people.

10
THE REALITY OF RELATIVITY IN MEANING

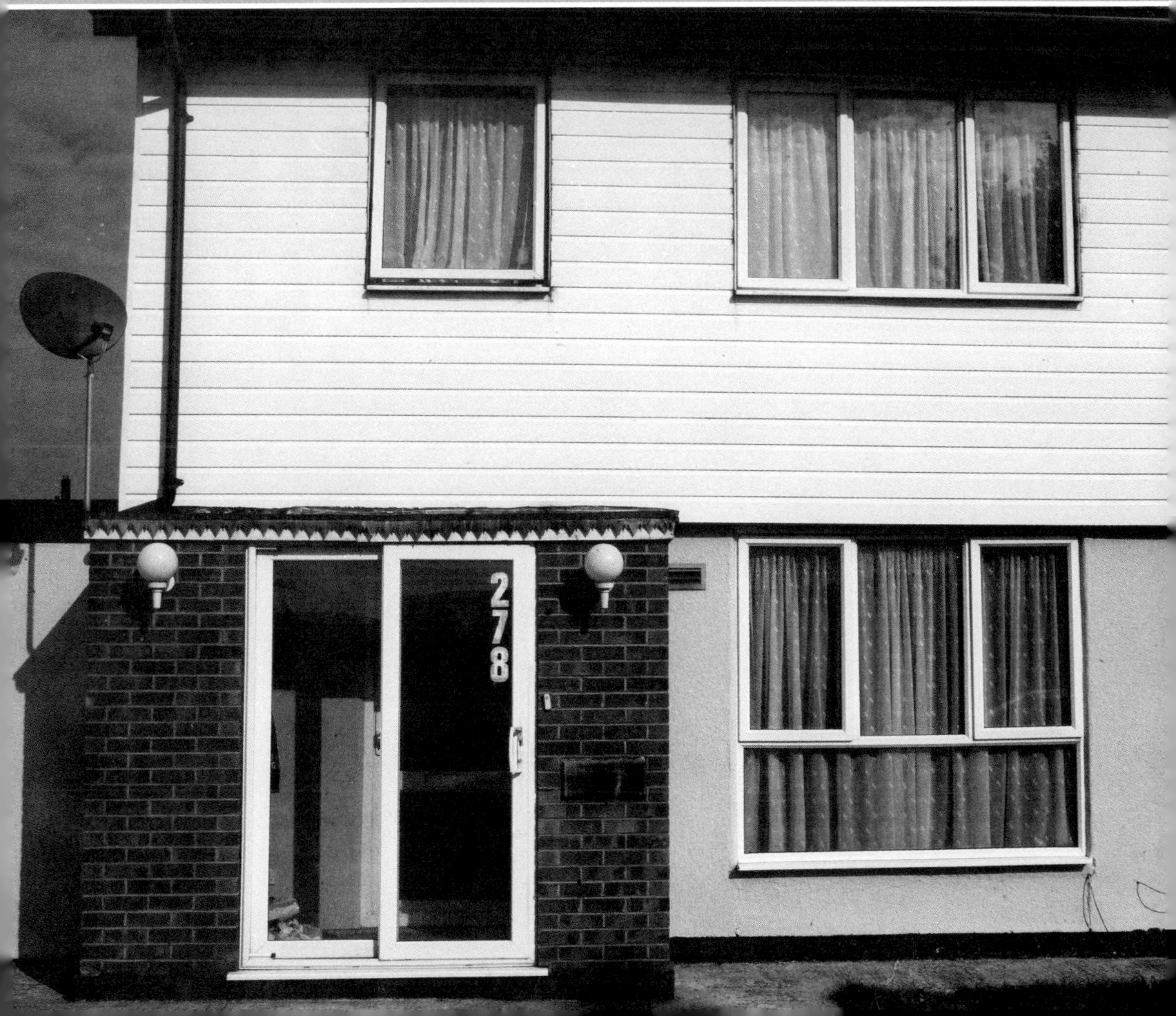

THE WORLD THAT CONFRONTS ME EVERYDAY

Every day, when I wake up, when I get out of bed, it is the world that confronts me—the contemporary reality in which I live out my day—that has an immediate meaning, an immediate relevance. I see that the fabric of this daily reality is filled with signs and symbols that radiate their messages to me without my intervening or having any influence on them, constructing the consciousness I have of myself and the world in which I live. Thus, embedded within the very physical fabric of my environment is a whole spectrum of signs, symbols that exist as objects, and which individually and collectively state to me the ideological outlook of the culture from which they derived.

My daily world is crammed full of objects that exist on different physical scales, with completely varied materials, shapes and functions. For example, any street that I walk down is full of objects, buildings, cars, street signs, shop window displays of various kinds, to the extent that even people are perceptually reduced to the level of objects. In fact, as I walk down the street the entire physical nature of the environment is revealed as an overt statement of the ideological parameters on which the dominant, institutional culture is founded.

Fundamental to the institutional culture is a consciousness of social power that is ultimately deterministic and which is communicated to people through the possession of objects. Thus, whether it be through the buildings I encounter during my day, or the domestic objects I use at home, it is by our own possession of, and desire for possession of objects, that the culture can demonstrate to us statements of the social power it has vested in those objects. The inter-relationship between objects and people is expressed culturally in visual languages that have achieved levels of sophistication, and which implicitly, and sometimes explicitly, are used by the individual to transmit their identity and social power to others.

MACRO TO MICRO

An important area of the work 'Macro To Micro' centred on the randomness of what we perceive, and how order is created by ourselves and then projected onto reality. Thus we can decide in advance at what different level of resolution we are going to view reality, and different levels will generate different complexities of information about the same thing. So in fluid, transient networks of exchange, nothing is fixed, nothing can be completely predicted as certain, for changing levels of resolution will alone generate seemingly quite different realms of meaning. Our everyday encounter with reality is in truth an encounter with a random variable, a highly fragmented random variable which we order ourselves. In contemporary culture this is expressed as a jungle of multichannel fragments that become signs, that we can extrapolate into clusters of meaning that give us the perceptual models of what we want to see, and thus from one event there may be as many versions of what happened as there are witnesses.

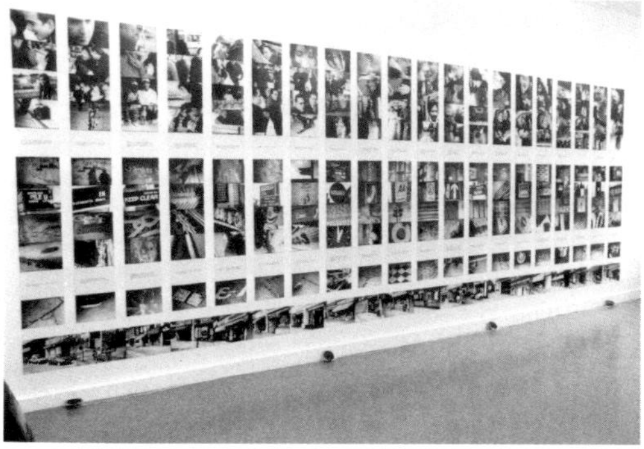

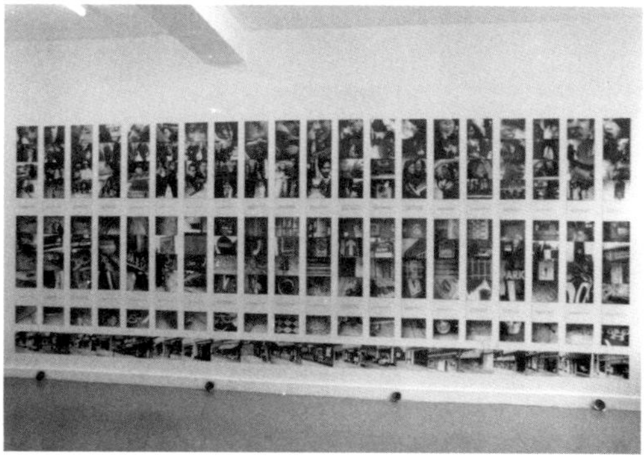

The installation of 'Macro To Micro' at the Laure Genillard Gallery, London.

VISITORS TALKING ABOUT THEIR EXPERIENCE AT LEEDS CITY ART GALLERY

SW Yes, well, looking at this can of soup, the last one.
—Well, that reminds me of the old TV series, the American TV series, the Alphabet Soup, it reminds me of Superman comics and such like DC comics, in a way alphabet soup was something that was never available and only later introduced, it's something which I associate with everything tasting the same, all soups have the same distinctive taste, just change the colour or change the consistency it's also the object itself.

SW Yes, so we are looking at this can.
—Yes, well this can reminds me of multi-nationals taking over the, the food industry and just giving you churned out anything, you know eating letters, eating words, it shows how ridiculous food can be when you're eating words and you can play with it, eat your favourite book or whatever, but it's also a sign that the artist can latch on to anything and make money out of it, and this was a person who worked for advertising and so he associated things with names, associated art with names, and so he went in and just tried to rip off the art industry, could have been anything, could have been Campbells, could have been Heinz, it's totally arbitrary.
SW Do you think Campbells was ripping off the food industry.
—They were making the food industry.
SW Yes, like ripping off the consumer or something, so you think perhaps the artist and Campbells were in it together.
—Its all very, yes gimmicky, I mean the way they're making food into shapes, just you eat it, and the artist has latched onto one of them, just to I don't know.

SW And now we are looking at the can of soup here, what immediately does that bring to mind.
—I think the fact that it's vegetarian soup, and I have got a vegetarian in the family, fairly homely sort of connotations I think with this one, and a couple of days ago I went to a photographic exhibition and there was a can of soup, pouring out, the jug was pouring out tomatoes into the can and I think it just conjures up advertising, how we are really being got at by the media.
SW So you are thinking it's a sort of modern image, a sort of McLuhan…
—Yes I think it has a certain modern image, I think it makes me laugh a bit, I think it slightly humorous that people should bother to do a picture of a can of soup.
SW And you said interestingly that it's about being about us being got at by the media, how does that come through do you think in this particular picture…
—Well it just seemed to me an advert for a can of soup, nothing more or less, and it's amusing that somebody would present that as an art picture.
SW Perhaps it's vegetarian that has a significance for you.
—Family significance nothing more than that really.
SW Does it give you an idea of modern living, of convenience.
—Of quite yes, yes it does very much so, you know condensed soup, more than one use, I associate it with the food business of which I am quite interested, I don't particularly appreciate it as an art form.

SW Yes, now we're looking at the Campbell's soup can.
—Is it, its olden days, anyway old, it's an old label anyway.
—No. cos there's no weight on it at all.
—No, when I get Campbells, my meat balls, they don't have all this on it.
—That's just the drawing isn't it, to describe itself it does look like the 50s.
—To me it looks old anyway.
SW Yes, well, it probably is quite old, do you think it's like a modern way of eating or…
—Yes, modern, it's modern, know what I mean, some human being hasn't got time and you need to get something to eat just like that.
—It'd be easy.
SW Sort of convenient.
—It doesn't take long to warm up or anything. It's like a convenient picture.
SW Is that what you eat?
—Yes, meatballs, Heinz's soup.
—Campbells.
—Yes, the label's got a lot more better nowadays though, got more colour in them and things like that.
—Just convenient that picture isn't it.
SW That's interesting, you think it's just convenient, I mean do you think it's better eating just out of tins like that.
—Yes, it is when you're on your own and things like that, but that, it's got no picture, it's got no colour in it, I mean I don't know whether it did when you took it, but…
—It's like going to the shop and it's a convenience, that's what the picture is, just a convenience. But it's alphabetical soup, vegetarian, whatever it says, vegetable soup, it's got no colour in, or picture what the soup looks like, I like a picture on mine, see what it's like when it's warmed up.
SW On the front?
—Yes
—Like its boring but convenient, you can just have it when you want it.

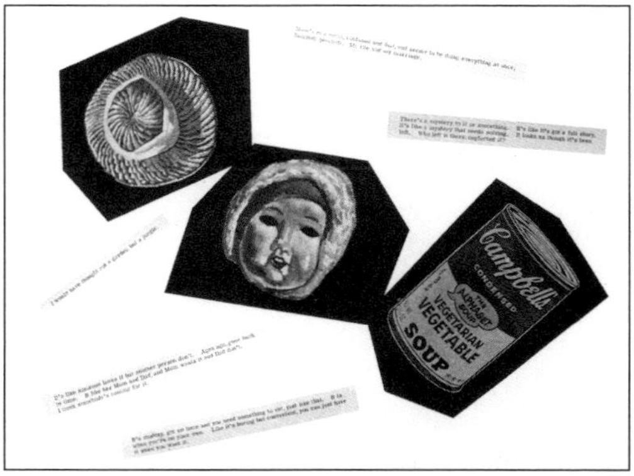

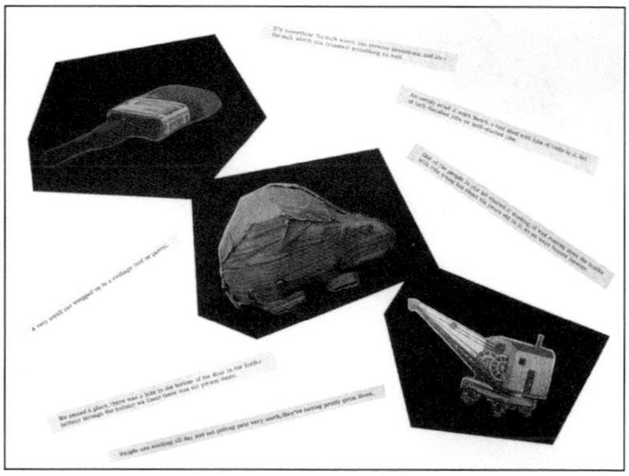

Display Boards from the work 'From Different Worlds' presented at Leeds City Art Gallery.

LAYERING PRIVATE LANGUAGE ONTO THE FABRIC OF THE ENVIRONMENT

A crucial role in the exhibition of language, of a group's private signs was that it defined a territory, it exhibited the difference between their values and beliefs, but this was not some separate island, it did so by transforming the existing fabric of the estate, that belonged to the world in which it was in opposition. The exhibition of language apart from 'Tagging' the environment took the form of dress codes, and behaviours previously associated with youth culture such as dancing, walking down the High Street in swaggering groups etc. Dress codes were an appropriation of existing inexpensive items such as chains, locks, studs and the famous safety pin, or ex-army surplus garments which were purposefully trashed, ripped etc., the result being to give new meaning by being put together in combinations and circumstances that were deemed unacceptable outside the group, but reinforcing on the inside.

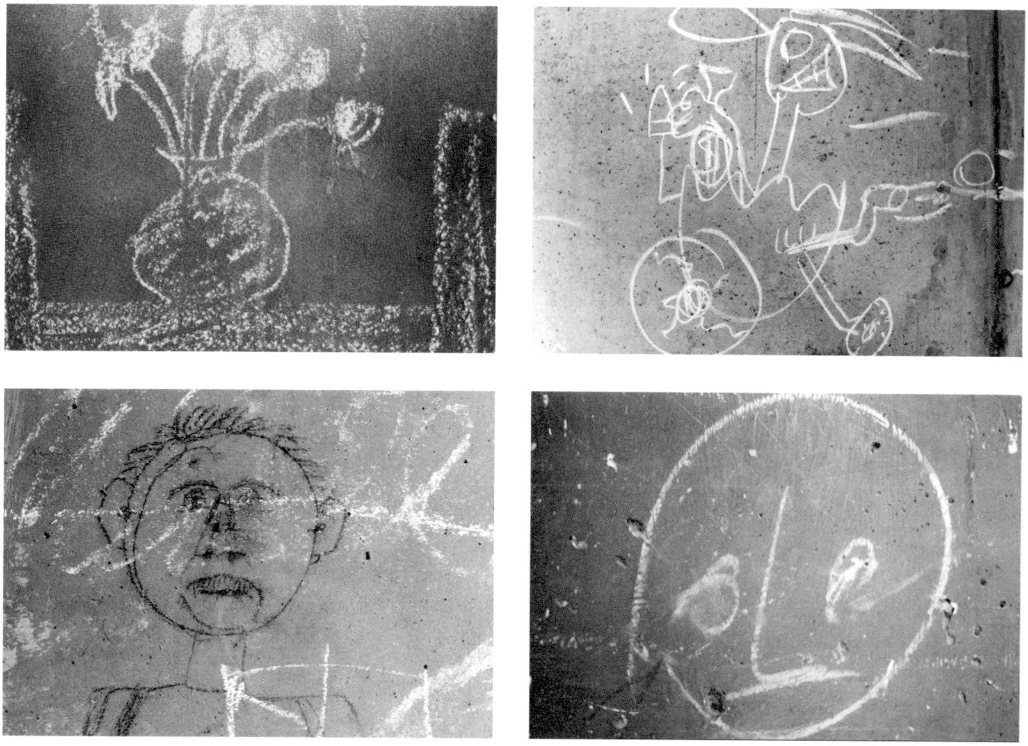

Wall drawings made by children in West Berlin at the base of the buildings in which they lived.

11

INSIDE THE MUSEUM: THE ARTWORK AS EMULATIVE ICON

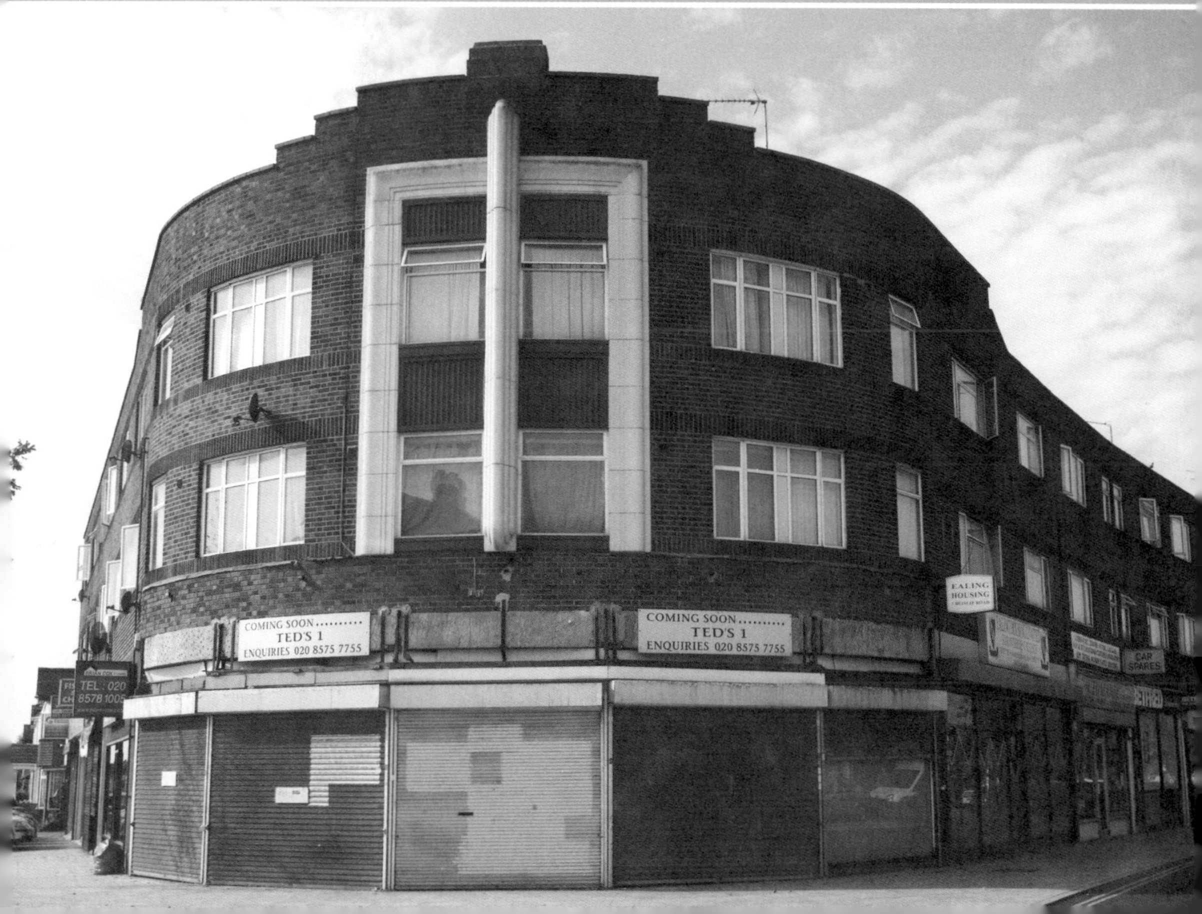

THE MUSEUM AS RESTRICTED CULTURAL SPACE

Conversation, Andrew Wilson and Stephen Willats

AW Art can be self-fulfilling in the sense that if it is validated by the museum then that is a validation for that art's continued state of existence and development.
SW Well, very much so. I think that the museum is this highly restricted space but also we have to remember that it also represents the idealisations, projections and beliefs of the culture. These are the beliefs of a certain section of the culture and a section that is authoritatively in control. On entering the museum one is entering into a highly determined message and the objects in the museum are referenced to this message.
AW So you are saying that on entering into the museum you are entering into a map of how the dominant culture wishes to present itself?
SW Exactly that. Curiously enough most museums represent the past and the past is appropriated to the present by the present culture so the past proposes a sort of immortality—a continuum—to the present. I have always been fascinated by the way in which human beings make signs: to denote the past, the present and the future, and they coexist. But in the museum, the future is generally denied in the terms of any polemical vision and it is descriptive, in the sense that the future is referenced to as a kind of unchallenged continuum of the present. The idea of any polemical intervention, or of any idea of dealing with the issues of reality external to the museum (and certainly the kind of future outcome of those realities) is denied within the sanctum of the museum. The museum represents this idealised and highly tranquil continuum divorced from reality. So, in a way you are absolutely right. There is this self-fulfilling perpetuation within the museum structures and its contents, but it is highly mediated and is certainly not a casual event.

ATTITUDE CONFORMITY IN REACTING TO ART

Discussion between Stephen Willats and Michael Compton, curator, Tate Gallery

SW Would you like some sort of way of communicating more with the audience or finding out how they respond to things.

MC It would be extremely difficult because the field of art even more than other fields is a field in which people speak in terms of what they are expected to say, in my opinion, because art is so much about attitudes and so on the person you are speaking to about art is probably consciously or unconsciously thinking what would be an appropriate attitude to take, you know if you were cultured and so on you would feel that you ought to have a certain response to Mondrian or Malevich or to Picasso or more recent artists depending on your stance. And therefore you really cannot believe a word that people say about art in my opinion, and that is to say you can't believe it at face value you have to know the person quite well to understand what they are saying in relation to some particular work of art or some particular exhibition.

RESPONSE TO THE EXHIBITION 'TRANSFORMERS'

From a discussion with John Millard, Director of the Laing Art Gallery, Newcastle

JM It is quite difficult to tell but just before your exhibition opened at the end of the previous exhibition we had a visitors' survey done, and it surprised us actually, and presumably the findings carried on during your exhibition as well, that during that visitors' survey we identified as one of the bulge groups for our audience, had been clerical workers from Newcastle. In fact without knowing it, when we put together your exhibition we targeted one of the existing audience from the Laing and I know that they have continued to come for Transformers as well. It is difficult to gauge audience reaction. One of the things I did notice was how a few works, some works particularly attracted attention, I don't know if it is the same else where, but certainly 'Difficult Boy In A Concrete Block' in the Home section, and in the Night section 'Escape With Us Into The Night'.

SW I think there is a separation between the public's engagement with my works and their engagement with the world of art, for my works are developed as public works I mean the installation 'Between Straight Lines' was devised as a public work and it is a work for people that are not necessarily vested with the knowledge of the history of art. So these works are about communication, about engaging with people, and the strategies I employ are all about that, so it doesn't surprise me that a piece like 'Difficult Boy In A Concrete Block' maybe poses a lot of problematics for somebody in the art world who's concerned with modernistic theories about abstraction and so on. For here is a work about unemployment, directly engaged with an issue that concerns people in the world today and the way in which the whole piece is presented and structured is all about communicating to people about those issues, so it doesn't surprise me at all if people want to engage with them. One thing that came out of this from my point of view as the artist was that my original motivation to make an installation and an exhibition that demonstrated a model of practice, did in some way fail to communicate to those people that were in a position to further externalize these ideas within the art world, principally in London reviewers for art magazines and so on, they did apart from one or two exceptions fail to attend to that project.

GOING BEYOND THE ICON

Art as social process opens up the possibility of new functions for an artwork, by denying any object base, but as I have said this in itself renders practice beyond the boundaries of what will currently by legitimized by the institutions of the dominant culture. And this is what is difficult for the artist to accept, that when approval from the dominant culture's institutions is not forthcoming for art as social process, it does not mean that it is 'bad art' and should be discontinued, but it simply needs to be recognized that it cannot operate within the criteria of the institutions. Other criteria for success should be embraced that embody the work's social performance, and other groups of people sought who are outside the existing institutional set-up to provide a new critique for practice that is consistent with the ideological direction of art as social process. Instead of the cult of individualism, so central to approval within the dominant culture, mutually based co-operations should be sought with other artists also working within a framework of counter consciousness. Only when a strong body of work is simultaneously being undertaken by different artists operating outside an object-based territory, who are also in communication with each other, will the lure and power of institutional individualism be neutralized. For the pragmatics of sustaining an individual practice, to the extent that it has an effect that can extend beyond just a very immediate and personal context necessitates a community that is as strong as the dominant culture's institutions and which can provide a real support.

12
RETHINKING THE ICONOGRAPHY OF ART

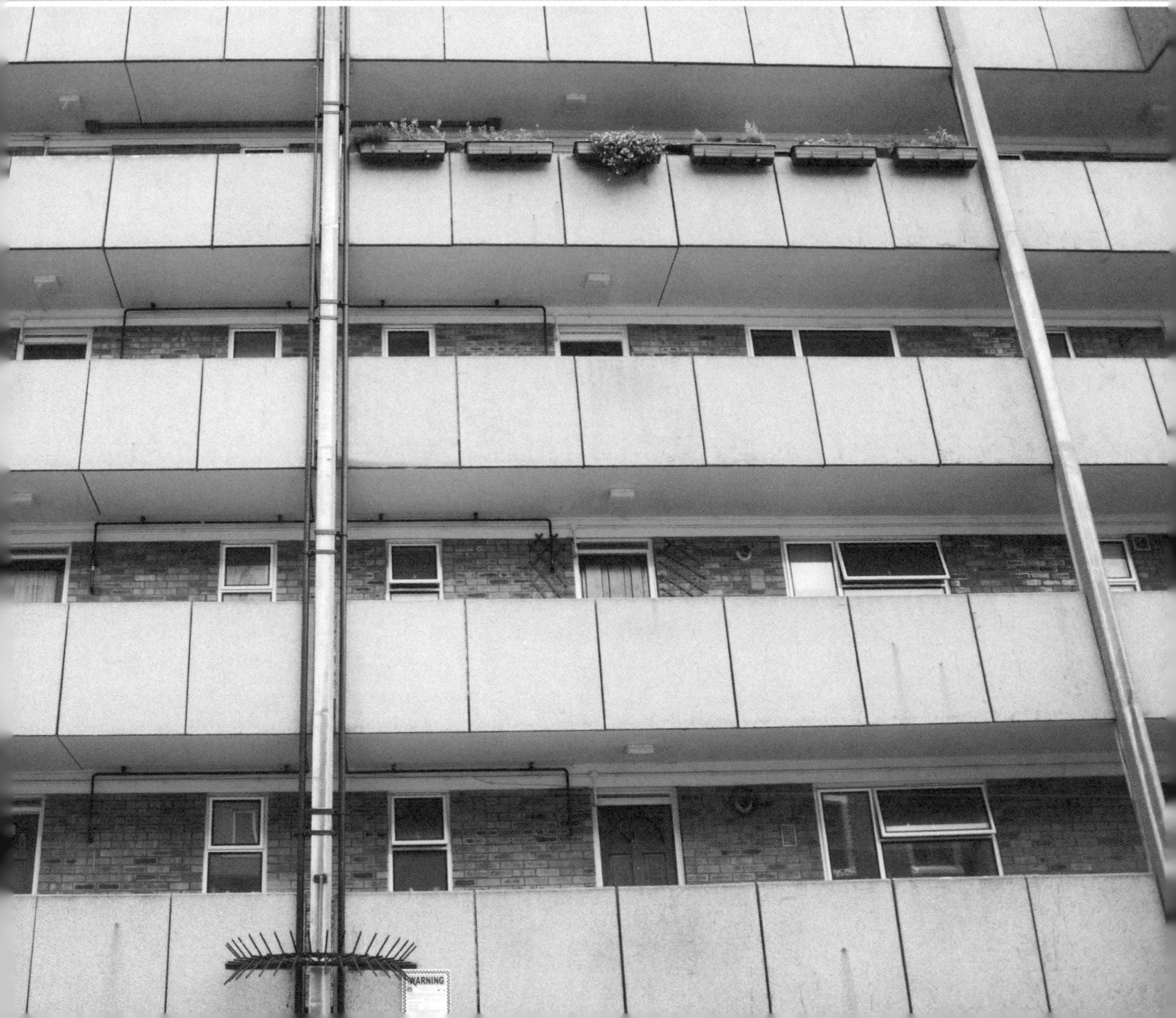

THE FAILURE OF STYLISM

Artists have attempted to give their work inside art institutions a social connection in a number of ways, the most important being by the synthesising of images and objects from the street, and then presenting them as art objects. Another strategy, and one that was doomed to fail immediately, was the taking of art works normally bound to the inside of these institutions and then repositioning them on the street. When this was tried they simply could not be read by the audience and more often than not were destroyed. Unfortunately the preoccupation by artists with the images of advertising also fails to achieve a cultural meaning beyond art institutions but for completely different reasons. The thinking was that by recycling the imagery of advertising and, in the process, transforming it in an artwork artists could build up a semiotic language that would have the availability of advertising strategies. Artists mimicked the visual composition and coding used in advertising but only the stylistic visual formats of single frame presentations, representing images that were devised and deterministically employed by the dominant culture, as refined art objects.

These attempts to widen an artwork's meaning by re-using already idealised images, those of the dominant culture, have been doomed by that very fact. As previously stated, the dominate culture's idealised images are object-based, reducing people and social relationships to objects and property; so the imitation of these images by implication renders the artwork object-based as well, it simply becomes stylistic representations of advertising. Both approaches towards seeking greater social meaning do nevertheless typify the growing awareness by artists that they should seek to resolve this issue.

EMBRACING COMPLEXITY

The idea that seems to be rigidly fixed in art administrators' and artists' outlooks when talking about engaging with the so called 'general public', is that people can't or don't want to handle 'complex', 'difficult' concepts. From my experience when working with vastly different communities such a notion is plain rubbish! However this idea does still persist despite everyone's disclaimers especially when 'targeting' working class communities and the resulting patronising, simplistic attitudes and overtures that attempt to involve the 'general public' in art are easily seen as just that, and quite naturally rejected. The traditional 'middle class' attitude towards the 'working class' embodies just this trait, where the simplicity of language routed and fixed in a particular context is perceived to be less rich in meaning than the elaborated codes of the upwardly mobile. The psychologist Basil Bernstein showed in his work in the early 1960s that meaning surrounding a narrowly derived language tied to a specific context, is indeed richer than a loosely defined language tied to nothing in particular. However such a restricted language does require a prior knowledge of its references. Thus contextually routed languages are simply not transferable without some orientation and recognition that the meaning is related and relevant to one's own priorities. And this is the dilemma for the artist, that unless his use of language is seen to contain relevant meanings for individual members of the 'general public', nothing is going to happen at all, it is simply a matter of context.

PUNK AT THE POINT OF ORIGIN

This was a psychological capsule, defined as a territory by layering onto the fabric of the building marks, what later in the 80s would be called 'Tags', that were important points of reference for giving the feeling of being on the inside, and also for keeping other people out. Sometimes interventions were made directly into the material fabric of the building to create holes, or bits of the building were used to form barriers, especially at the end of corridors, or in the stairwells or in the sheds. In my work on the Highfields Estate I eventually followed groups into the wasteland where they had constructed camps out of items discarded, or that could be removed in the outside world to create a realm in which they could hide out of the reach of the prying eyes of authority. A variety of objects were transported through the separating wire fence and into the wasteland to be given a new meaning in the context of the camp. Seats from abandoned cars, sections of corrugated iron, pots and pans are items you might expect but many of the things found there had required a complete change of function, such as embodied in the can of 'Evostick' glue which in one context is for sticking material together, but in the other world of the camp fire became a catalyst for anarchistic wild behaviour. Cars were stolen and driven into the wasteland and then set alight, the rusting hulks being left all over The Lurky Place as monuments to the group's behaviours.

'Punk' as an exciting outburst of alienated protest, a revolting revolt against what was seen as the increasingly corporate, clone-like normative norms and values of the dominate society, became highly visible on the street in the late '70s. As I first experienced it in West London suburbs, the discernible origins of what became formalised as Punk made their appearance around 1976–78. To me then, Punk was a way of life, a locally generated culture based on contextual values and self-organisation, that was an energetic rejection of the authoritative, imposed, universal idealisations projected by the world of the 'professional', which were supported by a validating criteria that was quite out of the reach of most people, certainly those living on the housing estates in West London. This validating criteria was socially exclusive and expensive but was held up as a prerequisite for legitimising creativity, determining what was acceptable, i.e. good, and what was unacceptable, i.e. bad. But such notions were irrelevant to Punk in its original form, for what was now to become important was the meaning creativity had within the restricted context of the community in which the creativity arose, maybe in reality just a few friends in a front living room or an outer suburban housing estate.

The DIY ethic that became the basis of Punk went beyond music, beyond the DIY recordings it became known for, and extended into publishing xeroxed fanzines, which at the outset while following local bands were also 'news based' but new for a restricted group from a particular place, e.g. one fanzine titled the Sunday Mirror came from Hayes in West London. Another important territory of expression that again originated out of what was available to small groupings were dress codes that eventually got to the point of involving the production of clothes through outlets such as Kensington Market. Of course, underlying all of these cultural manifestations were tangential attitudes, language and behaviour, that were in response to the new political agenda that was beginning to kick in as momentum got going for the 1980s.

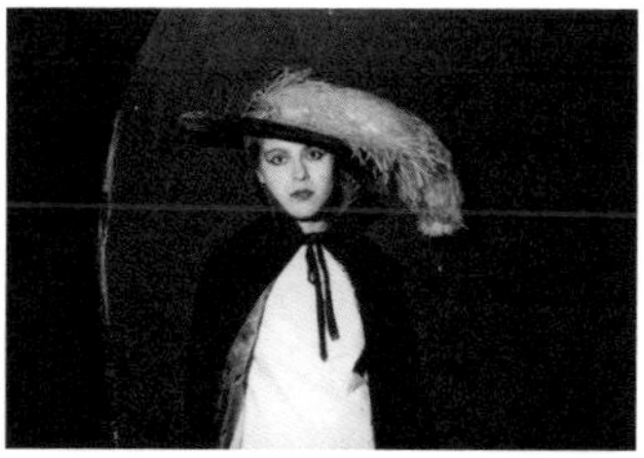
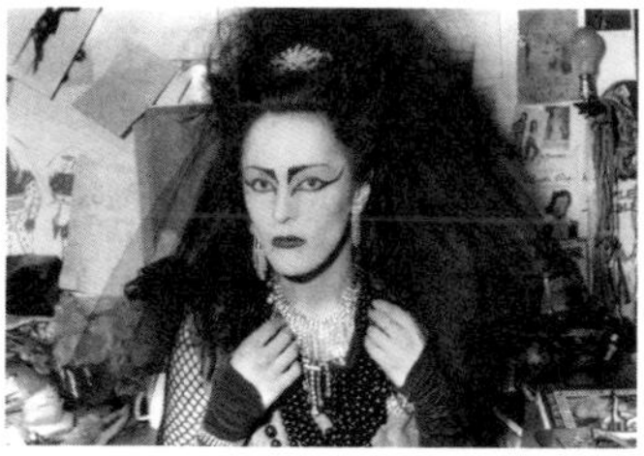
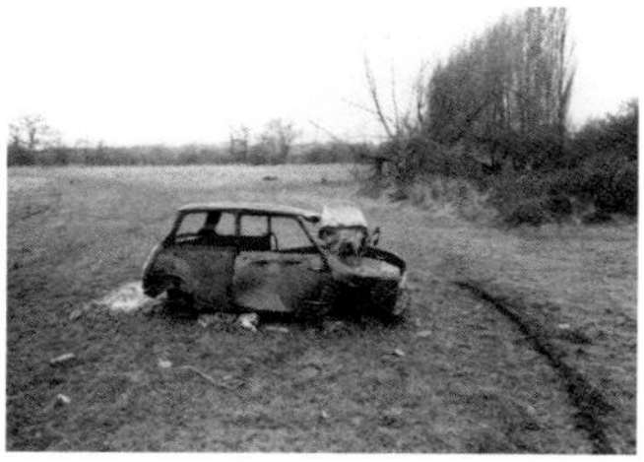
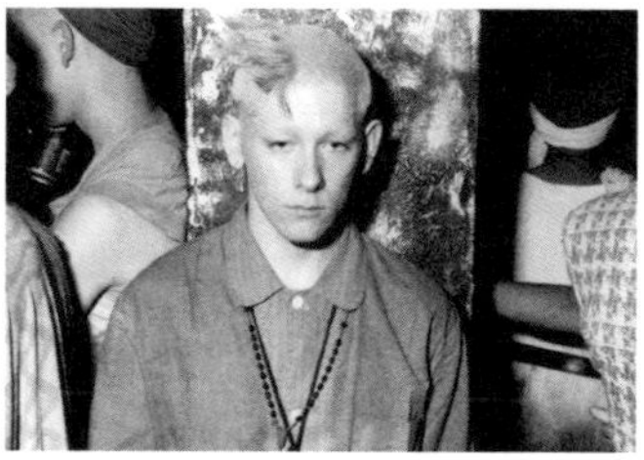
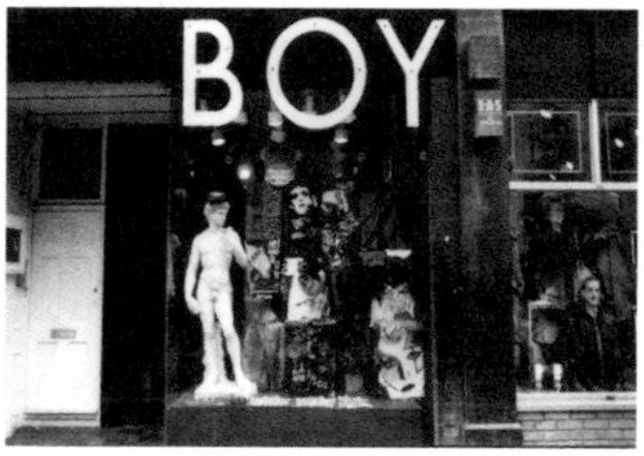

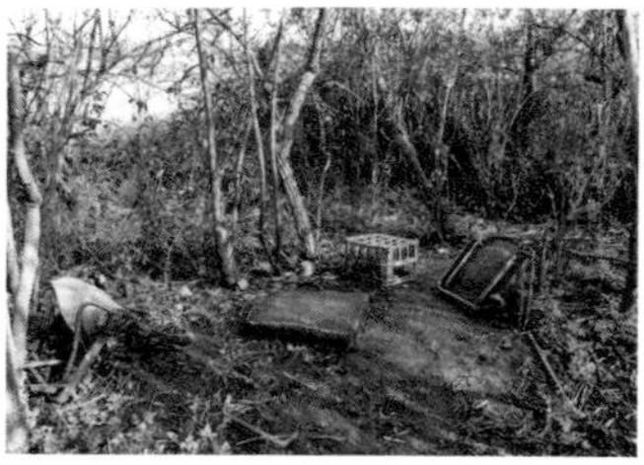

Top left, top centre, below left: At the Cha Cha Club; Below centre: Boy in the Kings Road;
Top right, below right: Inside The Lurky Place, Hayes, West London.

SUBLIMINAL MESSAGES OF OBJECTS

From an interview with Hans Ulrich Obrist

When I was in Berlin in the late seventies I was working in people's apartments in South Berlin. What I noticed was if I was in somebody's apartment and they had objects around them, these were objects that made people feel modern, just objects from today. A lot of the objects were quite monumental in a way. They were in a domestic space, a social space, but the objects themselves were like the building you were in and I began to see that these objects had a sort of inherent architecture so I began to think of a symbolic relationship between the architecture of domestic objects and the building in which they were contained. This led to an ongoing series of drawings which are to do with these objects and buildings.

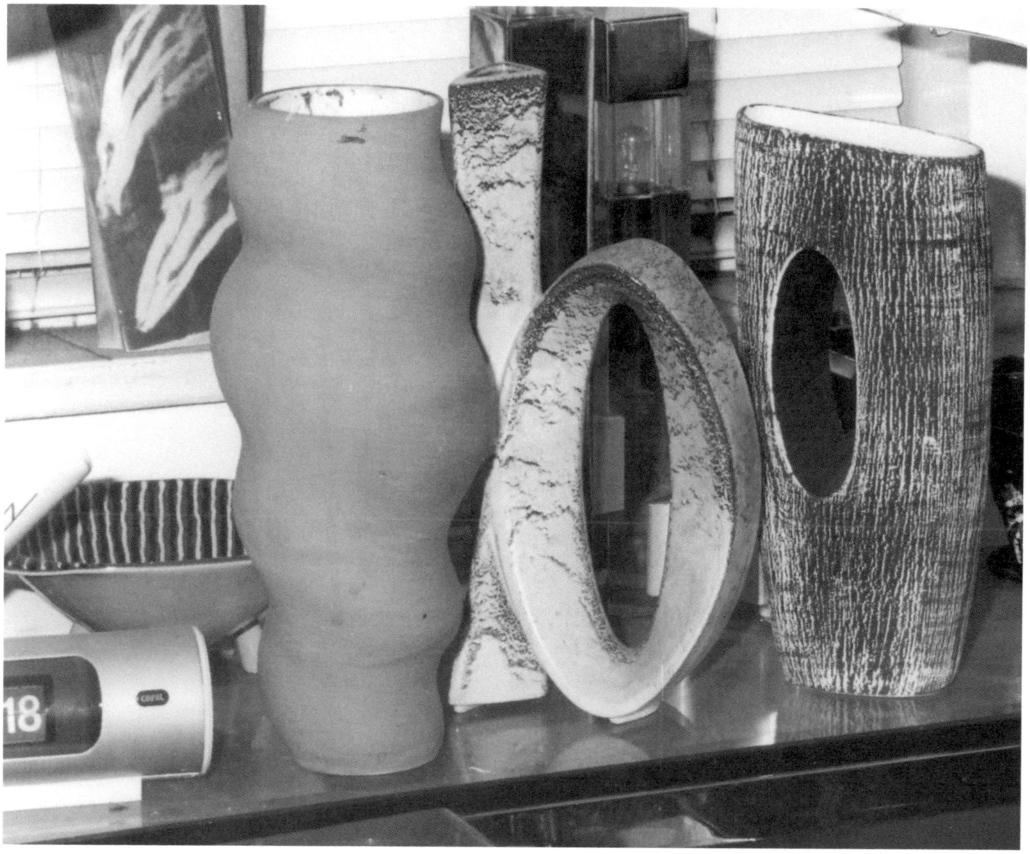

13
PROPOSING A SOCIAL MODEL OF ART PRACTICE

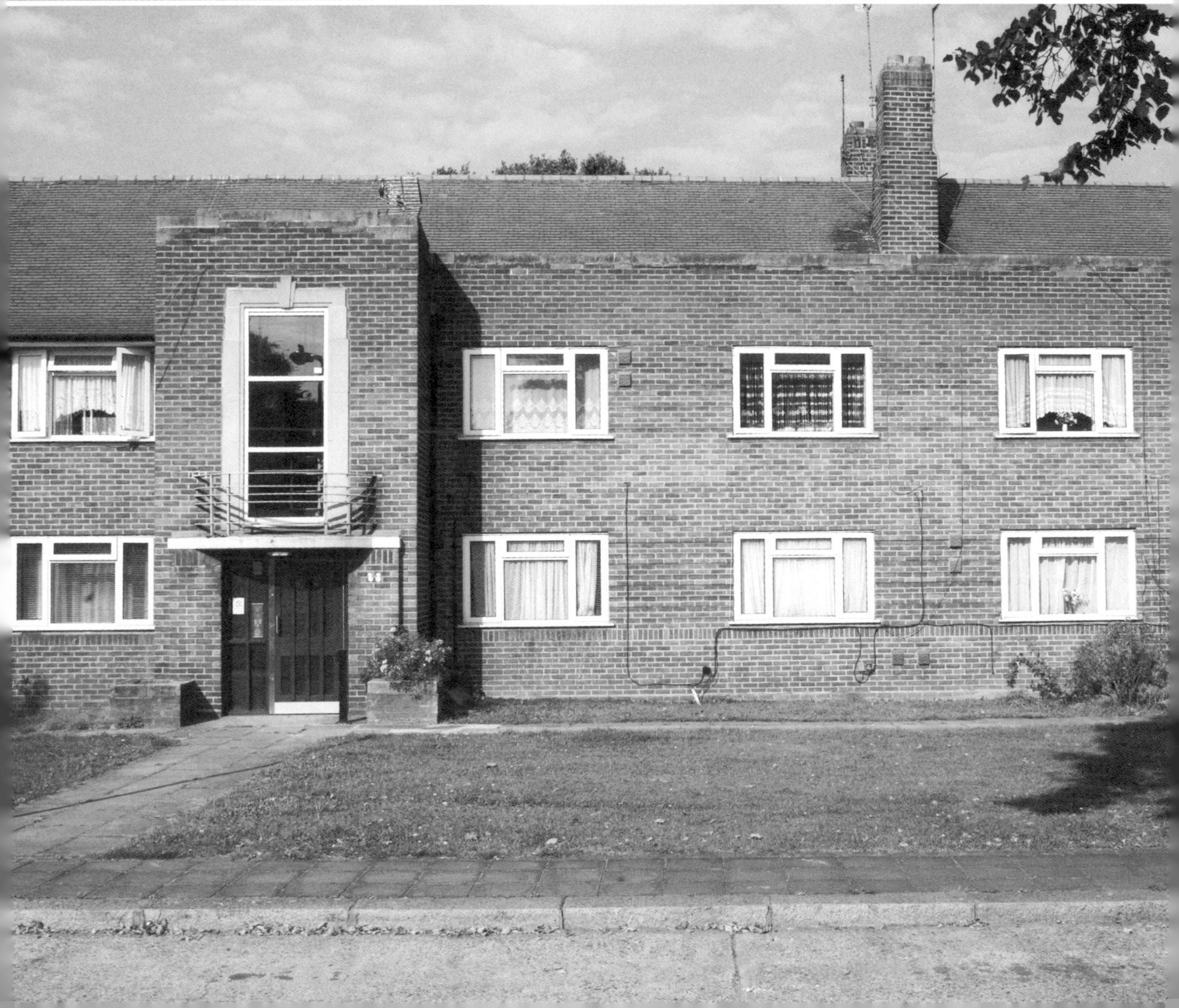

A SOCIAL MODEL OF ART PRACTICE

What I think is urgently required now, and has been neglected for so long or submerged in emotion, is a clear, pragmatic understanding of how the artwork can be effective, in a cultural set-up that is so obviously biased against instigatory developments materialising. The gap between the artist's intention and the cultural performance of the artwork obviously needs to be closed if effective intervention is to be realised. It is the artist who will have to articulate a coherent social model of his own art practice, that takes into account relationships between the intentions given to a work, the context in which it is presented and the composition of its audience. The relationship of the artwork to these three variables should be definitely clarified and seen as positively influencing the process of its realisation.

Artwork that seeks to instigate changes in the way we perceive the dominant value structure, so that we can engage in a more person-based consciousness, must establish links with social reality. In this case a consistency must be sought between the consciousness that underlies the artist's practice and the methodologies employed in the artwork itself, since the more the work is directly related to the lives people lead, their problems and their aspirations, the more central its meaning will become. Integral connections between three variables will be essential. 1: The artwork. 2: The audience. 3: The social context.

The closer the artist can bring the perception of reality encoded and forwarded through the artwork, to the reality experienced by the audience, the more powerful are the inferred meanings for that audience. Thus the references loaded in to the work by the artist should be transferable by the audience into their own experience, to parallel situations they've encountered. So the artist will have to act strategically and centre the representations made of the counter-consciousness of self-organisation directly in parallel with the representations held by their audience of the dominant deterministic consciousness.

ART AS A SOCIAL PROCESS

It is through the strength that a community can give to the artist in this respect that the actual pragmatics and will to realise the making of 'art as social process' can be stimulated to progress at the same pace as theoretical developments. Within the present social climate with its ever increasing ideology of property and conformity, the artist must seek to find personal reinforcement from other cultural activities associated with expressing a counter consciousness. One obvious outcome of such a redefinition of priorities is the prominence of previously hardly used contexts in which to work, such as the housing complex, the shopping parade, place of work, the social club or in fact anywhere that can successfully address the audience specific to the work. The change of status for the object, from being a pedestal fetish to an agent of social interaction, puts the emphasis firmly on the object being included in relationships between people rather than substituting for those relationships. This is an ideological matter of the highest importance, for the shift in the rationale of the artwork from object to audience puts it in direct opposition to the culture of property. Thus what is implied in culturally manifesting 'art as social process' extends well beyond the fact of the artwork itself, into the kind of society that will receive and recognise this art as legitimate practice. Because 'art as social process' while coexisting with the dominant culture, is through its demonstration, a model of a counter consciousness for social relationships based on self-organisation and mutualism.

With the pressing need now for an art based on concepts that address the present rise in authoritarianism and culture of objects, there is a real sense of urgency in the realising of different and new paradigms for the artwork based on a counter consciousness. 'Art as social process' offers a powerful challenge to the dominant position of the object, a way forward in fact to the shaping of an art practice for the future.

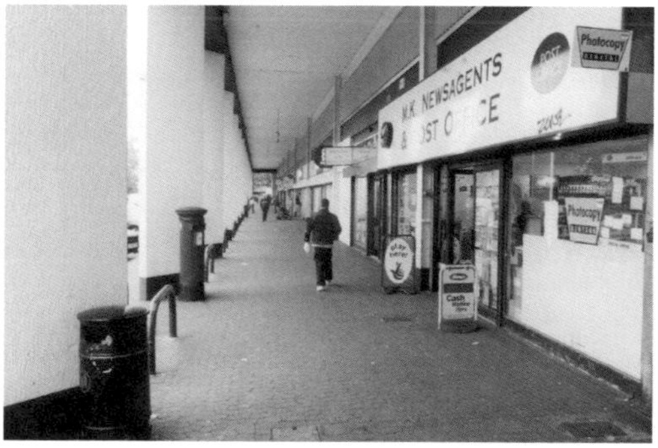

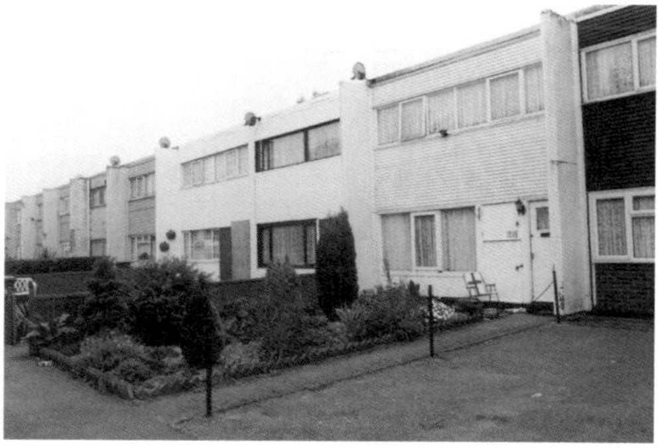

Two contexts in Milton Keynes considered for locating a work.

TWO SOCIALLY INTERACTIVE MODELS OF PRACTICE

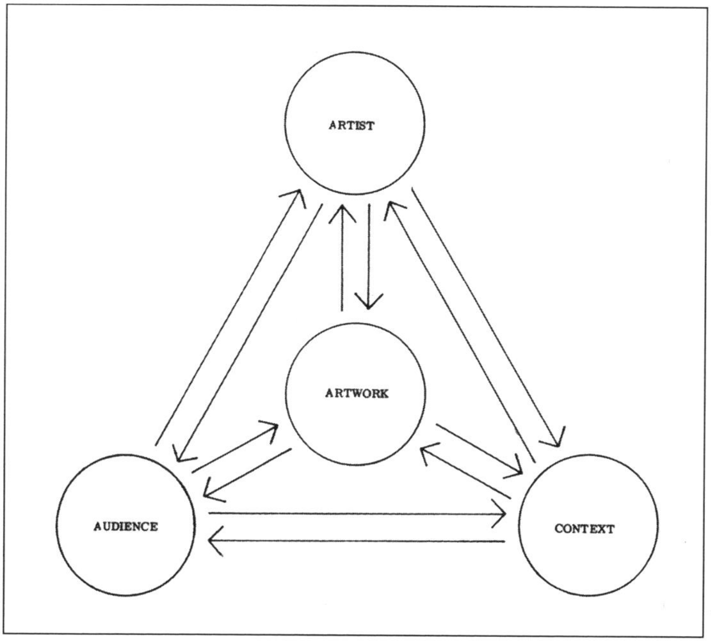

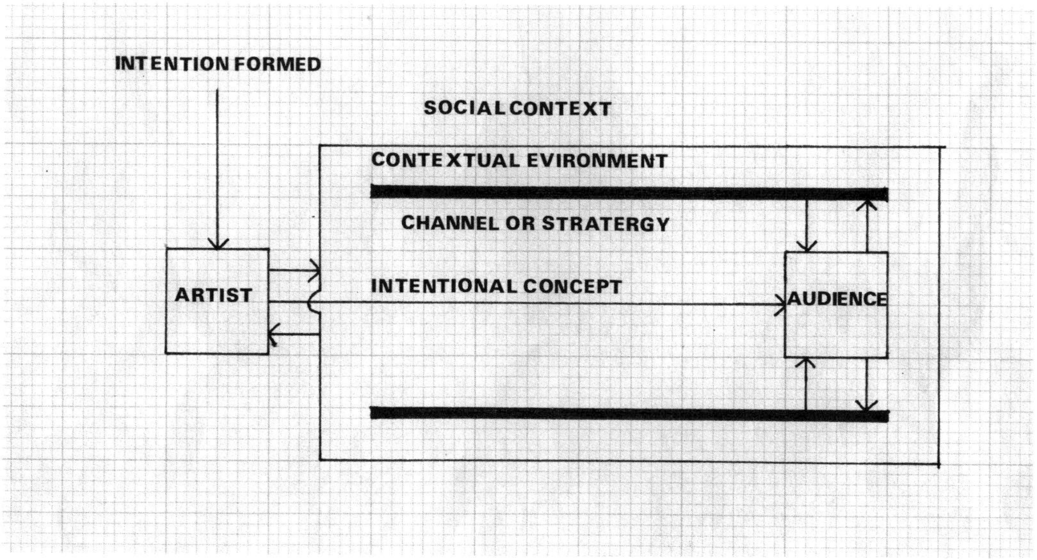

PROPOSITIONS FOR RELEVANT SOCIAL PRACTICE

From discussions at the Centre For Behavioural Art, London

A number of important ideas were forwarded that I feel are relevant to the debate today about what constitutes relevant practice:

1. A work of art could itself constitute a societal state, a model of human relationships.
2. A work of art could consist of a process in time, a learning system through which the concepts of the social view forwarded in the work are accessed and internalised.
3. A work of art acknowledges the relativism inherent in perception and the transience of experience, there being no right or wrong it taking the form of an open ended process.
4. A work of art operates as its own institution and as such is independent of specific art institutions.
5. A work of art could engage anyone, being available to whoever wished to enter into its domain through embodying in its presentation the means for people to acquire the necessary language and procedures to receive and internalise its meaning.

14

THE TOTALLY CONNECTED ARTWORK

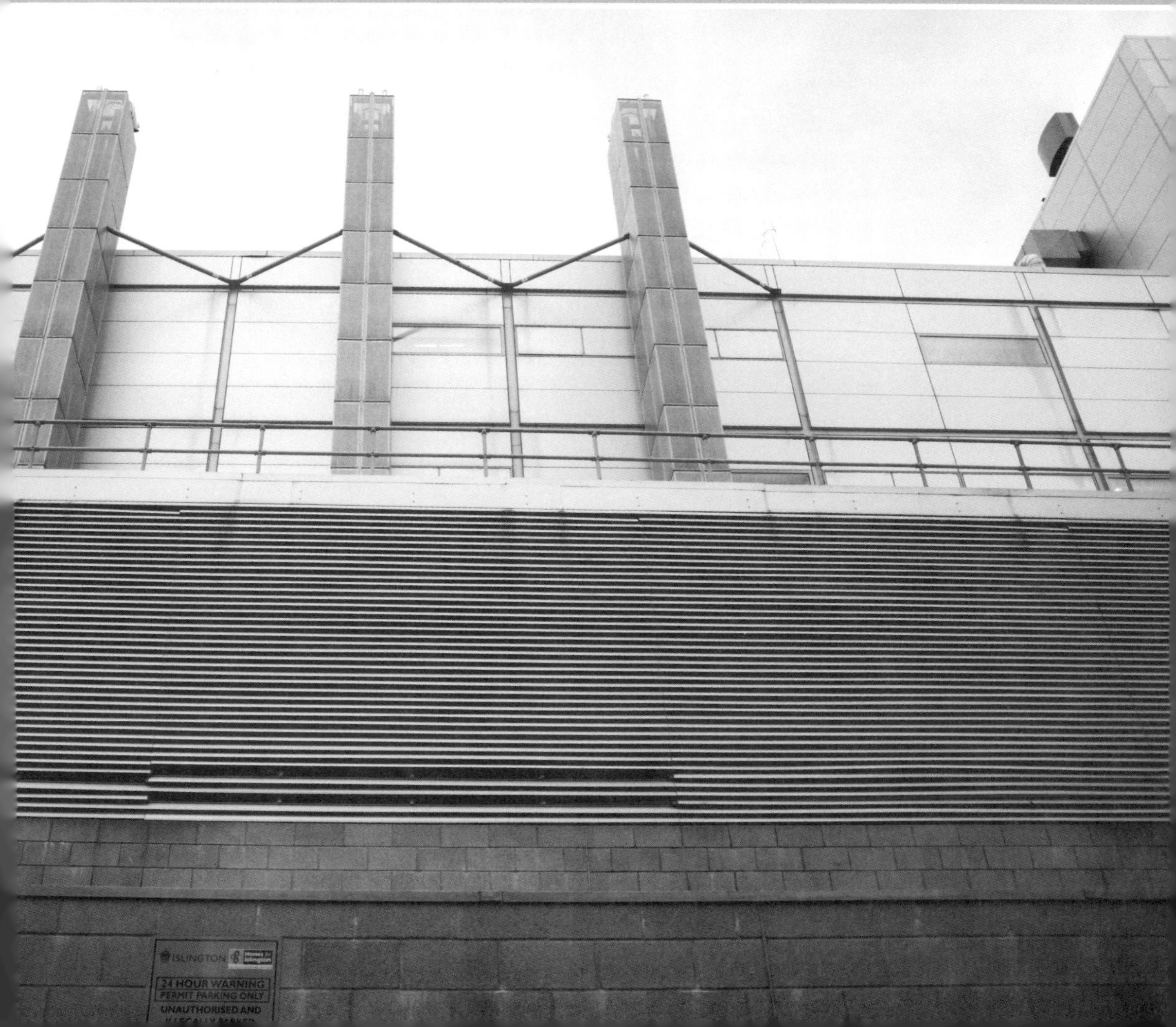

OPEN SYSTEMS

An open system of explanation between all participants in a network undermines the very foundations of authoritative, hierarchical, and exclusive frameworks. Perhaps, therefore, it is no accident, that there is a pressure exerted on the artist to maintain 'exclusivity', to separate practice from other practitioners, to declare sole authorship, exhibit a unique language. But it is an important initial step towards embracing the present to acknowledge that this pressure will drag the artist back into conflict, between intention and practice enabling meaning to be appropriated into value structures that will ultimately undermine belief in the potential ramifications of what is being forwarded. Only when networks between artists are fully independent of the existing value structures projected by the institutional world of art, and a consistency between intention and practice perceived to be true in the presentation of new art work, will the artist be able to move the agenda of art forwards to embrace the potential of networks of exchange, those same networks that are shaping the fabric of communication in society. An important starting point is the procedure and process of explanation which I would strongly argue should be undertaken as a matter of course by the artist, of both existing and possible art practice, the procedure of explanation being directed towards other practitioners to create an open network of exchange.

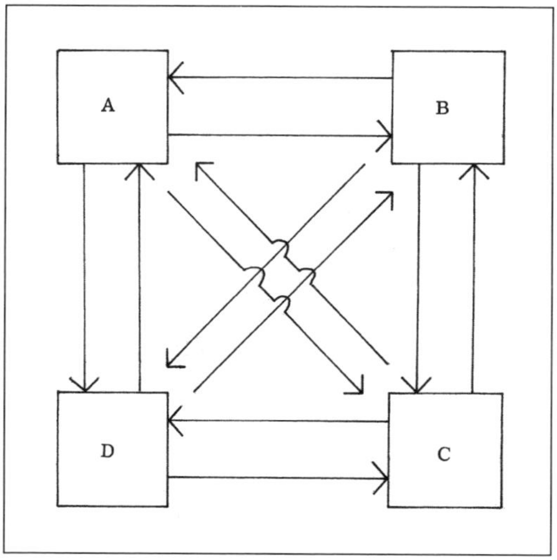

A basic model for a homeostatic self-organising system, showing total coupling between elements, A,B,C,D. Elements can achieve a Effector/ Affector condition as a result of the total coupling.

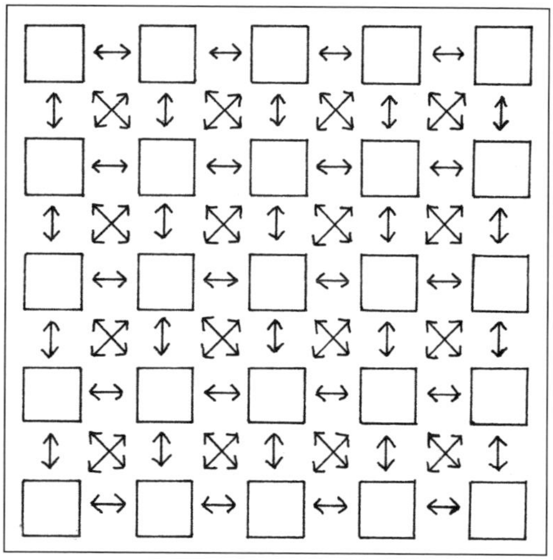

All nodes are linked to all other nodes in the system as a result of total coupling, creating a one layer network.

THE BASIC NETWORK MODEL BEHIND TWO LONG TERM SOCIAL ENGAGEMENTS

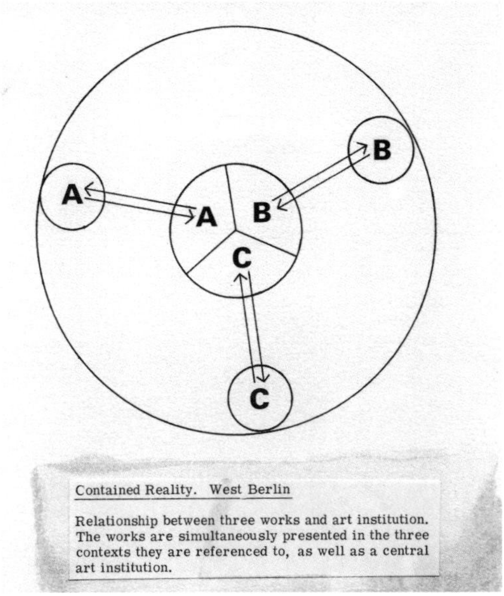

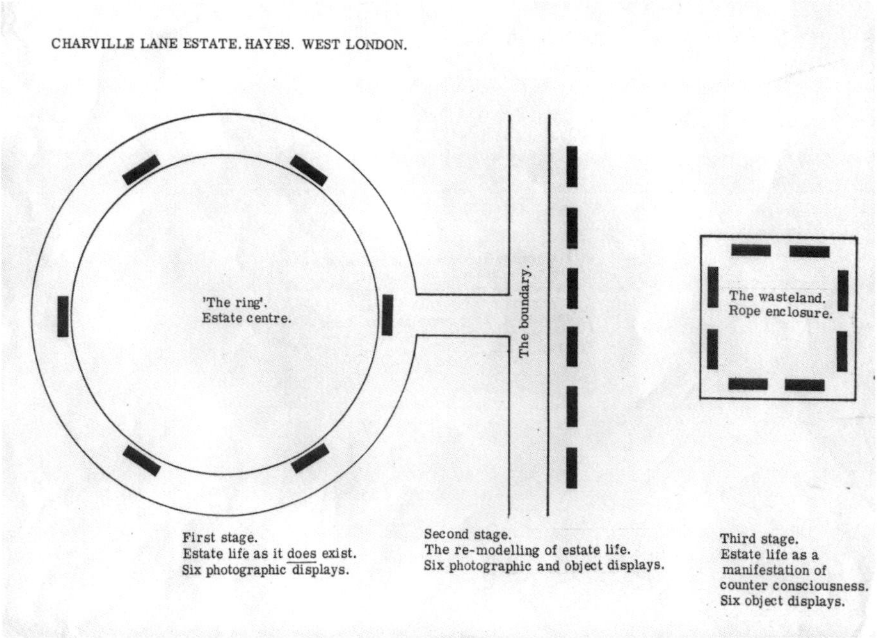

Diagram of the three main stages of development of the work 'Two Worlds Apart', Charville Lane Estate, Hayes, West London.

ARTWORK AS A COMMUNITY SOCIAL RESOURCE

After a number of experimental works I first established a truly interactive model between myself as the artist, audience and context in the formation of the 'Social Resource Project'. This work conceived as an abstract conceptual model in 1969 became 'The Social Resource Project For Tennis Clubs' in 1970 through my taking the conceptual work into the actual reality of four tennis clubs in Nottingham, the clubs being the context for the work and the members the audience. The work was to establish interactive channels between the members of the four clubs and involve them collaborating in re-modelling the existing rules of tennis to manifest what they considered were the real needs from their membership. The eventual outcome of their participation in a structured sequence of events over a month long period was their development of a new model of tennis which they played as a tournament for the Willats Cup under the devised new rules. In this work I made extensive use of visual references drawn from four clubs, photographing items within the club environment that were identified for me by members as having some special meaning. A resulting contextual imagery followed made up of photographic montages with linked questions, that were specially created to enable members to externalise to other members what they felt about those items. By meeting members of the club before creating my presentation of contextual imagery I was able to centre it on what they felt they would respond to, and make an absolute connection between the work's meaning, its context and its audience which was vital to their involvement.

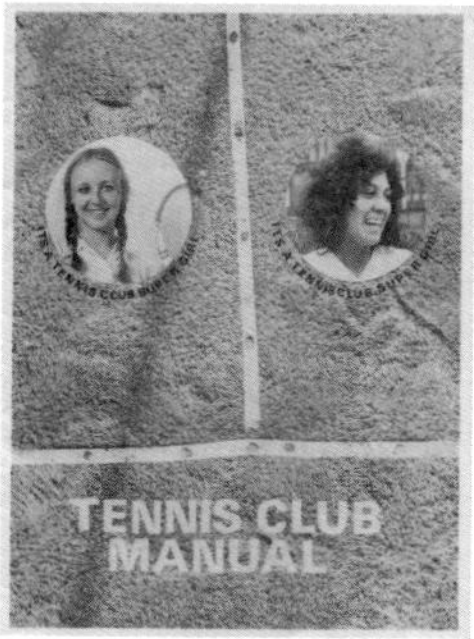

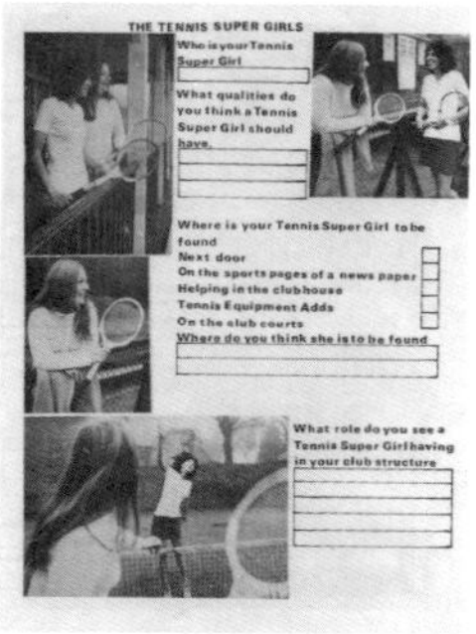

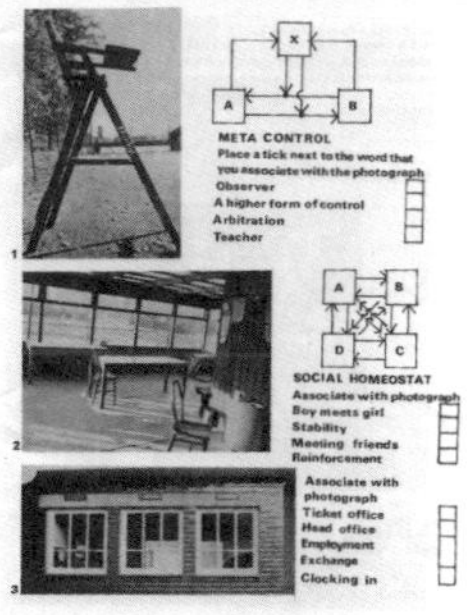

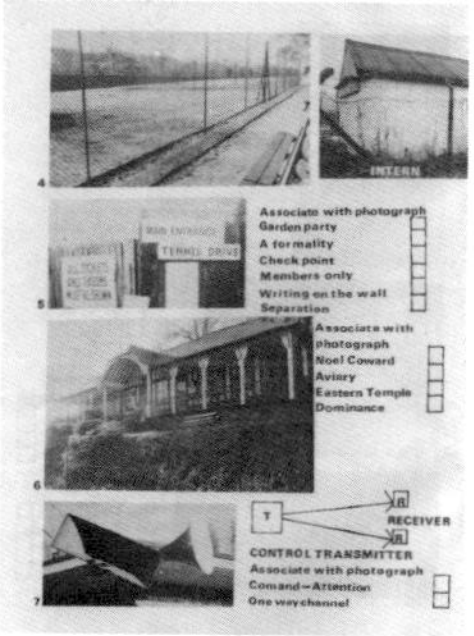

Pages from the 'Tennis Club Manual' presenting problem situations to participants.

ACCEPTANCE OF THE ARTIST'S INITIATIVE

Project Operators

I think when we got into working with people, we had this first meeting where we all met in Bewick Court where they lived, we all went up there from the Laing Art Gallery and talked to people. I was very heartened that they all seemed to understand what we were saying, that there wasn't a barrier, they all seemed very responsive, we talked about the exhibition, our ideas and so on, and they seemed to want to engage with us.

They must have wondered what was going on, but there was a willingness to engage with what was going on, and it was a voluntary experience, it wasn't something they had to do with any sense of penalty, they must have wanted to carry on with it, they must have found it interesting whatever they thought they were getting involved in, but we did take great care to discuss the idea of it as a work of art, and to fully discuss its ramifications with them.

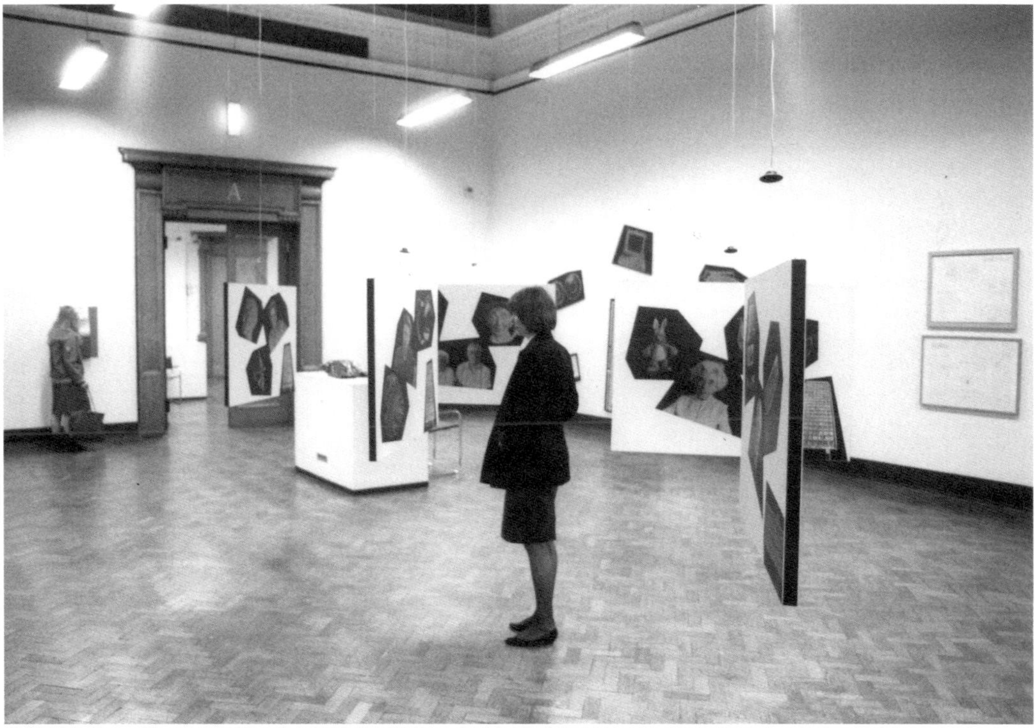

The project work 'Between Straight Lines' connected the Laing Art Gallery with residents and office workers in the locality and was presented in two adjacent buildings as well as inside the Art Gallery.

15
MAKING THE AUDIENCE THE RATIONALE

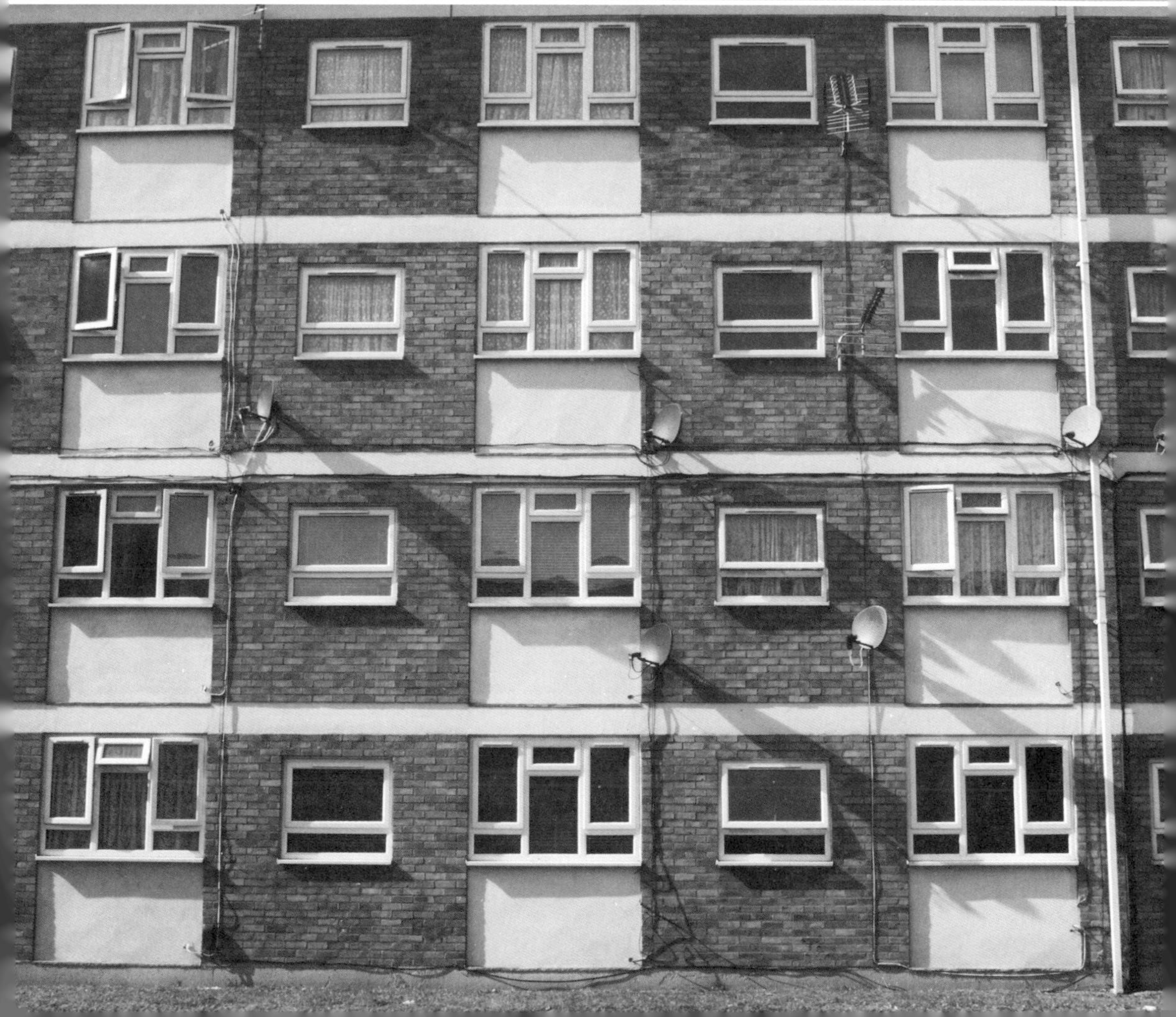

SPECIFYING THE AUDIENCE

One increase in the artist's freedom made by acknowledging the audience is that two fundamental strategies can follow, one pursued when the audience is seen as belonging to a fixed location or social group, the other directed at a more casual audience that cannot be specified. In the first strategy, with an audience that is definable by location or some other shared experience, their existing languages and shared references can be used by the artist to convey the message, the meaning of the work to the audience. The effect of this simple change of approach is far reaching, for the audience no longer has to acquire and learn the meaning of special art-based languages. When the audience cannot be so specified, and is more casually composed, then the second basic strategy becomes appropriate. This strategy uses references that are common to, and shared by, an audience with a wide variety of backgrounds, but who are nevertheless present within the same place—as would be the case with the average public museum. I would argue that if the artist is to break through his present social containment then it is to the wider audience that work must be addressed. Indeed the audience should be known in advance of the work's conception, pinpointed by the artist and given the highest position in the determination of the work's concerns. A prerequisite for an artwork that manifests a counter consciousness is that the separation which existed between the artist and the audience is closed, that they become mutually engaged, to the point where the audience become the rationale in both the making and reception of the work. In fact the acts of making and reception become mutually bound.

MOTIVATIONS BEHIND THE WEST LONDON SOCIAL RESOURCE PROJECT

One of the important motivations behind the setting up of the West London Social Resource Project was to show other practitioners in art concerned with its social function that an artwork could actively involve people from diverse social backgrounds, even though all of them had little previous involvement with contemporary art. To this end I purposefully specified that four 'classically' defined social groupings would determine the work's audience, and that in terms of the Social Resource project they were physically, socially and economically separated within the geography of West London. I felt that the potential dynamic created in the artist exercising the freedom to create work for a specific audience and context could only reinforce its meaning and social ramifications. It seemed absurd then and even more so now in the present climate of ultra conservative normality, that the artist is so bound by traditional roles that he/she is inhibited from exploring the new possibilities of making a work with an audience outside the enclosed world of art institutions.

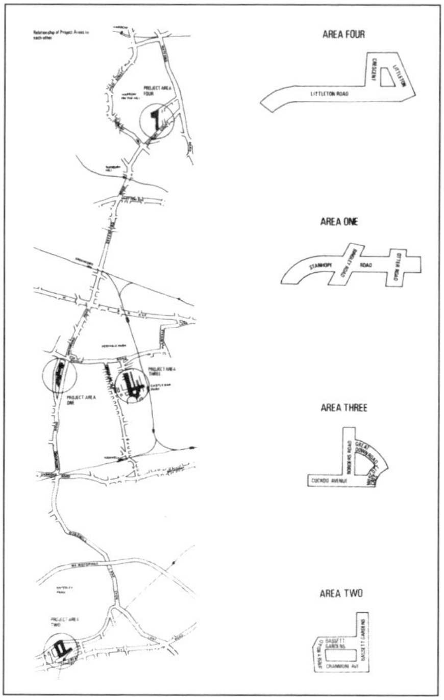

Map of the four Project Areas relationship to each other.

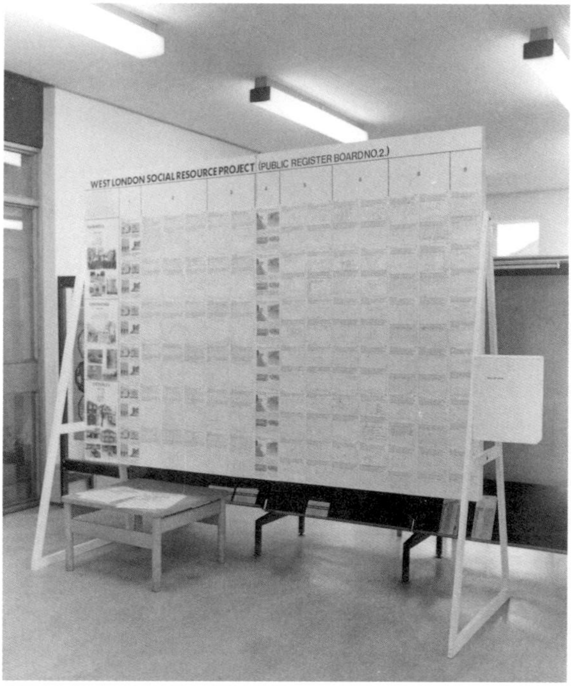

The Public Register Board, situated in Osterley Library, West London.

THE FORMATION OF PARTICIPANT GROUPS

In the West London Social Resource Project the audience was specified as members from four different but typical social groups residing in West London; these being Upper Middle Class, Middle Class, Lower Middle Class and Working Class social groups. The definition used to distinguish the groups from each other, was their respective, decision roles, within society. The selection of areas which represented the selected social groups was made after a number of reconnaissance trips into West London by the artist.

The decision to use a particular area for the project to function in was based on the following requirements. 1: The area's typicalness regarding its representation of a social group. 2: Its compactness. 3: That the areas were within reasonable distance from each other, in order that participants from one area had easy access to another. The project was initially planned as taking about three months to complete, though in fact it took nine months. This was due to the differences in time it took participants to complete various tasks.

In order to minimize any conflict between the project organisers' usage of language and that of participants, it was decided to use the existing languages, codes and frames of reference of the social groups involved in the project. The four areas selected in West London were as follows: Area One, Greenford (Working Class Group), Area Two, Osterley (Middle Class Group), Area Three, Hanwell (Lower Middle Class Group), Area Four, Harrow (Upper Middle Class Group). The project organisers gathered participants from a few compact streets in each area. The four participant groups were, in general terms, geographically, economically and socially separate from each other and saw themselves as such. Though all the participants had models of each other as a social group, these were simple and associated with kinds of social groups, rather than the particular ones taking part in the project.

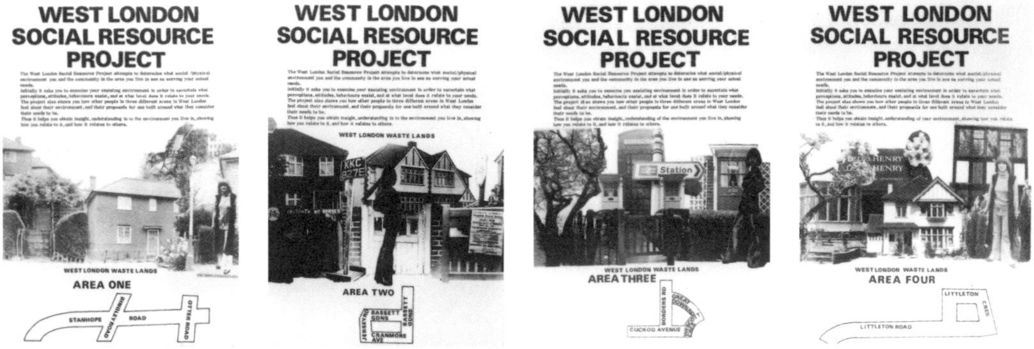

The four Project Area leaflets.

VISITORS' EXPERIENCES OF THE WORK 'VERTICAL LIVING' LOCATED INSIDE SKEFFINGTON COURT, HAYES, WEST LONDON

Visitor

SW Can you describe your first responses to the actual location, Skeffington Court, I mean when you first got there, if you remember we all went out in the car, can you describe this and how you felt about it.
LB Just the physical environment struck me as quite peculiar because it, because we had to go round those one, one-way streets and it did seem very isolated just from that point of view and, and then we arrived at Skeffington Court, which has, two storey blocks all round it and with the Tower over the top and it seemed curious to, to begin with I didn't see that the Tower would be that, much differentiated, from the other buildings around it and it seemed a bit arbitrary to isolate the Tower and use that for the project rather than, the whole complex. But, I think as soon as I got inside the Tower and began to use the lifts and to sort out how incredibly isolated each of those floors is from the other floors and then how, one side of a floor is isolated from the other side of the floor, I saw that as quite justified, I mean a good way to isolate it and, make a space for yourself.

SW Can you just say, if you can remember now, it's a few months since we actually did the project, but can you remember how you felt about going out to such a place and what were your first reactions on getting to the actual place itself.
LB Em. I remember the journey very vividly, and I was struck, particularly in the later half of the journey by the fact that one did seem to be almost literally entering a kind of no man's land and by that I don't mean anything very glib, I mean something very precise, in the sense that it didn't really seem to be anywhere in particular. Street followed street in more or less uniform succession and after a time you did feel as if you were marooned in the middle of a district which didn't seem to have any kind of local identity—everything seemed to be very regularized and anonymous and, I guess when I arrived at the tower block itself, because that did seem to epitomise everything that had happened increasingly on the journey out of London, it reached a sort of climax when we got to the tower block and not only the tower block but its surroundings because it's very homogenous architecturally, the block and the tower and the walkways and the flats which surround it and I got this extraordinary sense of isolation, the feeling that the people that lived there must of necessity, whether they liked it or not, be very sealed off from any other kind of context apart from the one they inhabited and that one seemed to be shorn of all character except a very predictable kind of 1960s character which has been imposed upon them by the architecture and it was striking, I thought how impossible it was for any of the residents really to personalize those surroundings very much, it was all laid down for them by the building itself.

16
THE CONTEXTUALISATION OF ART STRATEGIES

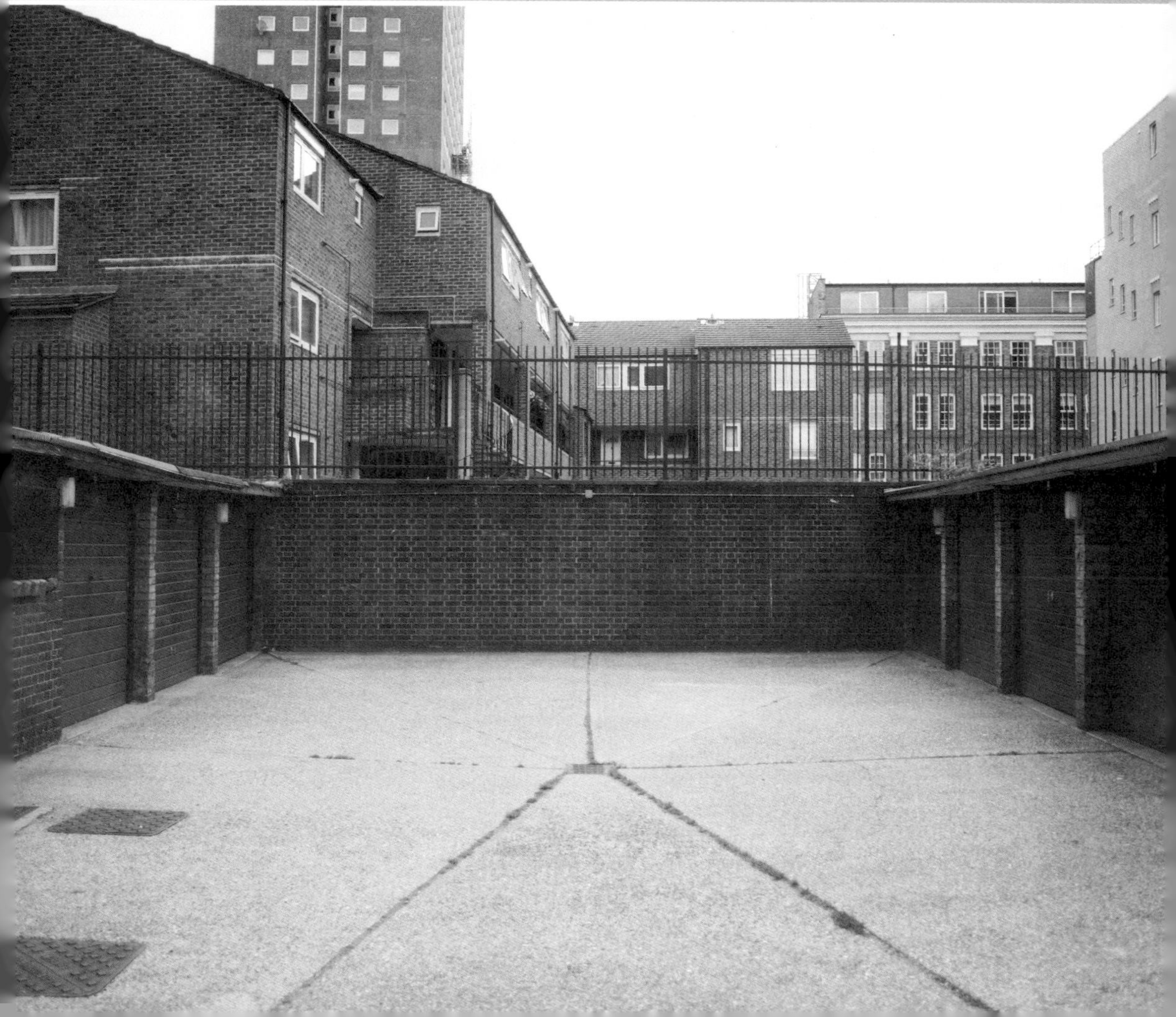

THE PROCESS OF CONTEXTUALISATION

With an audience that is definable by location or some other shared experience, their existing languages and shared references can be used by the artist to convey the message, the meaning of the work to the audience. The effect of this simple change of approach is far-reaching, for the audience no longer has to acquire and learn the meaning of special art-based languages. A similar and constant change is experienced when the work is physically sited within the existing world of the audience, through the use of public points of reference such as shops, libraries, schools, front gardens etc., that already fit inside the group's existing everyday routines. The language of the artwork is built from the references drawn out of the audience's own reality, and presented as images readily identifiable by them. This does not imply that the work is just descriptive of reality, but that these images form the basis for a remodelling of that same reality. The artist's intervention is to change what is perceived as normal by the audience, not reflecting to them what is already normal, but using normality to provide an access into what initially are likely to be difficult concepts to internalise.

The process by which the work is contextualised means it is loaded either by the artist or the audience (or by both) with references that belong to that specially defined context, and which have an established special meaning for the audience. Thus a concept is represented through references already meaningful to the audience, or, itself grows out of those references. The intensification of the artwork's meaning by contextualisation also increases its physical ties to that particular location. Then, if the same artwork is to be presented to another audience, it will require a complete reloading with fresh references appropriate to the new location. This dependency prevents the artwork from being misread, or appropriated into other criteria, value structures and contexts, the artist needing to examine a work's relation to each location afresh. For every new location the essential properties, languages and resources of the audience are pinpointed by the artist (or by the artist and audience in collaboration), then these are used to manifest the artwork from conceptual model into reality.

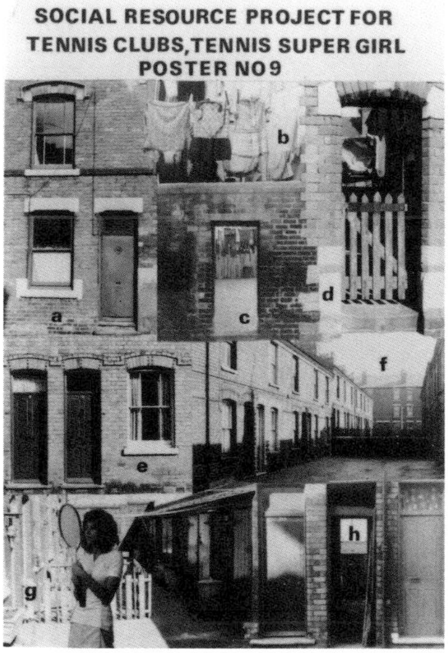

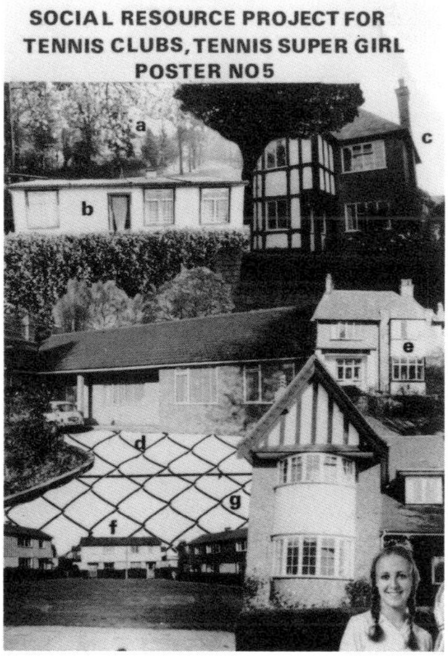

Two of the twelve neighbourhood posters that took their references from the environment of the four clubs and members homes.

TRANSFORMATION AND CONTEXT

An important element of transformation is the contextualisation of the space surrounding the transformer. The transformer loads the space with references that they find meaningful, thus converting what is impersonal, perhaps even anonymous, to somewhere personal, relevant, a statement of their own sensibility and identity. For example, within the bare, pre-planned anonymity of grey concrete housing schemes, residents have found their own way of contextualising that environment, in layering graffiti on the wall surfaces, displaying signs and messages of their existence as well as leaving objects, the debris of their activities, all over the ground.

Similarly I use the contextualisations in my work, to present the audience with a 'symbolic world' that parallels their own, which feels familiar to them. They can then load that world from their own framework of references, thus making the representations of my 'symbolic world' directly relevant to their own experience. This process of contextualisation in my work enables the audience to reconstruct their perception of normality into a counter-consciousness. But I also see that contextualisation is an ideological as well as a pragmatic recognition of the complexity and relativity of the individual's psychology. Thus the embodiment of symbols that can be seen as directly concerning issues of modern living is crucial in my work, for they are more likely to be contextualised by the audience.

Contextualisation by the transformer is an active state, going completely against the universality, the passivity and reductiveness of the dominate culture. The punks or night people fed their own references into impersonal surroundings, transporting and transforming objects so as to create a social and physical environment in which they could freely express their own sensibilities. It is a similar cognitive action that I want the audience to undertake, not only within the framework of my work, but also, and more importantly, within their own lives.

'BRENTFORD TOWERS' DISPLAY BOARDS MADE WITH RESIDENTS OF HARVEY HOUSE

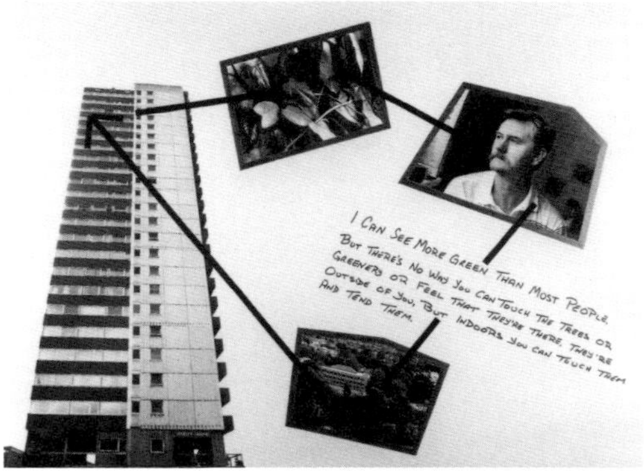

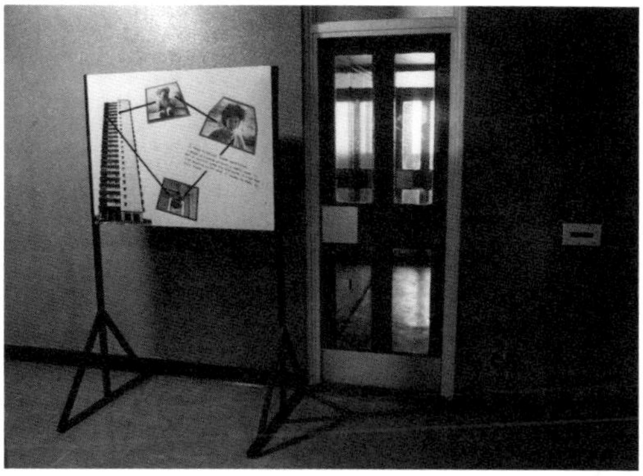

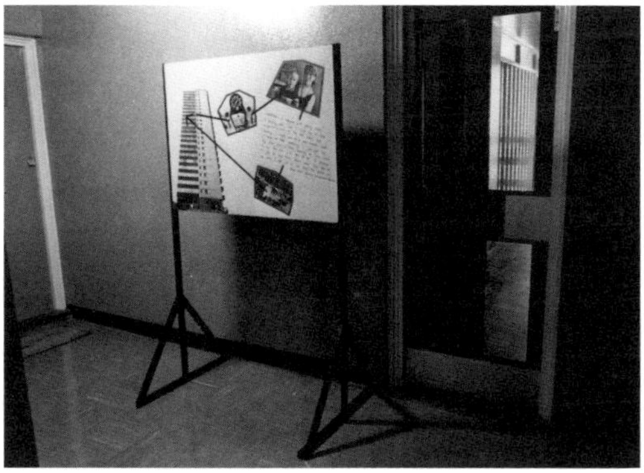

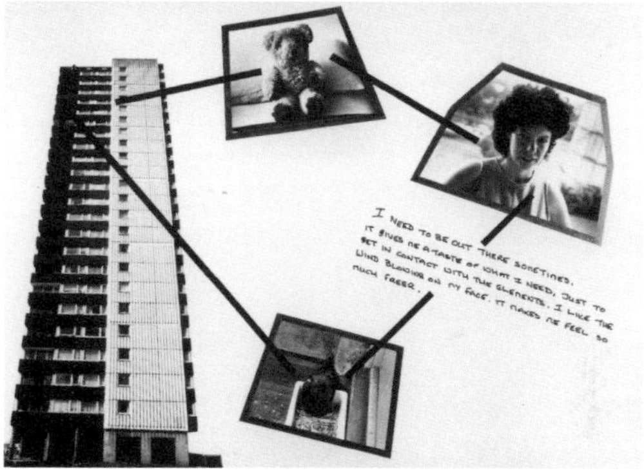

The Display Boards were made in residents' living rooms and presented on the landings throughout Harvey House. The work was viewed by taking a lift to the top floor and then walking down fourteen floors.

PROTOTYPE SOCIAL RESOURCE PROJECT, IPSWICH 1965

Student

DB I approached Art School expecting to stay in a studio, paint, learn to draw and to be surrounded by finished objects done by myself which people would admire as paintings, sculptures, not really thinking about what I'd do afterwards. In the course at Ipswich 1965 the most surprising thing was the fact that we spent a long time out of the studio, in the streets dealing with the general public, and the members of the public on such projects as to whether we could help them at all, with what use we could be to them, and there's one project I remember in particular when we went to a new housing estate which was being built in Ipswich, we went along, knocked on doors, got various responses, some good, some bad, asking if there was anything we could do which would help them in their present situation, the one response we got more than anything was the fact that there was no clear street signing, things like the way to the shops, how to get to the play area for the kids, the way to the launderette, so we simply went back to the Art School, made up a load of very temporary street signs some quite imaginative, some very basic, took them back, stuck them in the various streets and I think they stayed there for quite a few weeks.

DB I don't remember the questionnaire too clearly, what I remember is certain questions I asked like, being as it was a new housing estate, there were various sort of houses there painted, the doors were painted in particular colours, favourite colours, favourite colours for curtains, this sort of thing, cars outside, and I remember asking such simple questions as, favourite colours, how would you have your house painted if you had your choice, what's your favourite colour car, what particular colour would you like to sort of view out of your window and just basic stuff like that. Going further than the street signs when we actually constructed these various signs and things they were just straight forward sort of signs which were quite ordinary, you could read quite clearly, but then when I went back on the sort of drawings I'd done, very makeshift sort of signs we decided to sort of build some larger signs using purely colour as a directive. I mean trying to stop people from going in a certain direction by putting a great red sort of square up in front of them, sending them to a sort of play area by using such things as nice greens and things, launderettes were very basic sort of colours, we did a three dimensional sort of map using bits of material, clothing, objects which might sort of send them to the sort of shops, I mean another thing with shopping we constructed a construction made out of bottles, tin cans, dairy produce, shopping produce which would direct them to the shopping centre.

DB Well I can remember one thing very very early thing and the whole, the whole point of it was to get you out into the streets, right now we found that the majority of the people that lived in Ipswich didn't know any art students, didn't know what went on at Art School, just didn't come into contact with anything, sent to talk to people and do various things and to try and get their response, like before we were even talking to people there was one project where we got a map of Ipswich, I think we were blindfolded and had to throw a dart at the map, wherever the dart ended up in the map we had to go out with pick axes, shovels, spades, anything, dig a six foot hole and just get their response, see what people'd do, not talk to them just see what they'd do. I remember one of the sort of darts landed in the cemetery, grave diggers, and they asked them if they would help them dig the graves which they did before the police arrived, another couple ended up in British Home Stores, which is a big store in Ipswich, approached the floor and started to hammer at it with pick axes and shovels, the police were called and I suppose for a good two hours later the whole art school was full of police asking what was going on.

17

TRANSFORMING THE ROLE OF THE ART MUSEUM

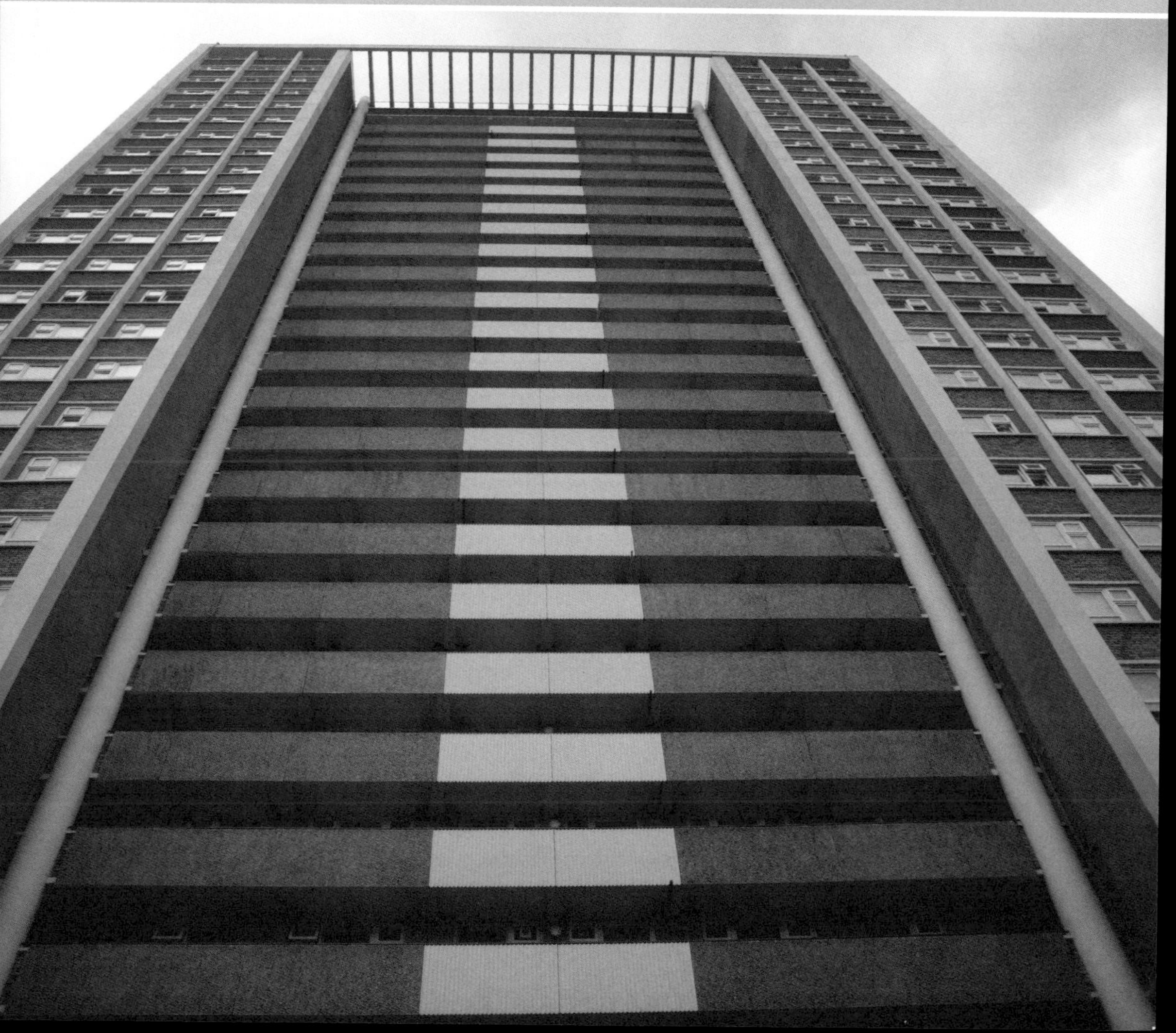

THE ARTWORK AS ITS OWN INSTITUTION

Stephen Willats in conversation with Andrew Wilson

AW Which is how you talk about Cognition Control, 1970/71: not a museum, nor a gallery but an agency which, as it were, facilitates things to happen, acting as a point of living, interchange between the audience and the creator and the various participants.

SW It is a moot point if we really need museums at all. Maybe the whole concept of the museum is increasingly less relevant to the idea of a culture that is embodying interaction and communication. It seems to me that there is this conflict between what the museum stands for and the orientation of the culture. The museum is based on the idea of the transmission of an 'object language' in which there is no interaction, while contemporary culture proposes a real possibility of interactive communication which is lacking in the concept of museum-culture. What I felt was interesting was to take people's expectations of what they want to find in the museum and turn them around, turn that on its head. Instead of them expecting a passive situation with authoritative works of art, they actually become engaged in a mutual social interaction.

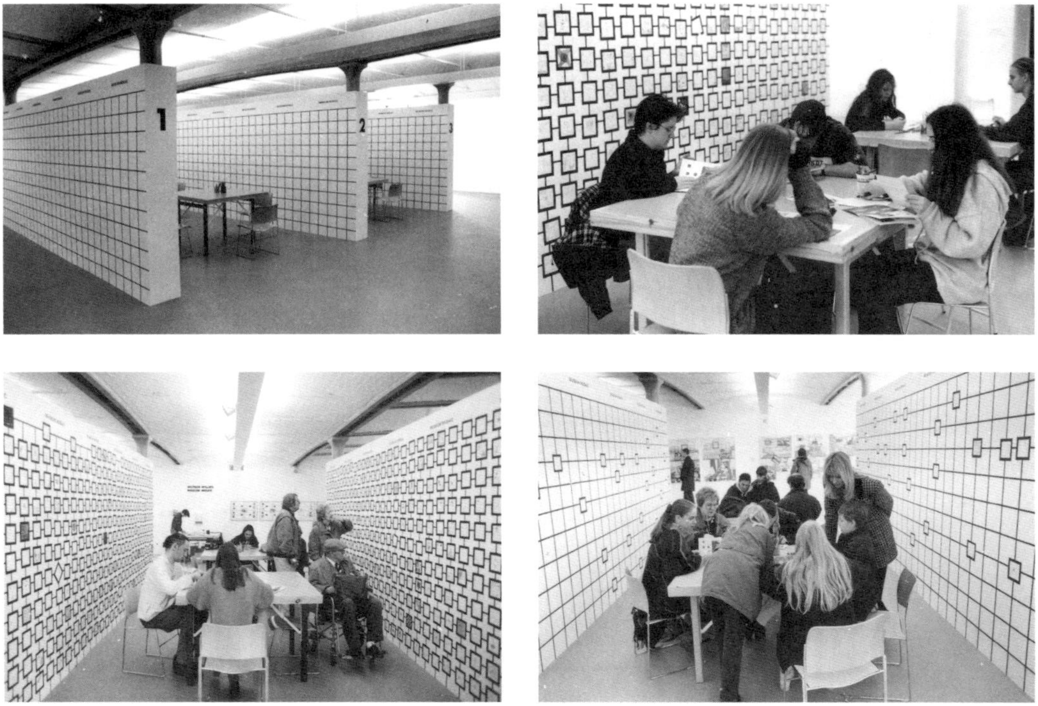

'Museum Mosaic', Tate Gallery, Liverpool.

THE CONCEPTUAL MODELS OF PRACTICE THAT RELATED THE ART MUSEUM TO THE SURROUNDING SOCIAL COMMUNITY

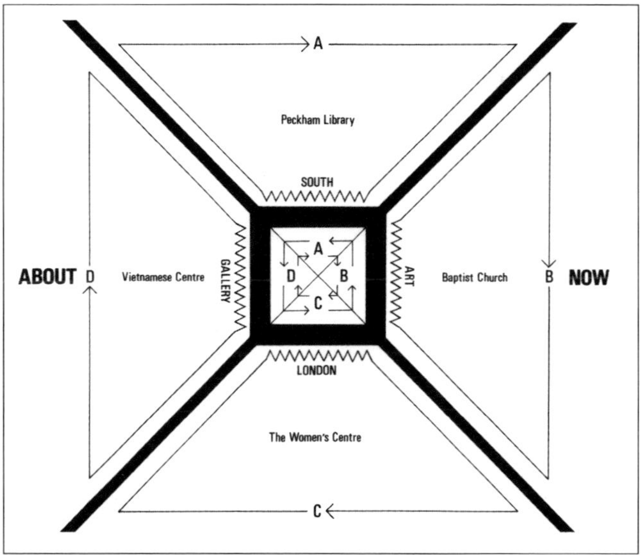

'Changing Everything' South London Gallery, London.

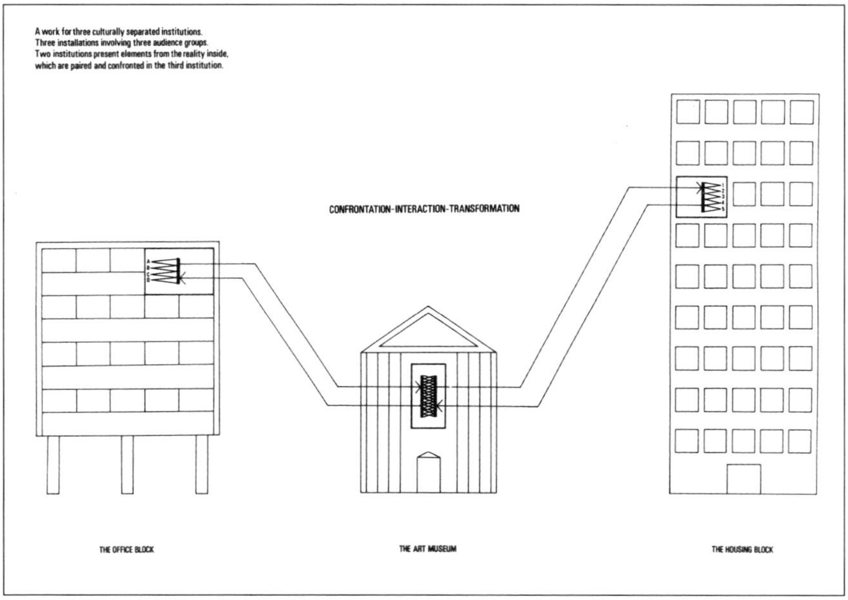

'Between Straight Lines' The Laing, Newcastle.

'FROM DIFFERENT WORLDS' LEEDS

'From Different Worlds' was conceived to open up the possibilities of a model of art practice that would involve the 'art museum' in a social interaction with the surrounding community. For my work embodied the City Art Gallery as an integral part of its structure and created an exchange of realities with two other symbolic institutions—the nearby tower blocks of Marlborough Towers and Lovell Park Towers.

The agents for my exchange of realities were the objects I found and photographically documented within three contexts, which I grouped into three categories, possessed, elevated and discarded. I saw these objects as existing in systems, but in different places within the same world, products of the same culture. At the same time I saw that the objects were culturally alienated from each other, by the social, physical contexts in which they were contained as systems.

I asked residents of the towers to isolate for me the objects that they considered important to their life inside their flat-possessed objects. Later I made a tape-recorded discussion with them in which they described their relationship with the objects they had singled out for me.

In the City Art Gallery I asked one of the Curators to select objects from within some of their paintings and I then photographed these details of elevated objects. Later I tape-recorded interviews I made with members of the public in the Gallery, about their associations with these objects.

Finally, I searched round the base of the tower blocks and photographed objects that had been thrown onto the ground—discarded objects.

All of these elements of the work took several months, the work evolving as a social process which involved many different people over the period.

To achieve a real exchange between the three realities, the installation was likewise divided into three parts. Two installations were made from the elements from the Gallery and were presented in the foyers of the two tower blocks. Conversely, the installation made from the documentations made in the Blocks of possessed and discarded objects was presented in the main exhibition space at the City Art Gallery. As a result not only was there a transplantation of the conceptualisations from one reality to another, but the only way to fully experience the work was to physically visit all three sites. This walk, the different realities found there and the buildings themselves were all part of the work.

The installation in the City Art Gallery consisted of five free-hanging display boards with photographs, with a constant recording being played of the person depicted in the display discussing the meaning of objects immediately around themselves: this presented the visitor to the Gallery with a set of simultaneous discussions creating a mosaic of sound. In the tower block displays photographs and text were juxtaposed on five free standing displays. I felt it important with these displays that they should not be seen as an aggressive intrusion in the foyer spaces by residents, so I purposefully made them vulnerable, so that they would rely on residents' acceptance for their survival.

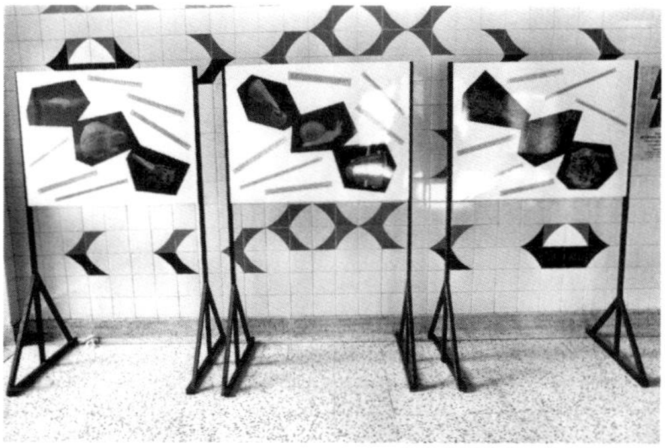

'From Different Worlds' Display Boards in the foyer of Marlborough Towers, Leeds.

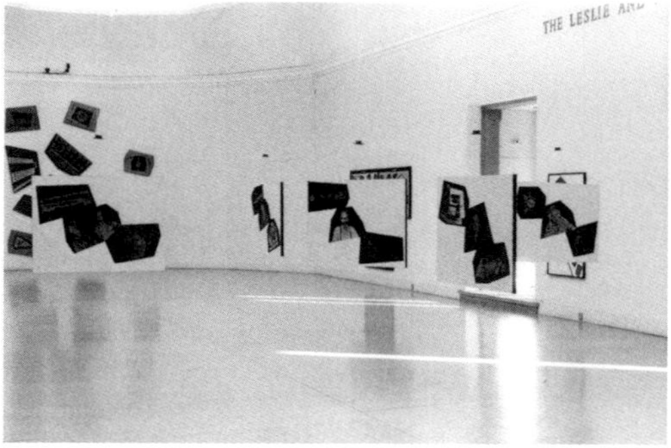

Installation, Leeds City Art Gallery.

AUDIENCE SELF ORGANISATION

My reaction was to develop models of the Art Museum that undermined the audience expectations of authoritative order by using the restricted space of the gallery to present a 'random situation' which required the audience to self-organise their own order. My intention was to break down any higher, authoritative barrier, institutionalised between artist and audience, and to recognise the relativity of perceptual meaning and creativity.

This idea of subverting expectations of 'order', i.e. norms and conventions of cognition and behaviour inside a restricted, predictive space, was realised through a series of sculptures and wall constructions, where sets of elements were self-organised and then left by people entering the gallery space. In these works any ordering made by someone was seen as valid, and left for the next person to take as their starting point.

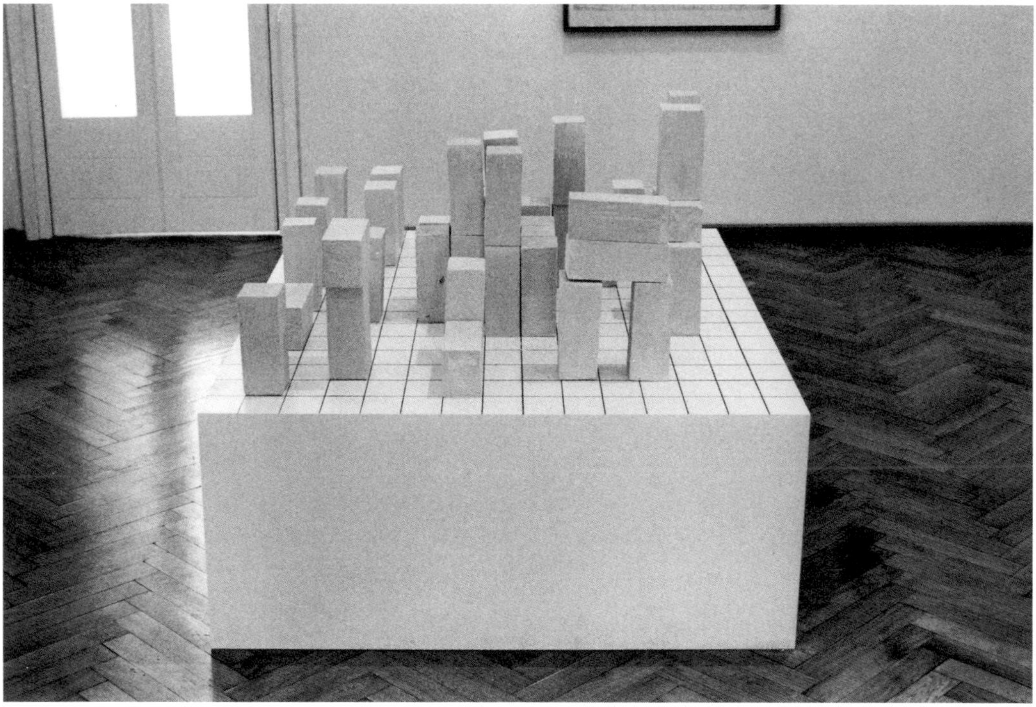

'Manual Variable' 1962.

18
THE ARTWORK AS A STRUCTURE OF EVENTS THROUGH TIME

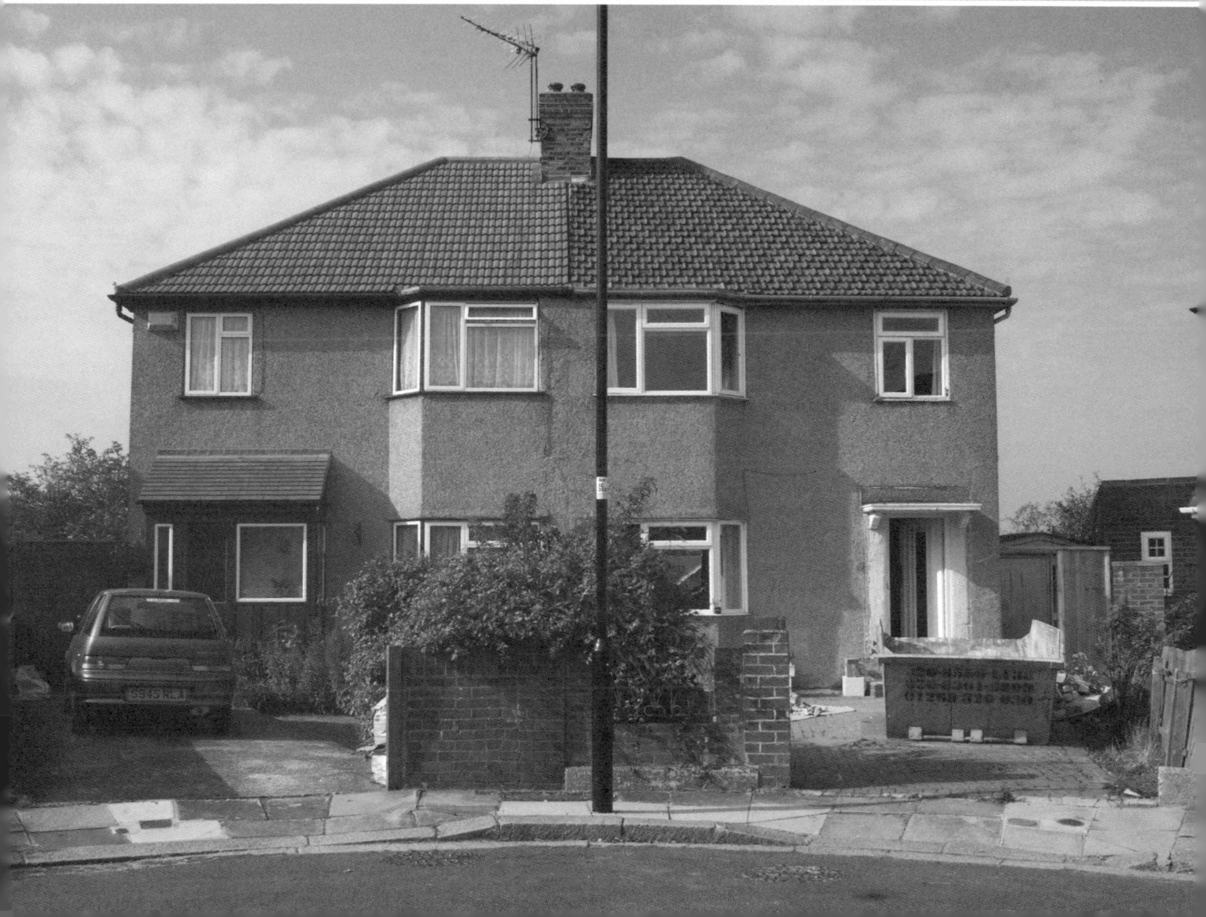

TIME BASE DRIVEN BY THE PRESENTATION OF THE 'QUESTION'

The work of art can now be envisaged as a process in time, a social process, a pragmatically structured sequence of interpersonal events through which fresh models of reality can be constructed by the actual experience of the audience. For example, when I ask a question I imply that I have an incomplete picture of some aspect of reality, the response demanded being to complete and fill in the missing parts, leading to an interactive sequential exchange in the organisation of mutual conceptions. Interactive channels are basic to society between people, and yet they are denied in the transmissional structures of the institutional fabric of society. It is for artists to shape the agenda by what they do next, and instead of being content with a marginal, alternative space for an art of social process.

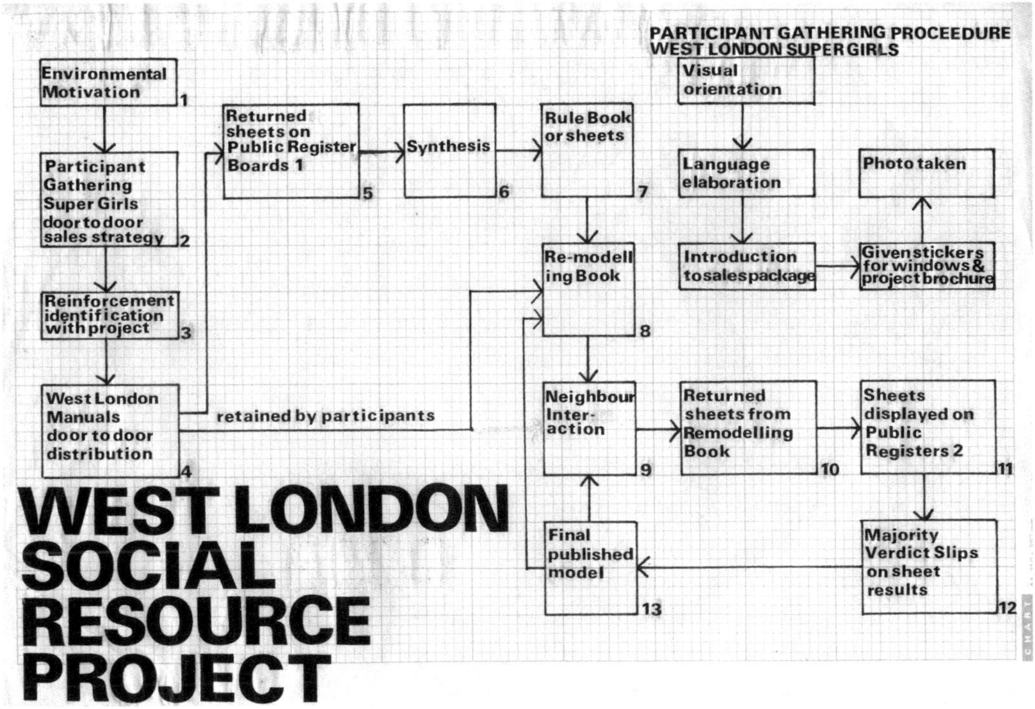

Flow diagram of events that constituted the 'West London Social Resource Project'.

MULTICHANNEL STRATEGIES

An important factor in the exclusivity of the art object is that it presents the audience with just a single frame presentation. Even if the single frame is to hold layers of meaning and so act as a cognitive process it will be incumbent still on the audience to keep coming back to stand in front of it in order to unravel its web of references. Motivation has to be kept up, if not actually increased, if enough time is to be spent unravelling the layered meanings which renders the single frame presentation wholly inadequate in forwarding new ideas and perceptions, for the audience is usually only able to attend once. Also the greater the difference between the presented concepts and what the audience accepts as normal, the more any positive response to engage with the work is going to be inhibited. For the audience to get to grips with what to them will be strange concepts they certainly need to engage with the same single frame presentation more than once, or better still to encounter a series of presentations that show different aspects of the conception. These suggestions immediately base the artwork in time, it becomes a structure of events that either sequence several exposures of the same images, or as a process that presents a changing progression of images.

As an evolving sequence the artwork is organised as an inter-related series of events that will progressively lead the audience from the familiar to the unfamiliar. A sequence like this becomes rather like a learning system, where a person acquires insight from one presented problem before moving on to the next problem, the interpretation of each problem being dependent on the insights gained previously. In this way a member of the audience can build up heuristics which enable them to look at increasingly more complex, unfamiliar and different situations. Problem B is dependent on insights acquired at A, C is dependent on insights gained at B and A, and so it goes on, situation A being closest to a person's existing frame of reference, and C being the furthest away.

Sequential presentations and repeated exposure have long been corner stones in advertising communication, and their particular interest to the artist here is that, in general, they have been developed to intervene in the audience's normal perceptions and behaviours. While advertising strategies are directly relevant to enabling the artist to break out from an otherwise almost inevitable institutionalisation and to positively intervene in the surrounding culture, a clear distinction must be made and understood about objectives. Those of advertising go in the opposite direction from my model of the artist discussed here, for advertising has its almost supreme function as the projecting and reinforcing of society's ideological parameters in the psychologies of people. The importance of advertising in the reinforcement of the dominant culture's ideologies has meant that a purely deterministic and descriptive technology has built up, and while it may be repugnant to many people, its effectiveness is not doubted. Hence I would say that the study of advertising communication is of relevance to the artist for the same strategies can be turned right around and used to free the psychologies of people and to enable them to be receptive to new perceptions and ideas.

It is not just the visual format used in advertising that wants to be examined, but the thinking that underlies the origination of those images, and right away there has to be acknowledged an inseparable relationship between 'time' and the positioning of individual presentations. The active, cognitive and sometimes physical involvement of the recipient group in the communication strategy is crucial to its successful evolution, for they need to be able to conceptually parallel the sequence of presentations. A link needs to be made by the audience between one presentation and another, carrying over elements from presentation to presentation, so as to build up, bit by bit, a new perceptual model. Instead of an image being considered because of its significance within a single framed composition, it is thought of as part of a moving structure of events in time that will evolve, as an active part of their internalisation, an audience's memory of the structure.

FROM SINGLE FRAME TO MULTIFRAME

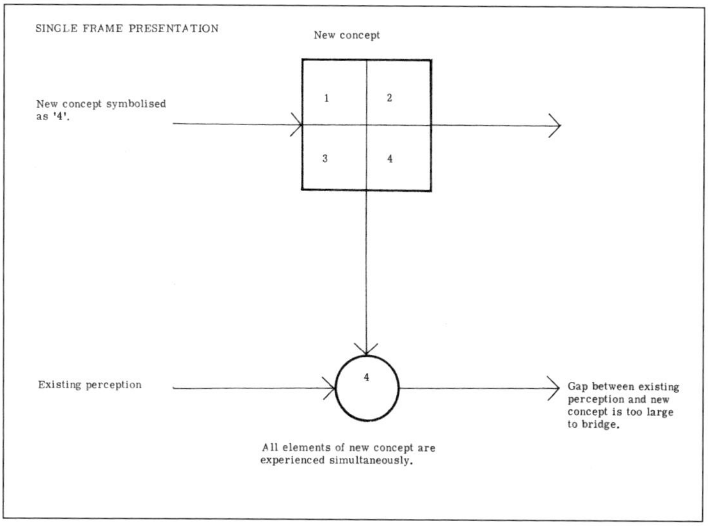

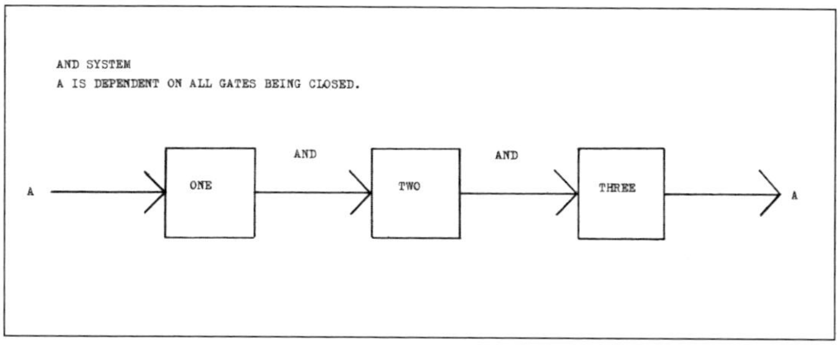

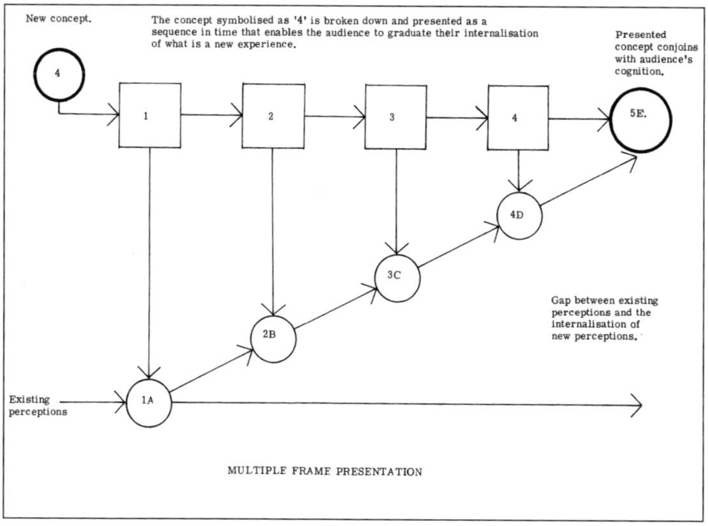

CONCEPT ACQUISITION AS PROCESS IN TIME

Sequences of references are laid out so that they can be found by a participant during the course of travelling between one Problem Display to the next. Participants use a booklet that has been designed to act as a key for the creation of connections between separately encountered references. By establishing links between the references they are formed into a progression that leads the participant to the next Problem Display where they are again represented in a polemical association

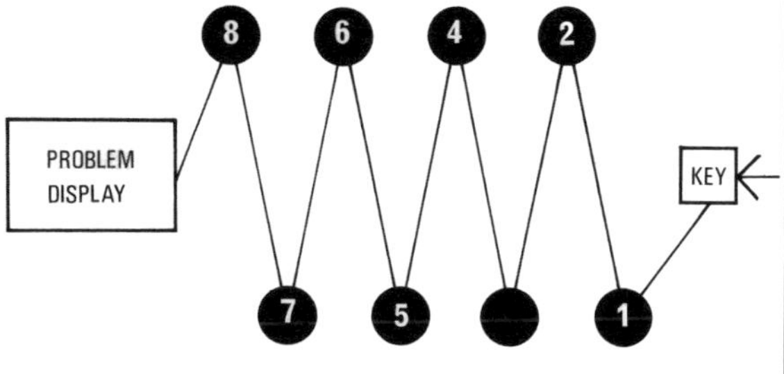

DISCRETE CONTEXTUAL REFERENCES

PARTICIPANT DOCUMENTATION OF POLEMIC

A multi-media documentation of a linear process that in some way dominates an aspect of daily life, is undertaken by each participant. Relationships between references separated by language and medium are made active by the participant's documentation. A variety of media are used, such as video, film, audio recording, photography, drawing and the collection of actual objects, so as to enact a process through time-with a beginning and an end.

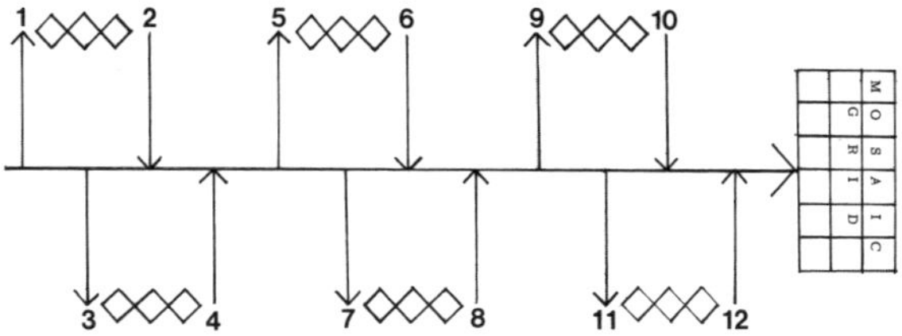

The references documented by a participant are later redistributed over a mosaic grid presented in the gallery, so as to reflect the multi-media nature of their working collaboration with the artist.

MULTI-CHANNEL MOSAIC

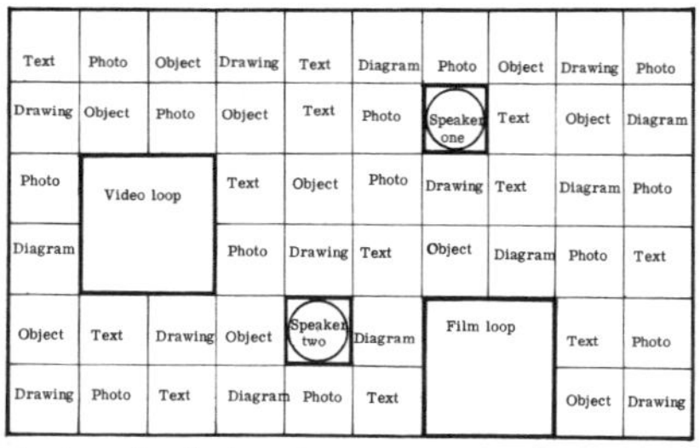

A dynamic concept frame based on a grid structure positioned on the gallery wall is constructed by each participant.

A variety of media will be used to document some linear process in each participant's life, and the results of this redistributed as discrete elements over the grid of the mosaic.

Three models that acted as parameters to the work 'Changing Everything' presented through the South London Gallery, Camberwell, London.

19

ARTWORK AS THE DYNAMIC SIMULATION OF A SOCIAL MODEL

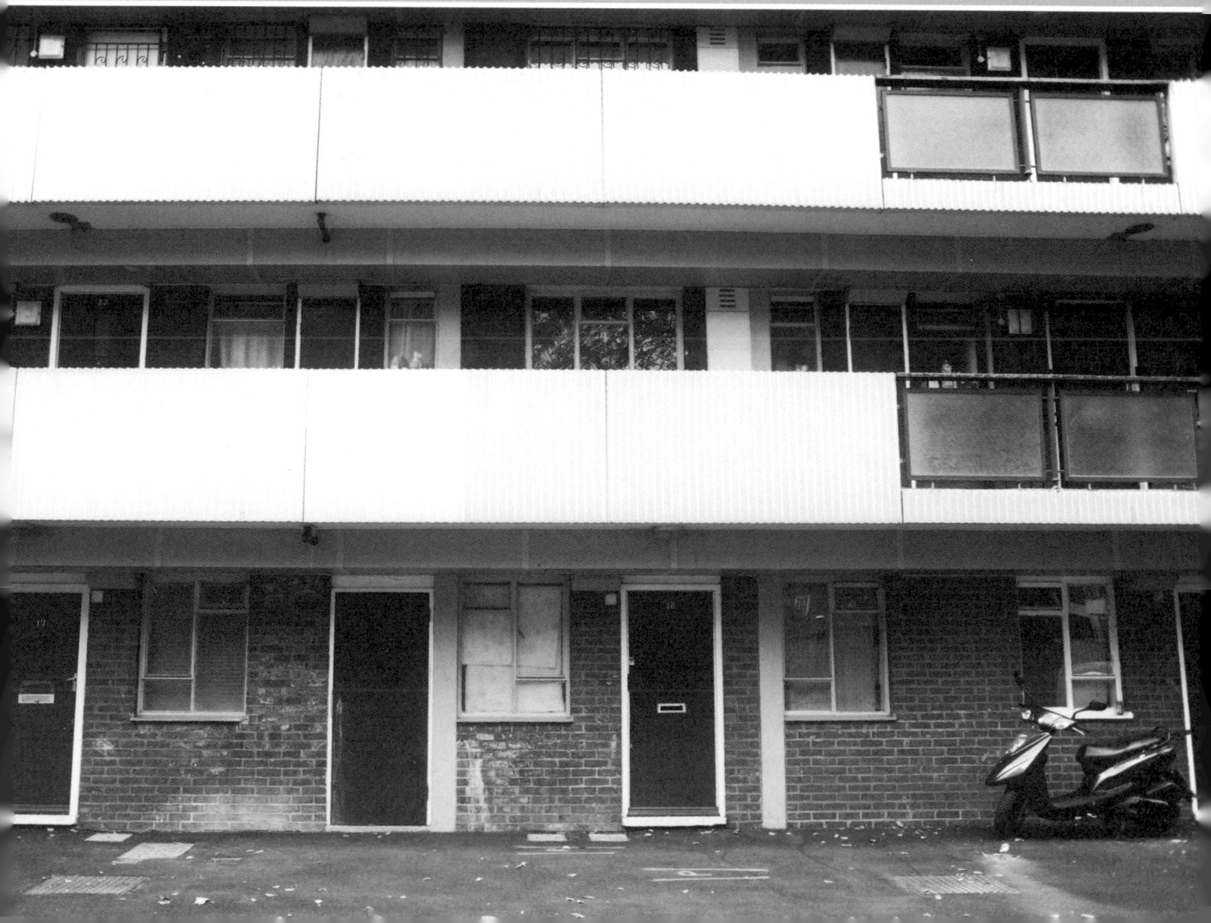

ARTWORK AS SOCIETY BETWEEN PEOPLE

More than being just a communication strategy, time can be used to take the artwork a step further and present it to the audience as a social model. By participating directly in the artwork's evolution the audience symbolically enact the social model on which the work is founded. The work is so activated by the audience that it dynamically shows the ramifications of the social model through time and through different conditions. To be really effective this symbolic enaction should take place within the fabric of the audience's life so that, as a social model, it can exist parallel with the dominating world of determinism, the world of authoritative possessions that people are led to believe is normality. In this way a work can evolve as a heuristic that is critical as well as interwoven with normality. So the artwork exists for the audience as a symbolic world, that re-models references drawn from a familiar daily reality, into a social model which can be measured against their own parallel actual experiences. In an evolving structure the symbolic world is dynamic, it likewise can evolve and be presented bit by bit in relation to the audience's ability to de-construct and internalise.

To present the symbolic world dynamically its total composition is broken down into sequential stages so as to present to the audience those parts that are nearest to their frame of reference first, before moving step by step on to more difficult conceptual territories. Thus, while still maintaining the audience's attention and involvement, the presentation of the 'Symbolic World' itself evolves from a descriptive to a prescriptive view of the world as it could possibly ideally exist. For example, relationships between four people represented in the same everyday situation can be conceptualised as both authoritative—the world as it does exist—and mutualistic—the world as it could and should exist. In a problem solving sequence the audience would actively recreate the next of the group, and in so doing they actualise the ramifications of the symbolism to themselves, and create a heuristic for getting involved in subsequent problems. Thus the internalisations made of the different meanings embodied in the stages of the 'Symbolic World' evolution are self-reinforcing to the audience, for they recreate each stage as a comparison with their own experience. The relationship between a time dependent artwork and the art institution is clearly going to be different from the traditional authoritative position of the art object housed within the art gallery or museum. It is self evident that these institutions will themselves have to become interactive social organisations to embrace such a development to a point where the audience will genuinely be their rationale and function.

Fundamental to this discussion of new strategies is that what we identify as an artwork changes from being a contained object to a structured programme of events over a specific duration. In this sense an artwork may have a 'beginning' and an 'end', and it would be the sum total of events between the beginning and the end that is the artwork.

CODES AND PARAMETERS

In developing a work as a social model, a relationship must be established between the parameters of the system, i.e. its underlying rules, and their manifestation in the real world as a coded structure of behaviour conventions. It is in the form of a coded structure of behaviour conventions that a social model will be manifest as an operational prescription, different ideologies resulting in distinct coding patterns. The establishment of formal relationships between persons is fundamental to coherency in the fabric of the social organization, regardless of ideology. These relationships result in the evolution of rules for interpersonal behaviour, that become norms or conventions, and which provide a criterion to facilitate interaction. These norms are specified by the group to fulfil such goals as the group's survival, ease and pleasantness of interaction. As such these norms form a parameter that underlies a social organization, and from which derives the structure of internal behaviour between members. Such criteria of interpersonal rules represent the ideologies of society, models of communication networks between persons forming the very essence, or control of the different social settings. As a social parameter, communication networks between persons depict how information is held within the structure, how commands are given etc., and represent the ability of a social structure to effectively organise and determine its own continuance. Thus different models of communication networks between people are associated with the parameters of various social settings. For example: the communication networks within the same small group configuration can be associated with quite different ideologies concerning the nature of a social setting.

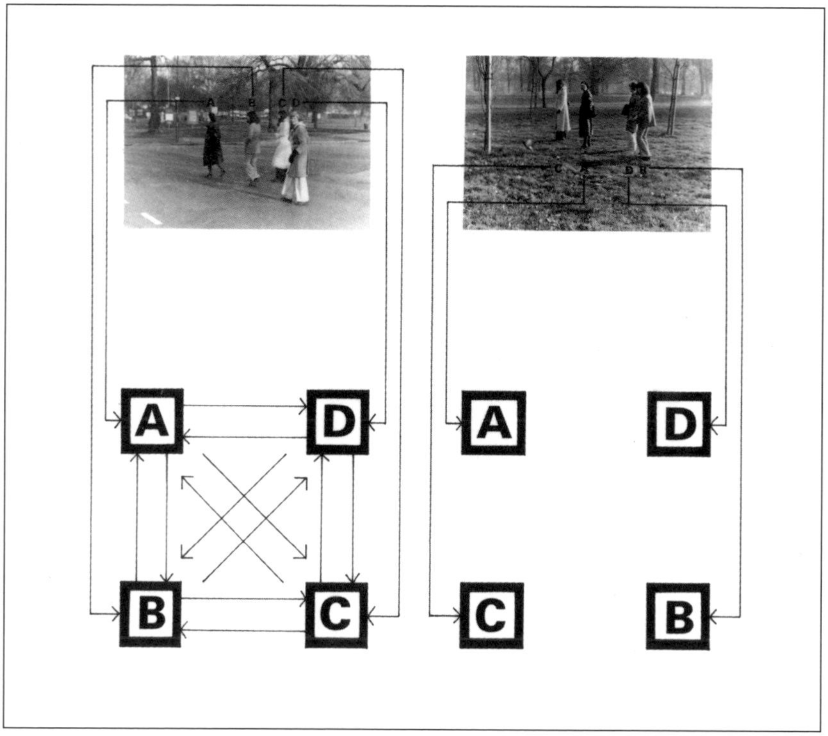

Connecting two diverse languages to create two pictures of the same reality, the photograph and the diagram.

CREATING A SYMBOLIC INTERPERSONAL TERRITORY BETWEEN PEOPLE

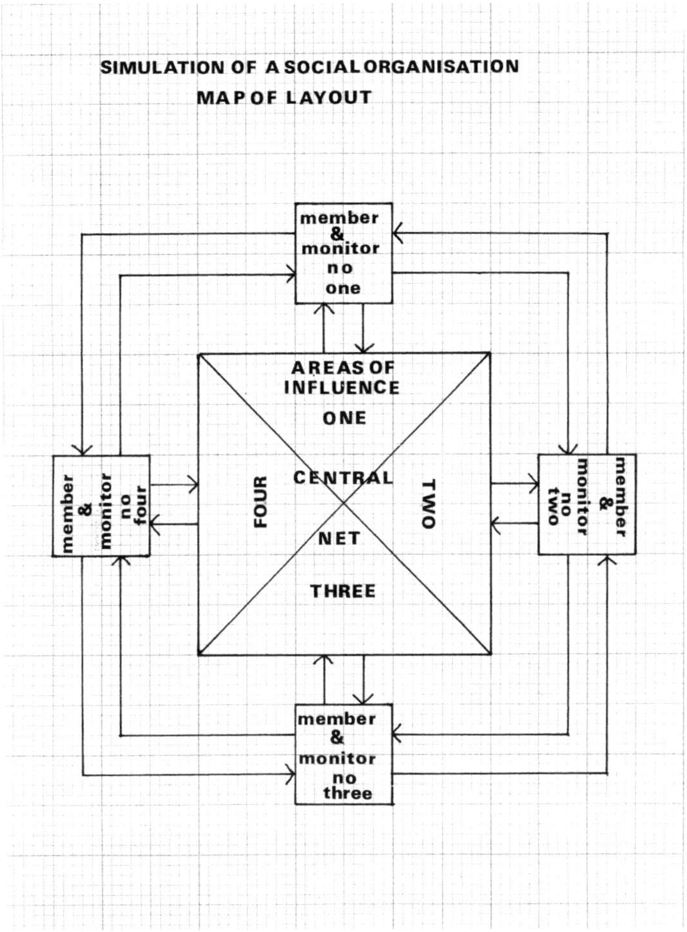

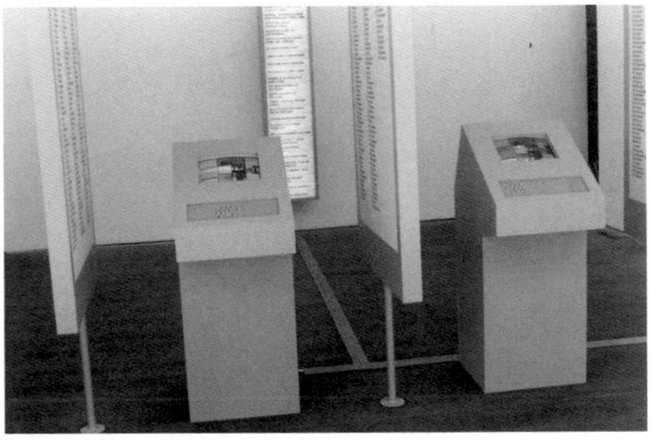

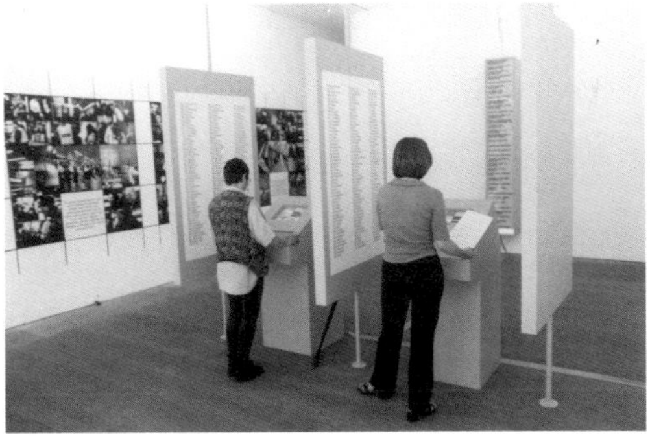

The simulation 'Free Zone' presented at Victoria Miro Gallery, London.

DEMOCRATIC ART

This model will operate on three different and developing levels: firstly on an individual personal level, then on that of the immediately surrounding locality, and finally on a broader level between the three neighbouring communities. Thus the action of the work is to externalise the implicit perception of individuals into the community, and make explicit their relativity by representing them in a dynamic state against each other and collectively, in a model of the consensus. The consensus model is made from the sum total of all the individual responses that are fed into the central core from any of the three neighbourhood areas.

The interactive interface is highly personal, presenting a dynamic model of reality to the individual that is responsive to the perceptual model they build of themselves and the directions they may wish to pursue in doing that, moving on to their relationships with other people and then to society. The fluid, changing relationship of reality is manifest to the participant visually through the interactive statements made on the visual display that is part of the console.

The work interfaces the private with the public, through a process that starts with a book of questions presented in the home and then leads on to the exploration of the same questions at a computer terminal situated in a suitable site in each neighbourhood that will allow open access. It is intended that the models developed by participants in the book will open them up, creating a conceptual freedom that allows them to develop imaginative heuristics which feed forward into the interactive dynamic world symbolically created in the visual display unit linked to the computer.

Important to the conceptual philosophy of 'Democratic Art' is the understanding that all representations made by individuals are as valid as each other, and consequently that there is a floating base line to the consensus. Thus the individual can feel the powerful freedom of their own expressions, and see at first hand their relativity in the collective consciousness of the community. In the process of this happening the work brings together the processes of communication that are increasingly shaping the infrastructure of society, with our personal need to externalise our own creative expressions into that infrastructure.

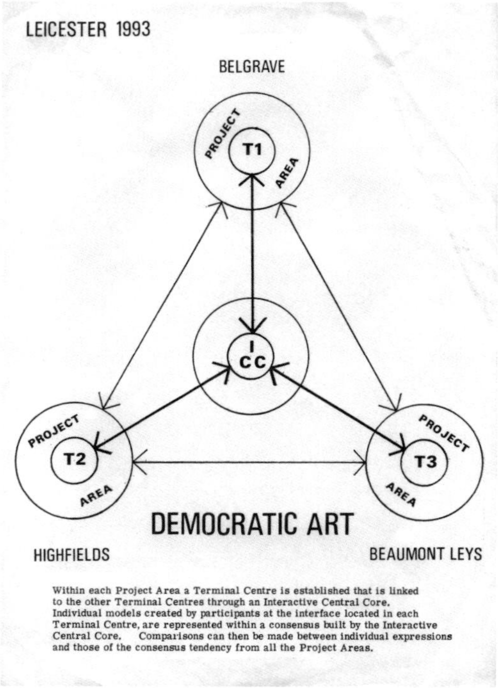

20
THE AUDIENCE AS PARTICIPANTS

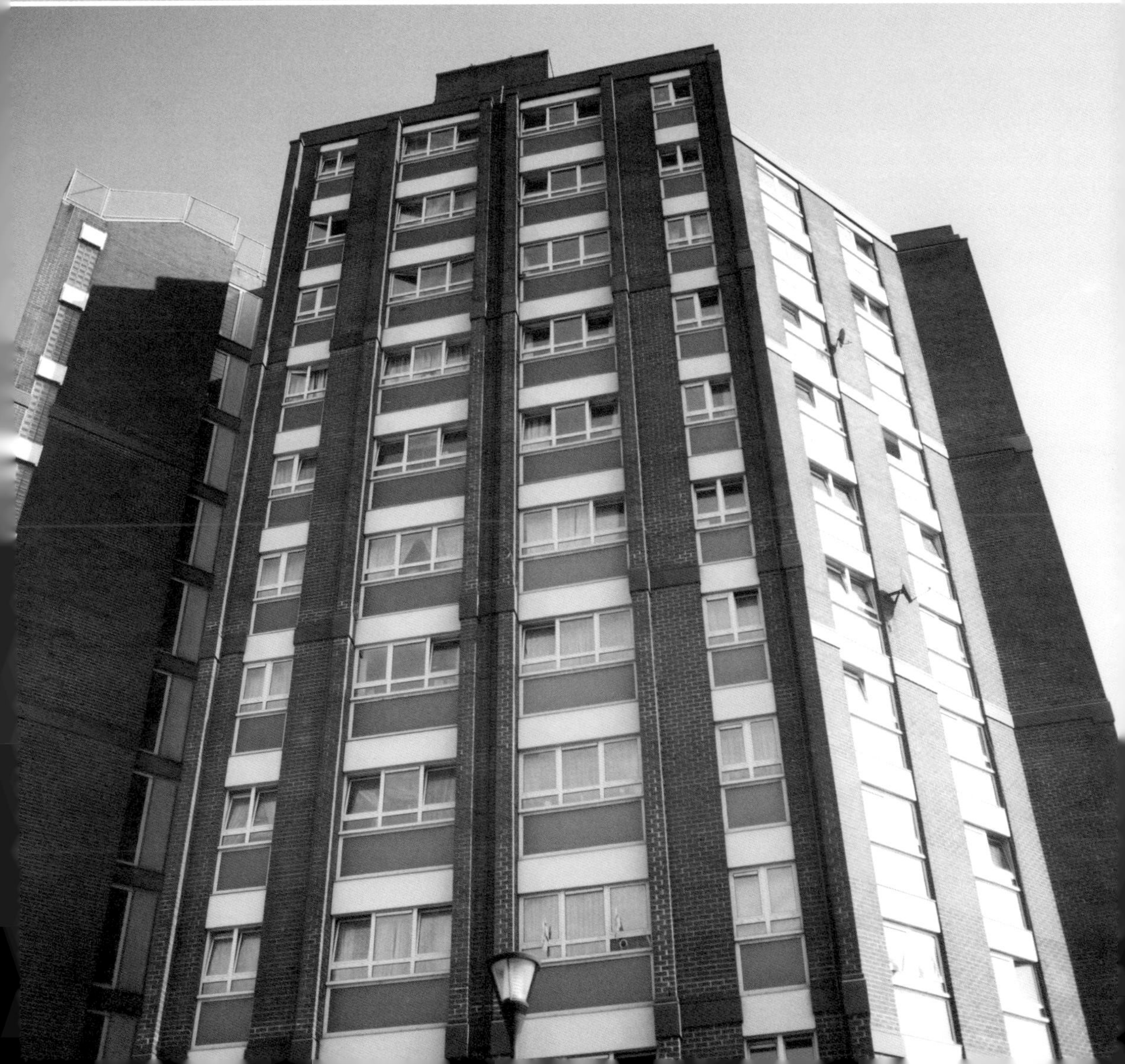

CHANGING THE STATUS OF THE AUDIENCE

The whole idea of the audience's active involvement is taken a stage further by internalisation being accomplished through engaging with actual 'tasks' of some kind. In a classical picture composition the audience passively decode the referential experience of the artist, the picture acting as an agent between this and their own experience. Now, it follows that personal experience is much more likely to initiate a change of perception than someone telling you about their own experience, and for this reason no communication strategy should be conceived of as having purely passive recipients, on the contrary the recipients should themselves activate the communication process. In fact, the more the audience can actively create the meaning for themselves the more relevant the presentations will become to them, hence the strength of presenting a series of mental, or even physical problems, to be completed in relation to a visual presentation.

The audience as 'participants' have now quite a different status in their relationship with a work, for the work's existence becomes totally dependent on people's involvement. One means of initiating audience participation is through employing the question, and using it as a fundamental vehicle for generating social interaction. The question implies that the 'asked' has an incomplete picture of some aspect of experience, by answering it the recipient completes the picture, in the process ordering and making their own perhaps implicit thoughts coherent to themselves before the act of articulating them to another person. Time dependent problem presentations will require much more attention and commitment from participants, especially as the presentations are to intervene in the real world, so a clear and relevant objective will need to be apparent from the outset. An audience which normally has attention to art as a low priority will only want to get involved in presentations if they see a likely outcome that is relevant to themselves, so immediately its functionality for them is their prime initial question. This condition must be especially important when the artwork is considered as an entity operating within the everyday fabric of the audience's world, where it has to compete with so many already established priorities. Here the artwork is presented within what a participant already accepts as normal, and yet it is ultimately aimed at pulling them out of that acceptance of normality, asking them to question the normality and ultimately to remodel how it will be perceived.

PROJECT AREAS IN RELATION TO A CENTRAL COMPUTER PROCESSING CORE, EDINBURGH SOCIAL MODEL CONSTRUCTION PROJECT

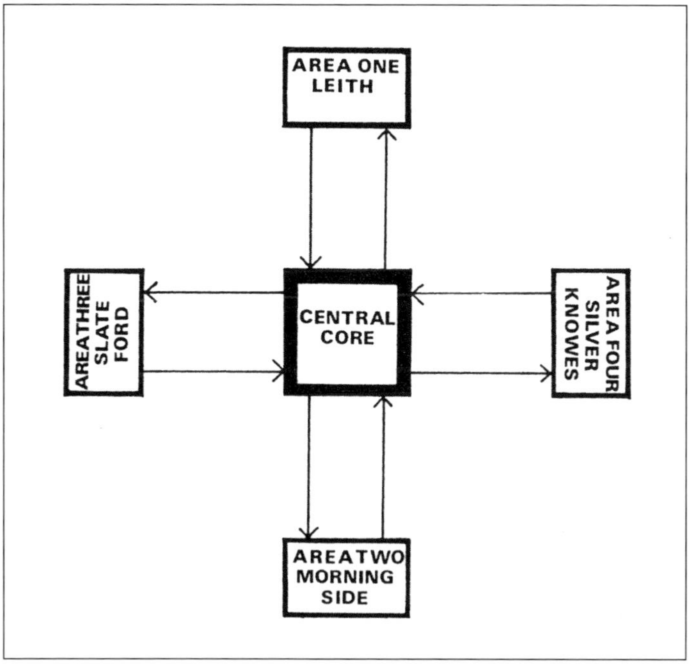

The basic structure of the work as a social model constructed around Cybernetic concepts of self-organisation.

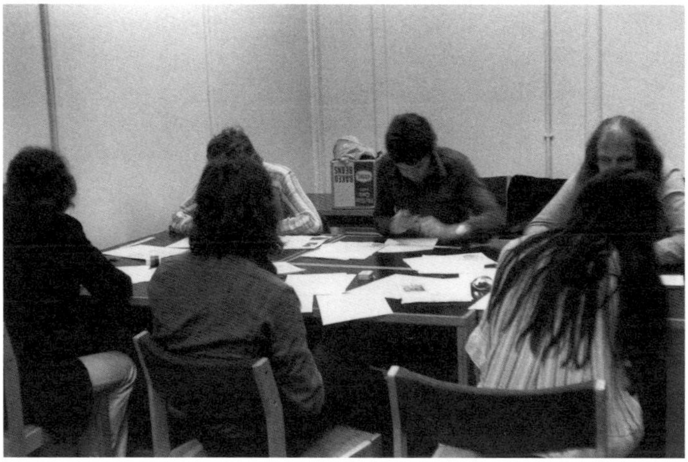

Project Operators working on processing Participant Response Sheets in the Central Core of the Edinburgh Social Model Construction Project.

A DESCRIPTION OF THE EDINBURGH SOCIAL MODEL CONSTRUCTION PROJECT

The project consisted of a self-structuring learning process made up from five interdependent Project States which were individually operational for one day. This learning process consisted of tasks and was aimed at enabling participants to encode their perceptions of social behaviour conventions, customs, and rules that were: 1: within their own social group. 2: between their social group and other social groups. This learning process consisted of an evolving information loop between participants from different Project Areas, and was established via a Central Core that consisted of a processing system located in the centre of Edinburgh in a room lent by the University. Each of the five interdependent Project States represented a cycle in the loop between participants and the Central Core. An individual Project State was linked to a Problem Category, these initially concerned a participant's relationship to intimate behaviour conventions within the family group. The Problem categories changed as the cycle of Project States continued during the five days the project lasted until they concerned formal and public behaviour conventions. During each Project State a participant was given three Problem Sheets on which were represented that task that they engaged in completing. These three Problem Sheets were of two different types, requiring different responses from a participant. The first Problem Sheet of the three had printed on it consensus tendencies made by the Central Core from the previous Project State's returns, beneath which were two Monitoring Assignments. A difference between Problems and Monitoring Assignments was that in the latter a participant recorded his perception of conditions as they existed, examining their origin, (For example: 'Describe how at present your family take their annual holiday') while in a Problem different conditions were postulated during the process of constructing a solution ('If all your family were on holiday together, what activities could you create for them.') Monitoring Assignments and Problems were linked as can be seen in the examples, a participant using the information recorded in a Monitoring Assignment as a foundation to construct a solution for a later Problem. Each Monitoring Assignment was linked to two Problems, the first concerning a participant's own social group's person to person interaction, and the second, inter social group, or other Participant Group person to person interaction. The list of consensus tendencies was also to be used by participants in providing solutions to Problems, especially those that concerned Participants other than from their own Project Area.

The actual completed Problem Sheets being processed by the Central Core were collected and displayed on Public Monitors located in the Project Areas. The Public Monitors showed the overall state of the project to participants and members of the general public.

As the basis of the problems used in the project learning system were adaptively chained (by using the solutions to preceding problems as a determining criteria for the selection of new problems), it was envisaged that the learning system would evolve a self determined hierarchy of information, the contents of which would gradually become more meaningful and relevant to participants as it progressed through the Project States' loop cycles.

THE ARTWORK AS ART INSTITUTION

In the early 1970s Nicholas Wagner established The Gallery London, it remains one of the only examples in this country of a type of gallery where the artist running the gallery sees it as a work of art—their own work of art. The exhibitions and the running of the gallery merge into one activity, combining to form an art work. My work 'Meta Filter', was one of a programme of collaborations made between The Gallery London and another artist, and represented the integration of two radical polarities in considering the artwork's relation to an institution. The Gallery London considered itself to be a work of art, and Meta Filter considered itself to be an art institution. Meta Filter was a dynamic simulation of a social model based on the concept of social self-organisation, enacted here between two people. These people, possibly never having met before, sat one on each side of Meta Filter and were presented with an evolving sequence of slides showing a group of people engaged in everyday activities. In association with each slide was a question directed at how the two operators saw various relationships within the group, and through the interactive agency of Meta Filter the two people attempted to construct a common perceptual model of social relationships. People from quite different realities, with nothing to do with the art world, could conjoin in their interaction with Meta Filter as they created their own language of participation to form agreements between themselves. The results of people's co-operation were displayed on portable screens positioned around Meta Filter, and the work itself was built in such a manner that it could easily be set up as its own institution within nearly any other social facility relevant to its audience, such as a supermarket, library, school etc.

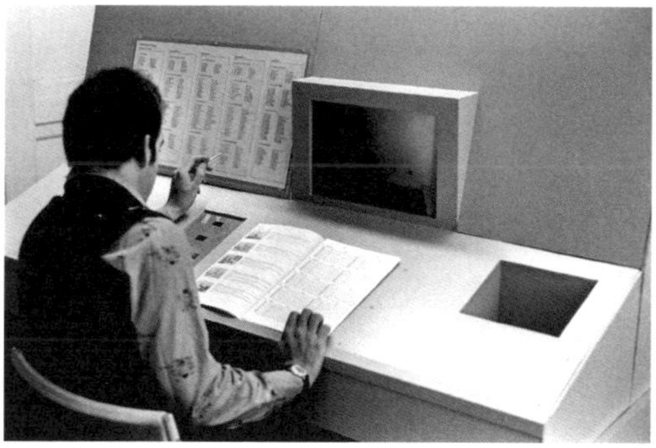

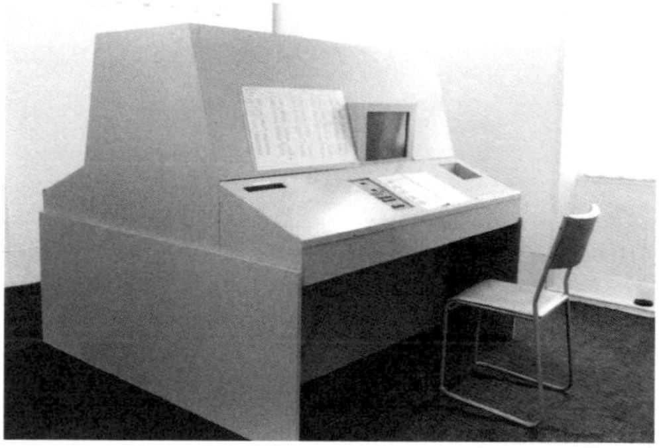

'Meta Filter' at The Gallery London.

21
PROBLEM SOLVING AS A CREATOR OF INSIGHT

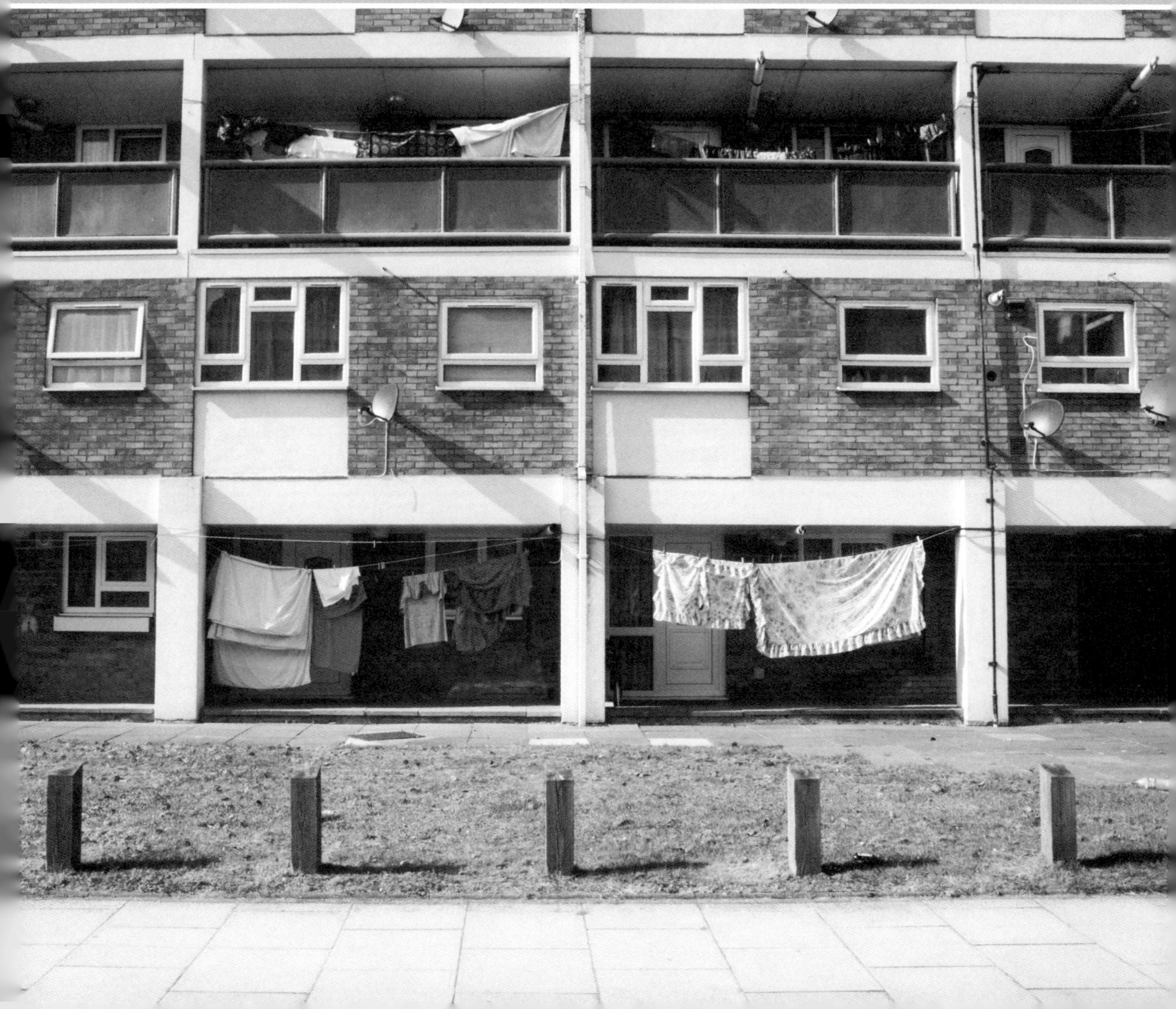

REPRESENTATION OF PROBLEM SITUATIONS

In developing a strategy for engaging an audience through a symbolic world, I have purposefully sought out polemical issues that will have a meaning to the audience. These can either be issues that are particular to a specific context, already known to the viewer, or are generally extant throughout contemporary life, and though they may not be personally experienced by the viewer, they will nevertheless be generally known to them. Both representations of a polemic lead to quite different encoded developments of the symbolic world; in the first instance encodings would be tied to a context available to that specific audience, for the contextual meaning would drop rapidly once outside it, in the latter instance general encoding symbols would need to be particularised by the viewer. For instance some of the polemical contexts that I have located and embodied in the formation of a symbolic world have been the tower block, the office desk, the waste land, the High Street chain 'life-style' shop, the early 1980s Post Punk private clubs in London. In selecting these contexts I was aware that not only does the issue, the polemic represented in the symbolic world need to be accessible, to the audience, but the language used to convey the problem situation must also be accessible. Three contrasting directions to this important consideration about language are as follows:

1. The existing language of the audience is used, especially language that is tied to a restricted context or routine. This of course would be directed at an audience that was already connected with the context from which the language was derived, so would be an appropriate approach when the work was destined to operate in a specific location, with a specific audience, both being known in advance. Then a high degree of engagement and internalisation can be expected, but when the audience is not specified in advance, i.e. if the context is not known, then this approach is not appropriate.
2. To embody the 'meaning' of the work in an encoding language that is universal and generally available within society, i.e. as in the case of projected idealisations, stereotypes, so here the work is put into a language that is above and beyond contexts, and requires the audience to actively contextualise the encodings, particularising them into their own experience.
3. The audience acquires, or learns, the special encoding language of the work either in advance or as part of the process of entrance into the symbolic world.

Giving a time base to experience the symbolic world, perhaps even representing it as a journey, opens up the possibility that a language is acquired from an initial access point, that is then picked up and leant as part of a problem solving routine. But in all three language considerations the more familiar, the more universally known by the audience is the encoding language for the representations used, the more likely the outcome will be for lessening inhibition and increasing involvement. Thus in building the symbolic world around a polemic such as 'high rise living', its effectiveness is through measures of prior knowledge because you do not need to live in a tower block, let alone the one depicted in the symbolic world to be aware of the polemic concerning living in such a building, for this knowledge is common throughout the culture. So the element of recognition, at least initially, with something familiar, perhaps polemical, is very important not only to access but also for the subsequent process of filling the symbolic world with personal meaning.

THE PRESENTATION OF PROBLEMS

An interactive task orientated learning sequence could provide the subject with the means to accomplish them. This would be achieved through the provision of a mechanism which controls through feedback the relationship between the tasks encountered and the subject, and would be responsive to their ability to learn.

If the tasks were presented in the form of problems to which the subject provides solutions, the subject could be placed in a position whereby they established their own heuristics in providing solutions, progressing through sub-routine sequences as they were accomplished. The provision of problems that are going to be meaningful to the subject is important if solutions are to be elicited. Man has been described as a problem solving animal, and the presentation of problems sited in an understood context (i.e. a crossword puzzle, etc.) can be generative towards providing solutions, with no apparent vindication other than self satisfaction, or perhaps as an excuse to run through and exercise problem-solving facilities. Fundamental to problem solving/heuristics is trial and error, which takes place when a possible solution is trialed against a problem, the basis of the next possible solution being selected according to the amount of trial and error. From trial and error a subject can construct probability based models of possible solutions, developing the ability to construct applicable heuristics.

In a sequence of problems which gradually increase in difficulty, a subject is able to build heuristics from a frame of reference constructed from past experience with previous trial and error procedures, undertaken in providing solutions to problems in the same sequence. The construction of a frame of reference by the subject, which is appropriate to a learning routine, could be structured so as to represent the acquisition by them of the artist's intentional concepts which are built into tasks in the learning sequence.

The presentation to the subject of 1: an environment that as it evolved fed the subject with problems (A Problem Environment), and 2: a goal that utilized a basic drive such as survival, which could be used to maintain their attention, would open up the possibility of the subject developing heuristic problem solving abilities in order to maintain a stable position within the problem environment. For example, events in the problem environment would become problems when they varied outside the boundaries of the subject's predictive model, thus making the subject's relationship within the problem environment less sure, and thus less stable. The re-attainment of the stability of the subject requires the development of probability-based heuristics, which are trialed in an attempt to construct fresh predictive models of events that are causing the instability. The amount of variance that events generated in the problem environment have from the subject's previous predictive model's limits, would increase over a period of time. This would gradually increase the amount of difficulty incurred by the subject in constructing adequate predictive models to ensure stability; though increases in problem difficulty could be matched to the ability of the subject to provide solutions, through the possibility of sequentially dependent problems in the form of sub-routines, one problem having to be solved by a subject before another is presented, through the use of an over-all controller.

AN ART CRITIC'S REACTION TO 'META FILTER'

Extracts from Richard Cork's London Art Review, Evening Standard, 16 October 1975: 'Nice To Meta You'.

Meta Filter's subtitle is a State Of Agreement, which neatly summarises the overall aim of the project: to invite its operators to examine each other's solutions to the problems presented by the machine and then, if these answers differ, to work through a number of alternatives until a consensus has been reached. Right at the outset, then, it is important to realise that Meta Filter does not base itself on the conventional idea of a test or quiz, to which there is one definitive, award-winning set of replies. The whole point of the exercise lies in the interaction between its operators, as they come to terms with the challenge of finding a solution which accommodates both of the attitudes they hold. Since the problems all take the form of photographs showing people relating either to themselves, to groups, or to permutations of the two, the entire programme revolves around how we all behave towards each other in easily recognisable, everyday situations.

To begin with, the operators both press their start buttons and look at the identical photograph they find on the screen in front of them. They then find the same picture in the Problem Book lying on the desks, and attempt to answer the question printed by the picture. The first photograph for instance shows a girl sitting alone in an empty room, and the operators have to decide whether she seems apprehensive, relaxed, angry, forlorn etc. The word they eventually choose must be selected from a thesaurus of nearly 1000 numbered words displayed beside the screen; and the operators feed their choice into the machine by punching out the word's number on their keyboards so that they can see at a glance how greatly they differ in their answers.

The procedure is then repeated with both sides attempting to find new words which come closer to an area of agreement, until they finally settle for a solution which satisfies the two players.

Each session usually lasts about two hours, but if the operators fail to agree on any of the photographs, they remain stationary within the system and are required to sort out their differences with a new problem drawn from the same kind of group behaviour. Players who fail to see eye-to-eye could, therefore, take several hours to complete the exercise. If all this sounds impossibly complicated, let me hasten to add that the system becomes easy to handle after only one trial run. And the fascination of pitting your own interpretation of the photographs against your partner's makes the time pass very quickly.

PAGES FROM 'THE PROBLEM BOOK'

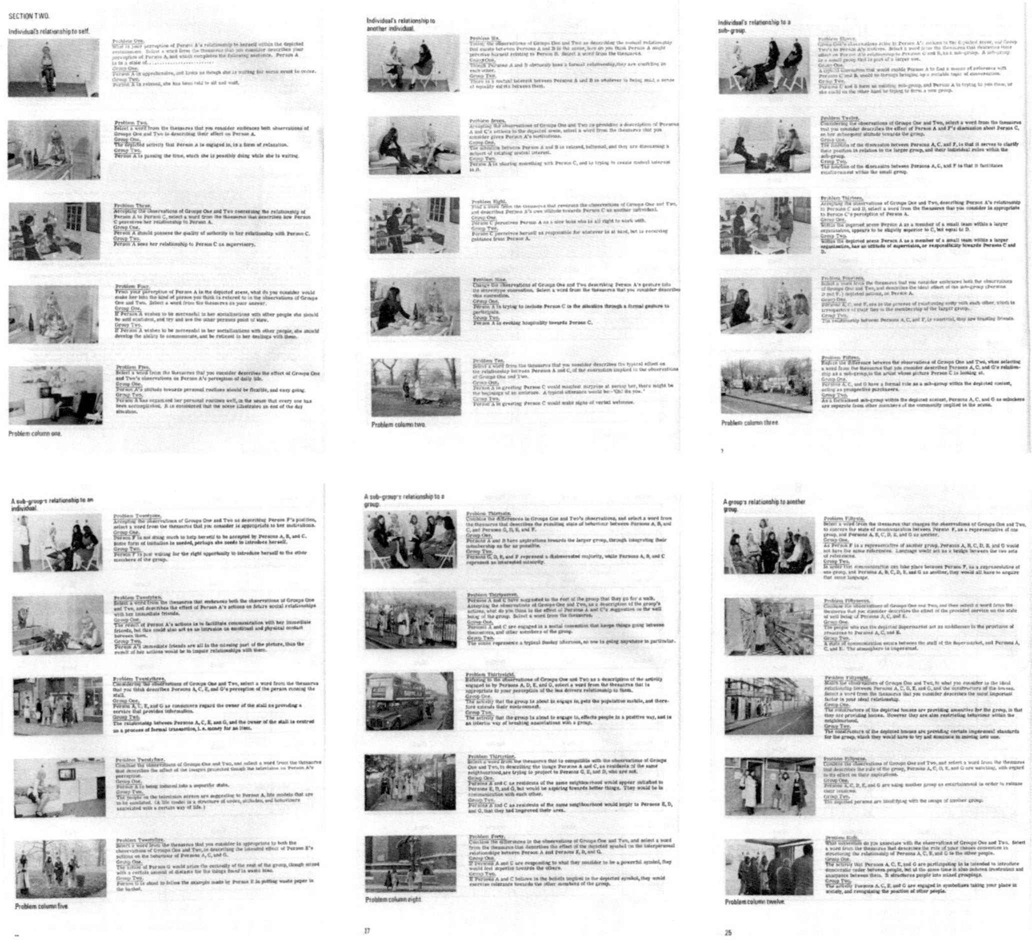

Each participant in Meta Filter was given a copy of 'The Problem Book' which they used to record their responses to the Problem Situations presented and their interaction with the other participant.

22

SECRET LANGUAGE

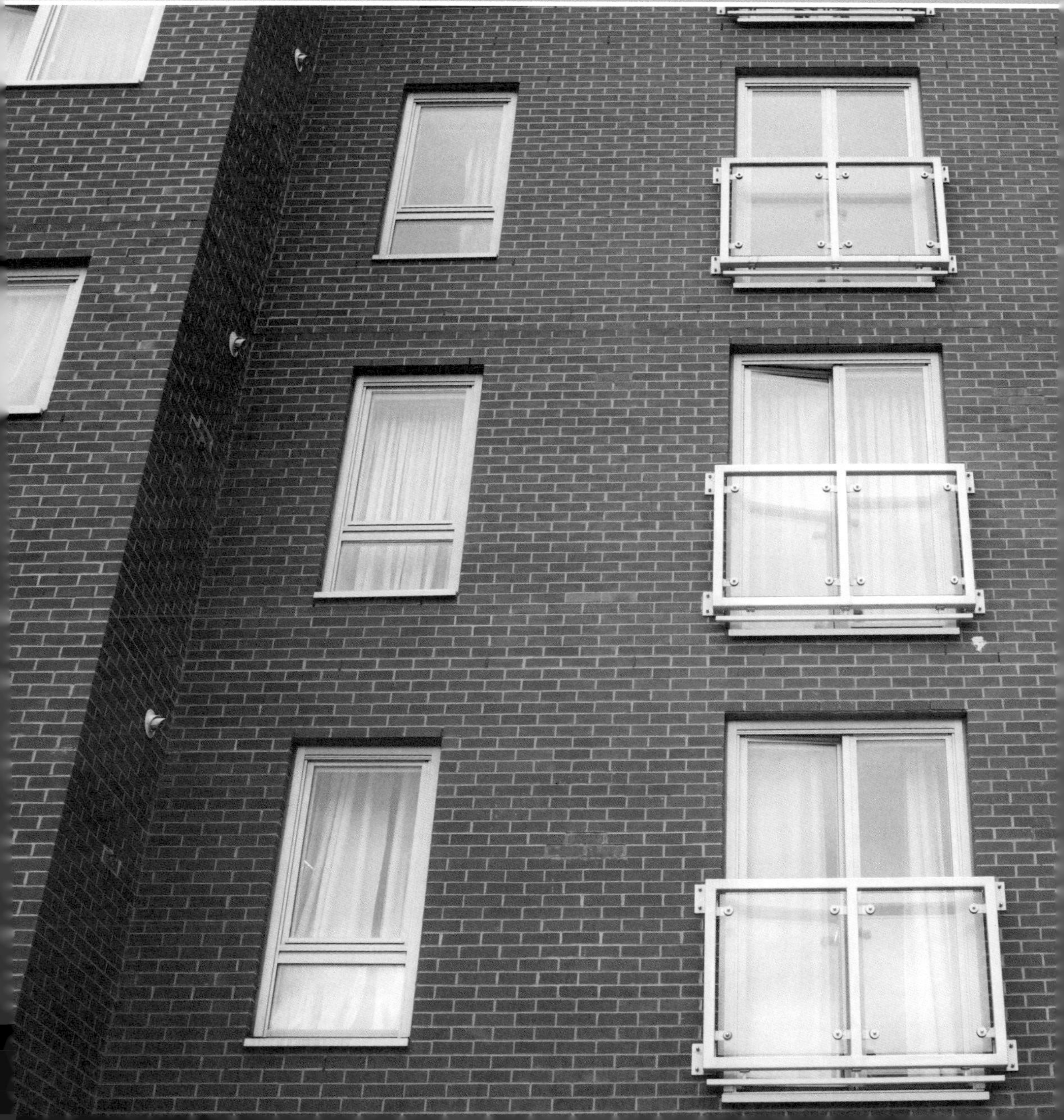

SIGNS AND MESSAGES FROM CORPORATE AMERICA

Contemporary life exists within a jungle of visual signs and messages that are vying with each other to influence our future thoughts and actions. One can go as far as considering that one's whole cultural experience is at some point mediated in this way, our engagement with cultural experience being a constant process of decoding what has been encoded and left / positioned by someone else. While it is easy to recognise the prominence that signs have in our experience of everyday life, the proliferation of signs, and whole systems of signs, that tell us what to do or who we are, is a largely unannounced feature of urban life today. A feature of this quietly spreading network of institutionally originated signs is their inherent reductiveness in the basic representation of complex reality. This simplification of complexity in signs towards a universal, basic object, reinforces an authoritatively-made distancing between people, between those persons that originated a sign and those that receive its message. These institutional signs are a 'secret language' that is articulated somewhere out of reach of those to be affected. Articulated by corporations, administrations and officialdom that generally inhibit the idea of the free expression of individual self-identity and creativity; but it is another 'secret language' associated with just this that has had much more public notice and attention.

This other 'secret language' is formed from highly personal expressions made public by people that are under pressure from the anonymity and passivity implied in the various forms of institutional signs, and state their opposition to its inherent determinism. This latter 'secret language' takes the form of sign systems that manifest the self-identity, the community and creative power of the sign maker. This 'secret language' is subversive, often consisting of spontaneous layerings made directly onto the very physical surfaces that radiate messages of institutional determinism. For here I include the material structure of the environment as a sign; for example, wood panelling, polished marble and unpainted concrete, all can have an authoritative, corporate message. Personal informal sign systems originate undercover, as a 'counter consciousness' that has been marginalised from the very normality projected by society, jumping out from behind its fabric to demand attention.

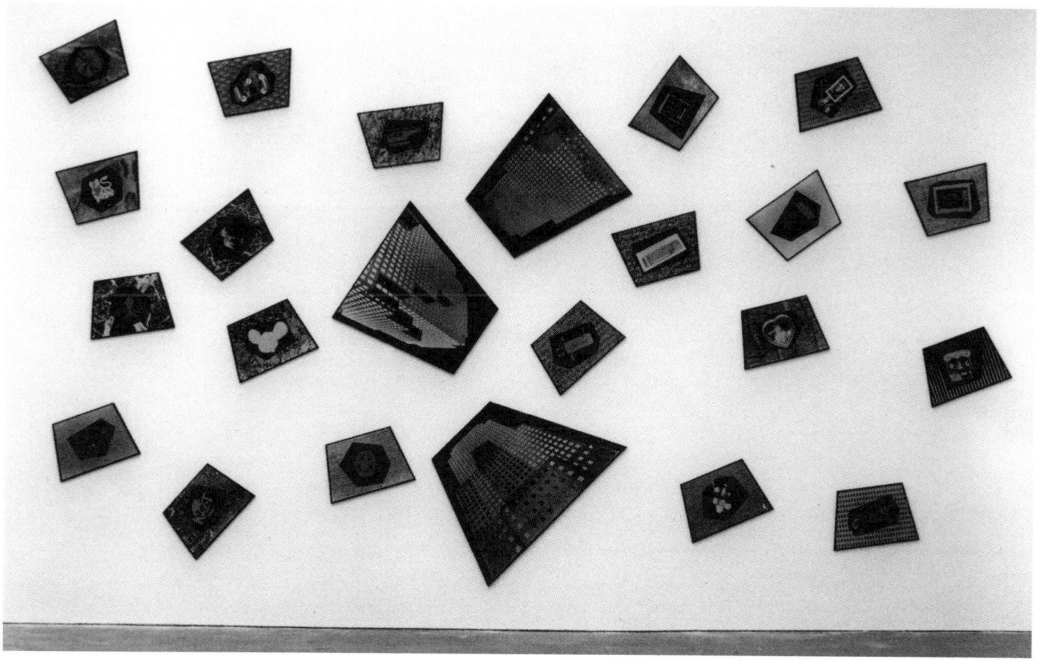

'Signs And Messages From Corporate America', presentation at the One World Centre, Manhattan, New York.

FROM THE OFFICE DESK SPACE AT MERRILL LYNCH, NEW YORK

In conversation with office workers

CG There are personal things they make us feel like you're a bit at home, like it gives you a little bit feeling that it's not all work, you can look at something, you can look at the pictures that you have on your desk, you can look, and everything means something to you.
SW Yes, so I mean that connection is sort of, do you think it relieves a kind of tension, or it says something.
MM Well, unicorn pictures are unique to me and they do, all four of them have been given to me by certain people in my life who've affected me, but they're the only things that hold any sentiment that are in that cubicle, everything else in the cubicle that I own, except for my pictures and my little cards that have been given to me by dear friends, they hold sentimentality, but the office equipment that I utilize to do my function at work, that holds no sentiment whatsoever.
SW Yes, I was going to ask you why you were involved with unicorns.
MM They're something unreal, and I sometimes like to dwell in the unreal, 'cos reality sometimes is, it's not good, and life sometimes deals us pretty bad hands and that life, that fantasy life that they come from is so beautiful that I just like to dwell on it and look at them and it's, it's just a mythical life, I know it's not real, I'm not, you know, I don't dwell on it I'd rather be there than here, I mean that would put me in a total different category, but I like to look at them and dream because they're such a perfect specimen and beautiful.
CG Yes, it's blank to go into a cubicle if there's nothing there, you have to have something of you.
MM The cubicle itself is not warm, so you have to make it warm, it's, when I first moved here I cried because I was so sad about the way it looked, it was so cold and we were facing the other way at the time, they had moved us around, it's a lot different now, you have to make it warm, because it's a cold environment.

THOUGHTS ABOUT THE DESK SPACE, OFFICE WORKER, WOKING

In conversation with office workers

KK I create my own little atmosphere and people can say, oh that's Kathryn because of the piggy mug on my desk, people associate because I've brought in little china animals of pigs, oh Kathryn likes pigs, so therefore you get presents of a pig mug, so people can always tell where I am, it's nice to know that, and with the Duck, that was a present from when we went on holiday to France and I felt if it's stuck at home nobody's going to see it, if I bring it in to the office and if somebody comes and says, oh that's nice, where did you get that from, then you say, oh we had this wonderful holiday in France and it's got a story associated with it, that postcard, the postcard on my window, that was where they had the sale conference this year in Tenerife, Sarah sent me a postcard so I put it up, so you try and bring your own personality to what is basically a very boring office situation.

SW So sometimes like these pigs and that, I mean, they extend you out of the space—in a way into another world, inner world.

KK People walk past and say, this is somebody, somebody with a personality, with a character, they might think you're wacky having china pigs on your desk but at least they'll notice you, the same way I call my little yellow stickies with notes on them reminders to myself, to me, they're just sticking them up on the window, pictures of authors or a Christmas card that somebody painted for me, yes, you try and project your own image you might have your own special files that people say, oh, that's Kathryn's file.

SW And also it's sort of personalizing perhaps something that's anonymous.

KK Yes, Kathryn the Secretary becomes Kathryn the Person who's got a fascination for pigs, you know, you can talk about something outside work, as I say, it's a way of bringing the outside world into work, but without affecting it, I mean, those pigs are very unobtrusive really, unless you're actually standing over my desk, the general person walking past wouldn't notice them, so you know, I wouldn't want, you know, big piggy display posters and things because then it's almost drawing attention to you, but it's nice just to have something subtle that if a person does stop by your desk, almost you're begging them to ask you, where do they come from, it's a way of, a sort of subtle attraction for people, as I say, I wouldn't want to be blatant and you know, hang up a picture of Richard Gere or something.

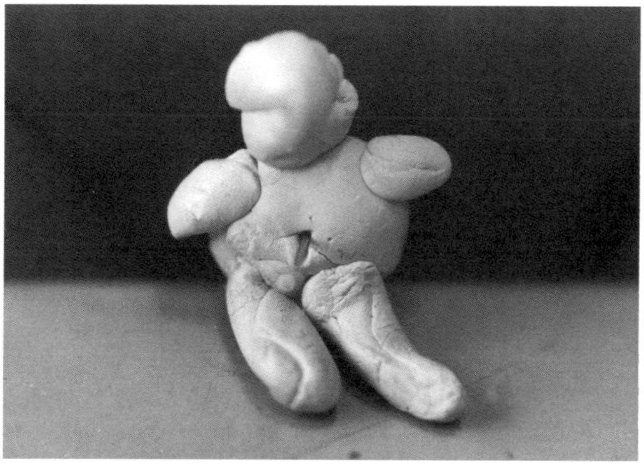

An image of 'The Boss'.

SIGNS OF PERSONAL EXPRESSION, DELANCEY STREET, NEW YORK

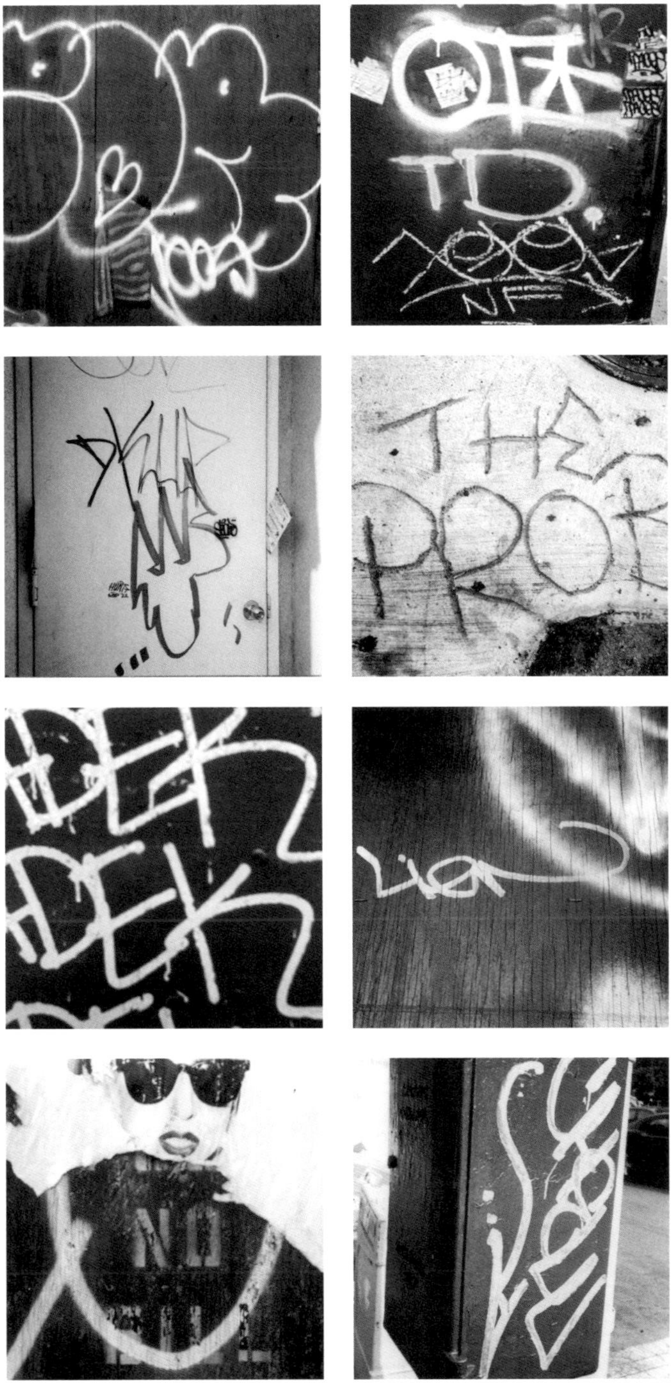

23
THE EXPERIENCE OF DETERMINISM

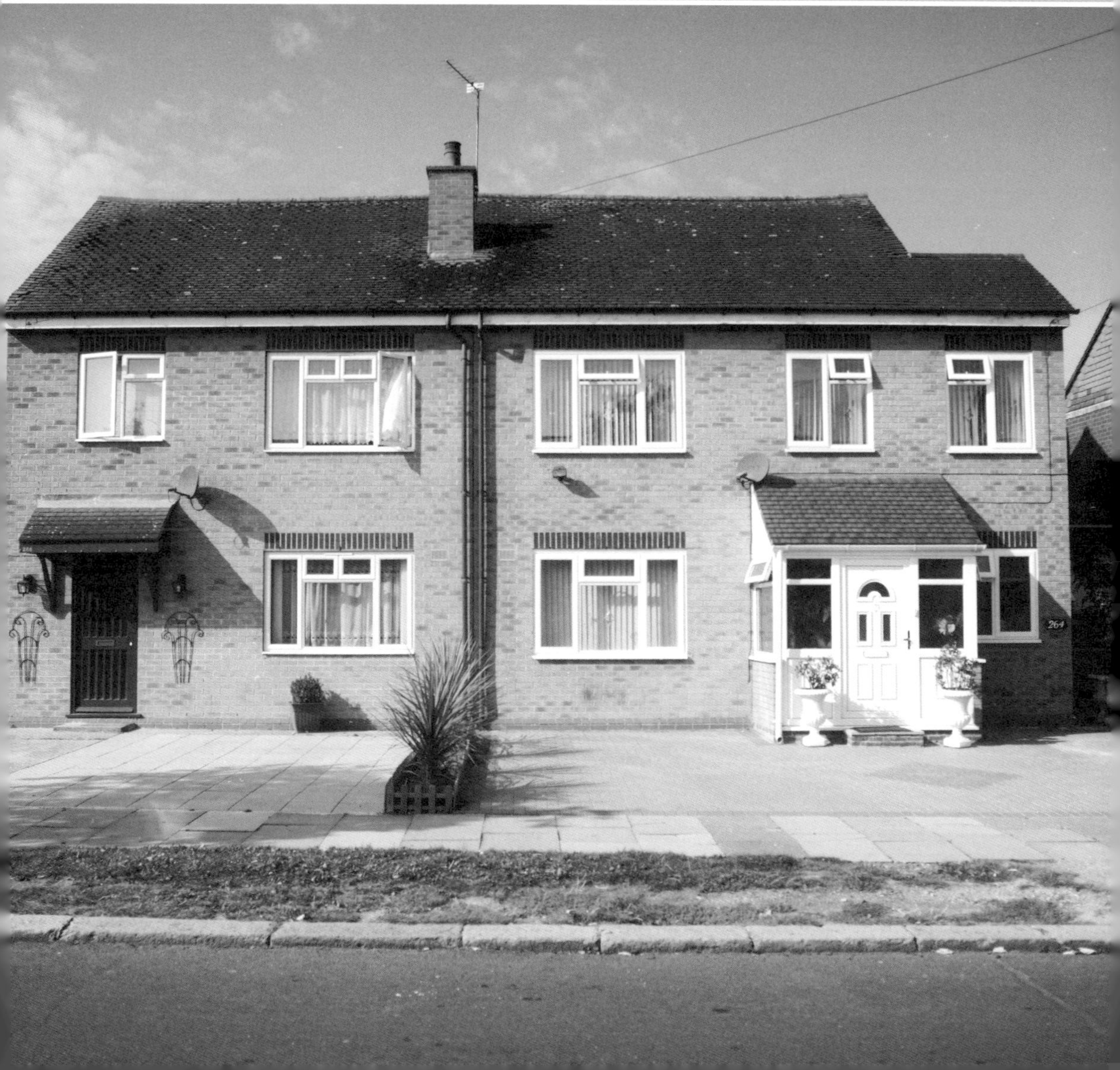

NEW REALITY LIVING

Buildings in our cities have long had the function of making public displays of a social consciousness, but particularly since the late 1950s and early 60s this has reached a new sophistication where all-embracing complexes have been planned to induce a particular morality and behaviour inside the psychology of residents. What has followed from this is an authoritative environment that I call 'The New Reality', which has had a major effect on influencing the personal and social lives of its residents, and become such a polemical symbol of modern life. This outcome arises from the simple message that flows from 'The New Reality's' very physicality of the building, that there is a separation between those that make and communicate decisions and those that are affected by them. This is encapsulated in buildings that reiterate the power of a higher authority, by not acknowledging in the building's outface the individuality, even existence of occupants at all. These now all too familiar estates of concrete slab and tower blocks that have proliferated throughout our cities are the new institutional icons that have become established as a normative feature in our physical world. For whether you live in one or not, they are still registered in your framework of reference for contemporary life.

Within the optimistic social climate that prevailed in the early 1960s an idealistic institutional paternalism took root, almost as a philosophy, which envisaged increasing resources, availability, and a new way of life for the future that was self-responsible and tolerant. In fact the idea of the 'future' as a dream that everyone was moving towards was very important, being in itself a validation for the professional architect and planner to actualise highly conceptual and abstract models into the environment as suitable for the envisaged 'modern' way of life. However, despite this optimism there was always the fundamental separation between the institutional idealisations of the planners, architects, and council officials, which they projected onto the building, and the actual lives of the people who had to live there. For residents were rarely given even a cursory consultation about the building they were being asked to live in, and they were certainly never able to feed their ideas back into the design. So, despite the liberal notions of the 60s, what was demanded from residents was an acquiescing self-responsibility, where they would accede to the social attitudes enshrined in the language of their building.

The regular, vertical or horizontal featureless surfaces of the buildings' outface, the cell-like interiors, the prison-like corridors, are the result of this thinking; the communal seats of concrete, the linear walk ways and concrete flower pots, all remind the residents of institutional power. The monumental massiveness, the immovability of the building—or indeed of any part of the domestic interiors—asserts a constant deterministic force on the psychology, and ultimately the behaviour, of residents. It guides them, pressures them, restricts them, mitigates against self-identity and self-organisation, inhibiting self-expression. The use of concrete and steel, with cold, hard, neutral colours and wall surfaces, contained in a factory-fabricated construction, radiates the constant message of conformity and permanent immobility. In the end it is the residents who are left with the building, it is they who must conform, or adapt their behaviour.

SEPARATION FROM NATURE

The exercise of control over the so-called 'natural environment' is a fundamental task of any society. In the 'new reality' this control is continually impressed onto the consciousness of people through encoding the physical environment into a highly complex structure of inter-related symbols that exhibit their separation from 'nature'. This control is emphasised by stating a high degree of society's technological achievement, expressed in the rigid angular structures, formed into blocks and towers, which then have highly defined boundaries drawn around them. So that the 'new reality' is not just physically removed from 'nature', but is also symbolically separated. Thus housing estate, office block complex, shopping precinct are all represented in the professional's conception as contained islands, which are given an added clear symbolic significance by a delineating boundary that states the difference between the order inside, and the dis-order of an external, remote nature. Here nature is perceived as a 'counter force' of entropy, a symbol of the untamed that is always moving towards anarchy, and is thus held as a potential threat to the stability of the infra-structure of society; it is therefore quite simply repressed. It is through the 'professional' that society is able to appropriate selected elements from nature and encode them into its dominate system of beliefs and values, neutralising what is considered its disruptive potential, and instead displaying them as isolated fixtures that are held up as its own cultural products.

The process of encoding the 'new reality' into symbols of cultural order is achieved through a combination of media and form, such as in the use of concrete, aluminium, glass, etc., and in the reductive design of hard, square, recurring, monumental shapes. All this is constantly impressing on the consciousness of the individual that someone else is exercising control on his behalf over natural elements that could disrupt the world in which they live.

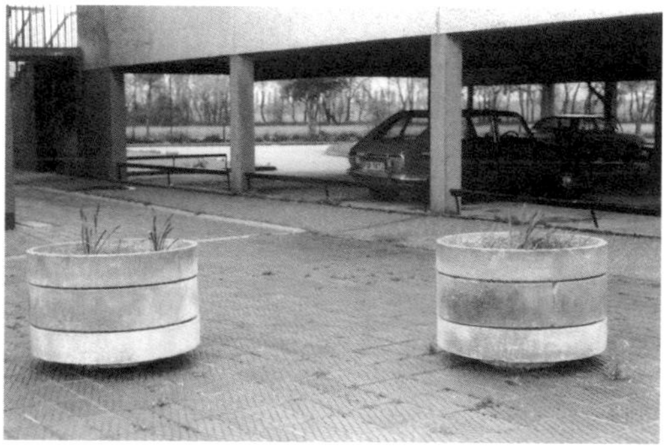

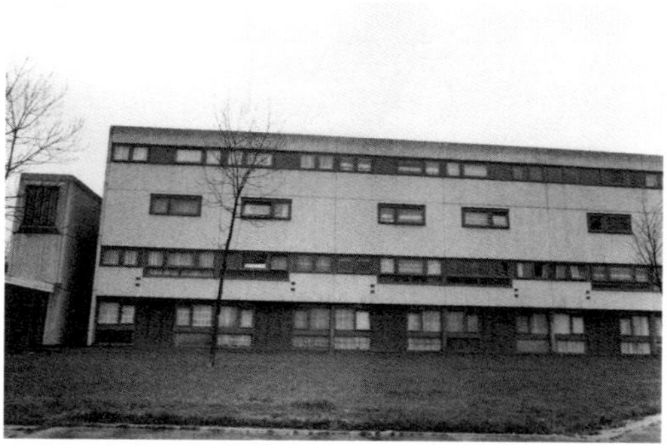

Estate environment in the Avondale Estate, Hayes, West London.

TRAPPED INSIDE THE BOX

Resident

PP It's the shape, the sizes of them and the way everything's, they just look as though the architect has just thought of shoe boxes and laid them on the site and just tried to organise us into these shoe boxes, even the rooms are just, everything's just completely square. I get the feeling on this estate that there's no nice curves or anything round, everything's just square and cold, even the rooms inside the house are square there's no nooks and crannies and little places or anything.

SW Do you reckon that, are you conscious of the fact that the architect is like trying to tell you how to live.

PP The architect he's tried to organise the life here, but he's not been able to organise it around anything central, we've got a big green that the kids are supposed to play on but they've taken the swings away from there they've only got a see-saw left and you can't have any community feeling when there's nowhere for people to meet and to communicate which there isn't on this estate, you just drift along the corridor and doors are closed, the architect has tried to organise our life here but he's not worked it out properly. The amount of people I've brought home and they've said, oh blimey, they've walked, walked through the corridor and said, oh blimey, it's just like being in the nick here.

I think that living somewhere like this can only do one of two things, it'll either make you totally depressed and suicidal, I mean there's absolutely no hope here for anything is there, you've got nothing, there is nothing, all you've got is a little box, a little box to exist in, or, it's going to make you aggressive and it's going to make you a right fighter.

No way do you want to stay in somewhere like this, I mean it's, it's got to instill in you the desire to get out, you've got to fight to get out, you've got to fight to survive basically in a place like this, you've got to fight to live, 'cos as I say these places aren't built to live in, they're built to exist in, to pack you away somewhere.

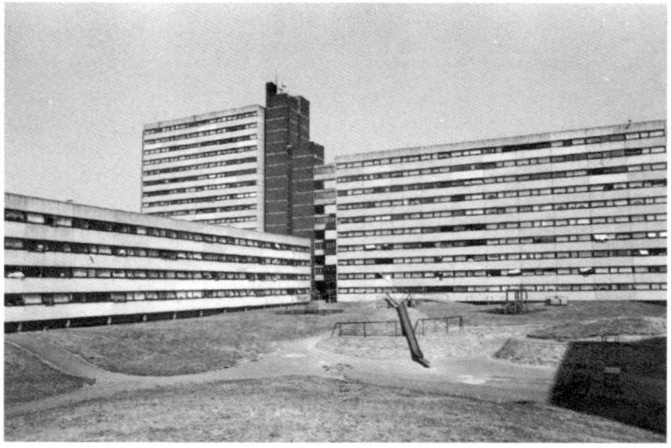

Homecourt, Feltham, West London.

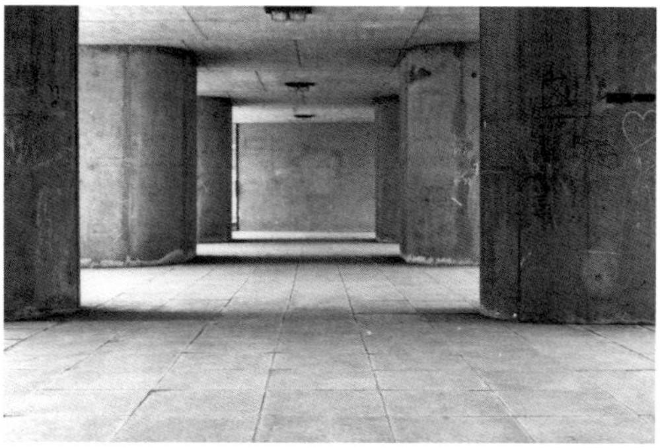

The Markische Viertel in Berlin.

STARTING AGAIN

Interview with Lisa Banks, Coffee Hall Estate, Milton Keynes

SW Lisa if you can say something about the house you're living in, how would you describe this house on this estate.

LB Concrete block and from what I know it was built with very low resources to accommodate the new city of growth, it's changed since, and at the time I moved in a year ago to this house, pretty bad state of repair, not a lot done to it and it needed to be just taken down to a blank canvas, all the flooring, all the wallpaper, the whole house had to be sterilised with Dettol, my kids couldn't live with me for about four weeks while I done it, they had to stay round people's houses.

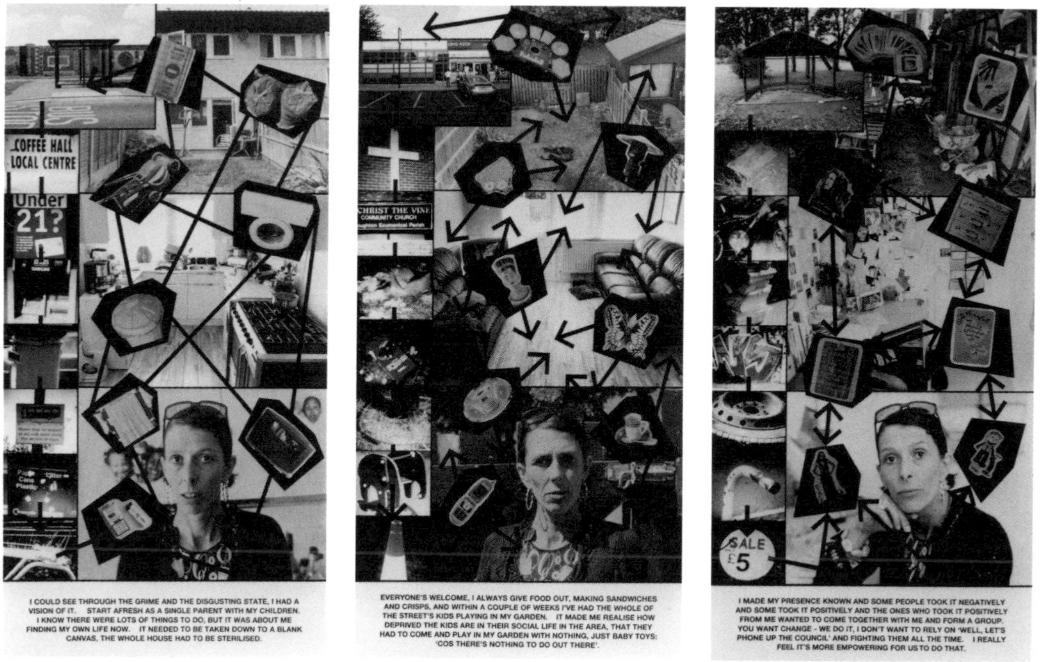

'Starting Afresh with A Blank Canvas', Milton Keynes.

24

THE EXPRESSION OF COUNTER CONSCIOUSNESS

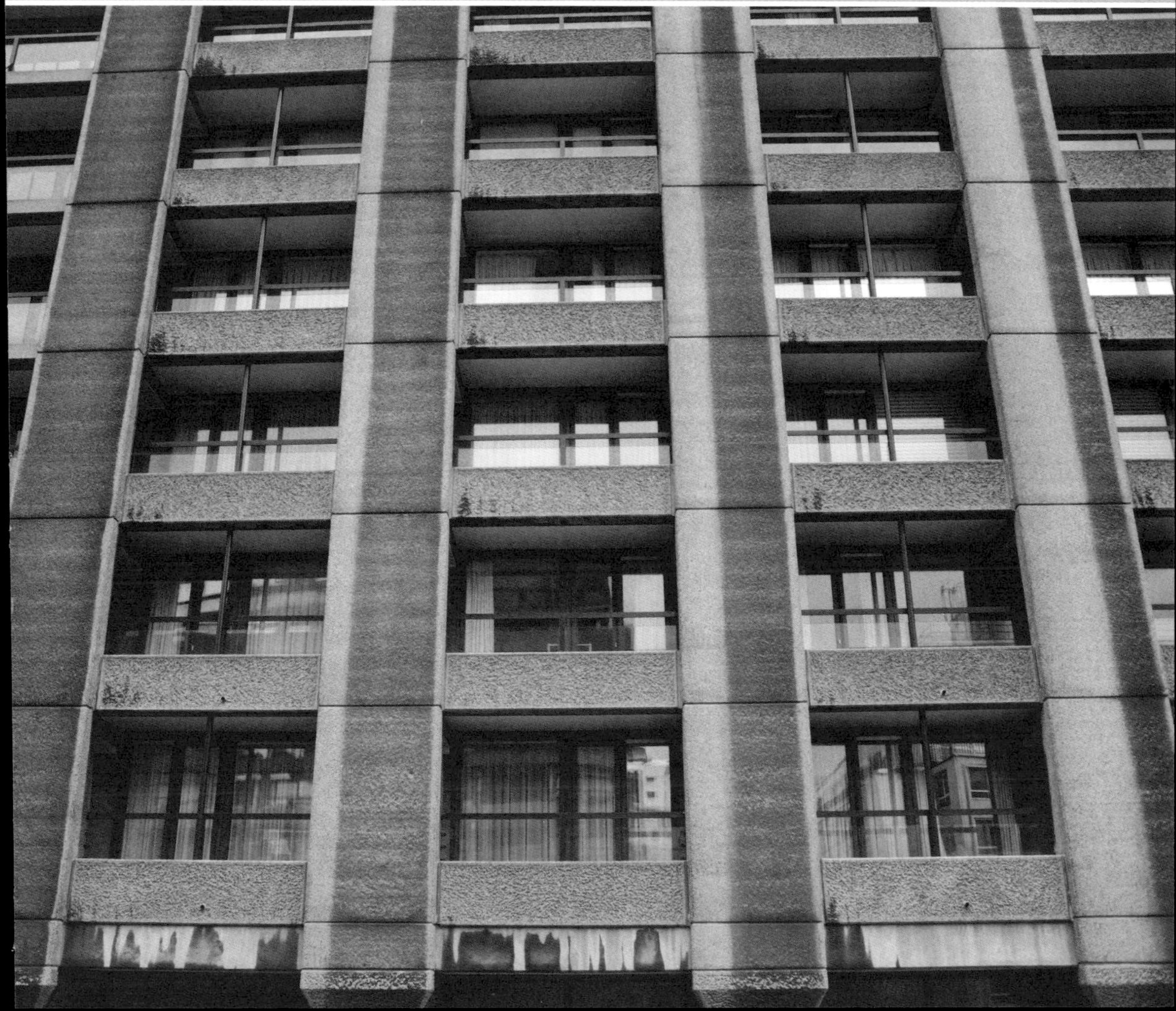

CITY OF CONCRETE

While the isolating effects of living within the 'new reality' are now widely recorded, what is not so documented is the response from residents. Their reactions demonstrate the creative power of self-organisation to register social expression by changing the language of their building. And this is what I have found important to the symbolism in my works—that this creativity meant objects existing in another dimension, as agents and vehicles to facilitate social interaction. The key to the new role of objects as agents is that their given, intended functions are transformed, so they can carry out quite a different role. It is this act which I consider to be so fundamentally creative and central to the concept of self-organisation expressed in my works. These creative acts take many forms, all of which express a counter consciousness of their own society, that is subversive to the building's given physicality and language.

The most direct expressions of counter consciousness, and what has involved me, are left as visual signs, messages about identity and community made on the surfaces of the building themselves, often recorded as rough spontaneous marks and gestures straight onto the concrete, symbolically destroying, or at least subverting, its deterministic message. What is denounced as vandalism by the authorities I consider creative acts of counter-consciousness, made to form and cement community—for these acts are rarely carried out by a lone individual, but are an agent, a catalyst for group behaviour. These creative marks, called graffiti in the authorities' parlance, are sign posts, points of reference, displays made by groups of residents for one another to stake out their territory inside the surrounding concrete.

EXPRESSION OF COUNTER CONSCIOUSNESS ON THE CHARVILLE LANE ESTATE, HAYES, WEST LONDON

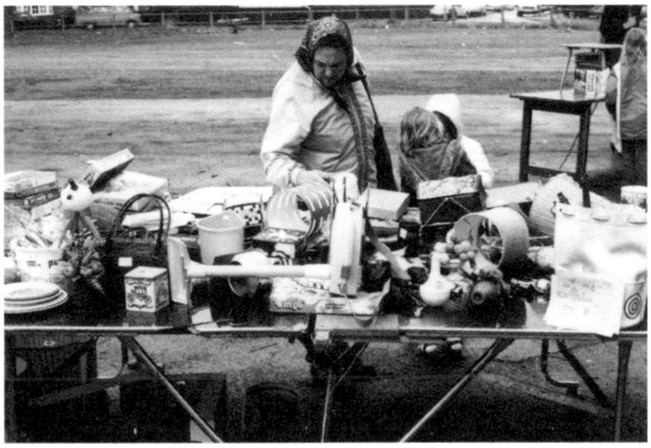

Mini market at the estate centre.

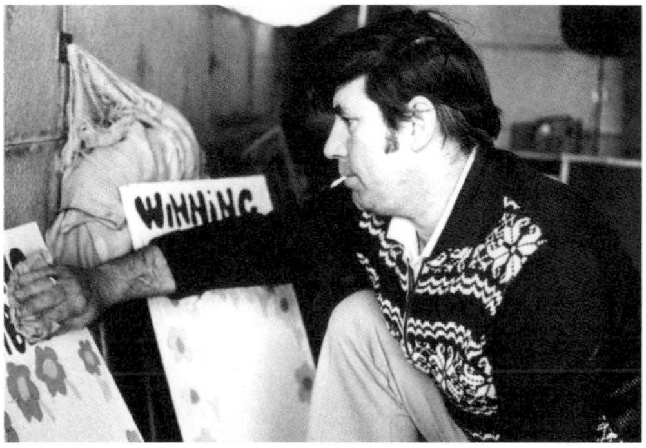

DIY notices advertising estate activities.

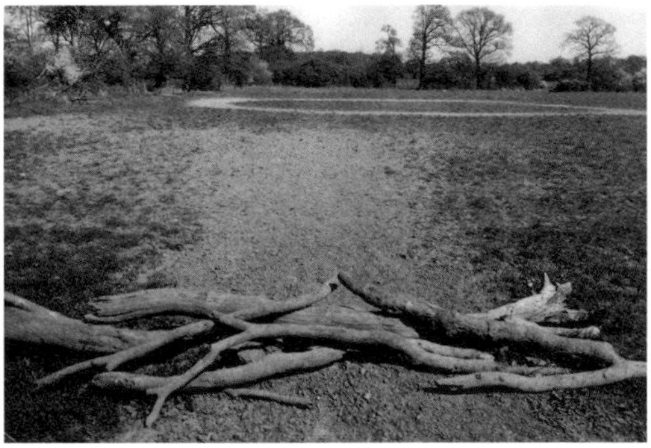

Horse riding in the surrounding wastelands.

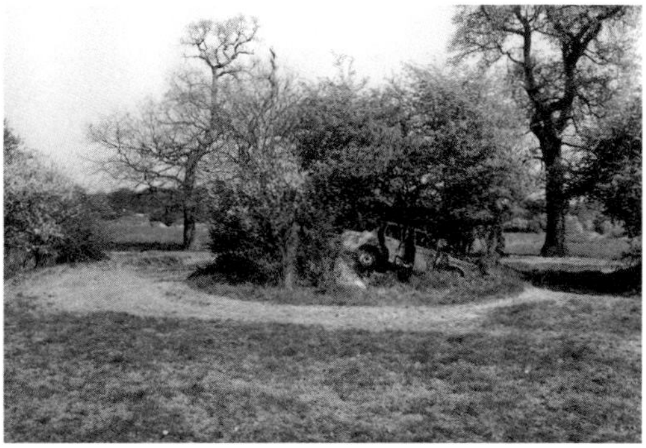

Appropriated car in the wasteland with racing track.

SYMBOLIC ENVIRONMENT

The epitome of all this was symbolised by the Highfields Estate in Hayes that had been built some ten years previously in 1970, but had now become an extreme example of the stigmatised environment, dilapidated and decrepit, that is commonly associated with modernist housing blocks and suburbs. In reaction to the isolation, and lack of expressive opportunities, bands had been spontaneously set up in flats when parents went out, in the sheds and garages, or in vacated boarded up empty flats, the boarding being broken down to gain access. The language layered onto the estate environment, graffiti, interventions directly into the material fabric, made in the corridors, on the stairwells, and in the sheds etc., was also an expression of DIY that at that moment in my mind linked into Punk, in that it was a language created and used to separate those in the group, the community of friends, and those outside, normal society. The language layered over existing manifestations of the society they felt alienated from, marked out a territory with what later in the 1980s would be called 'tags', signs that not only denote to others that an area has been taken over so "keep out", but importantly are there to bind the group together creating a context in which they can feel safe psychologically, protected by the display of symbols.

ANOTHER CITY

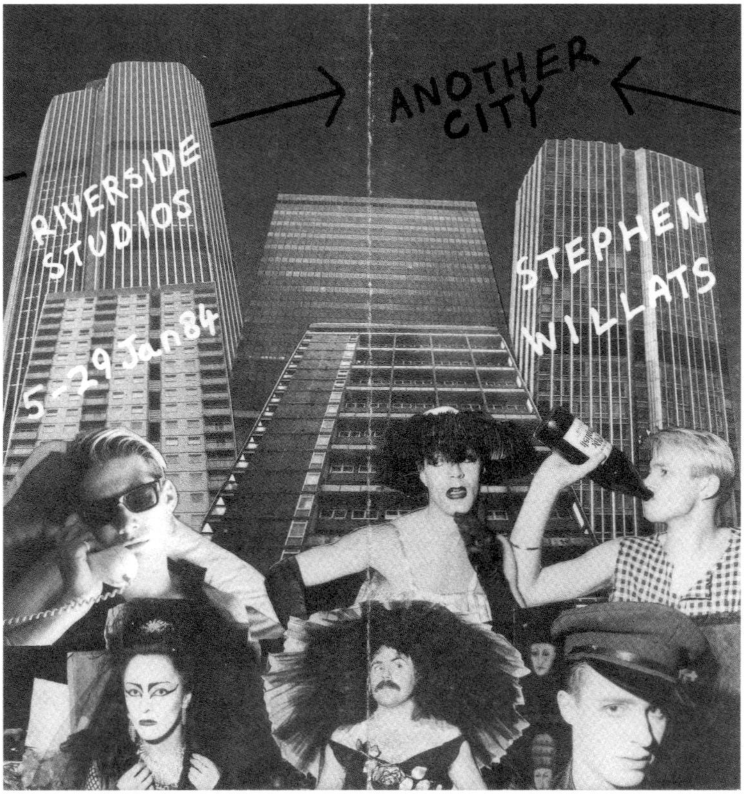

Announcement card for the exhibition at Riverside Studios, London.

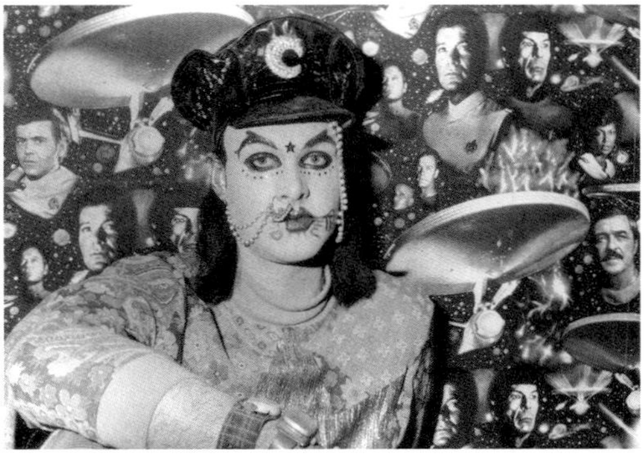

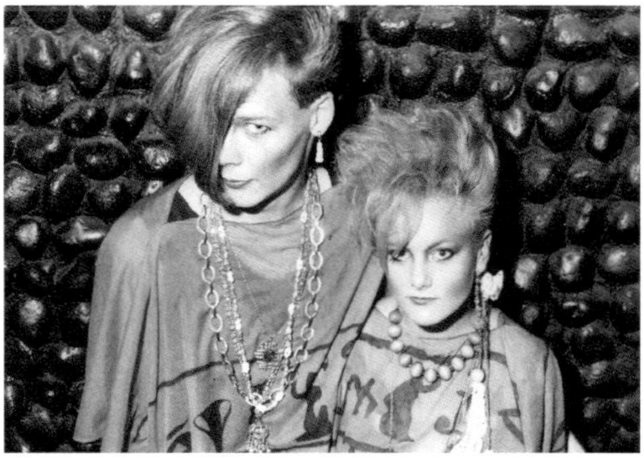

Futurists from the night world, early 1980s.

25

REPRESENTATION OF POLEMICS

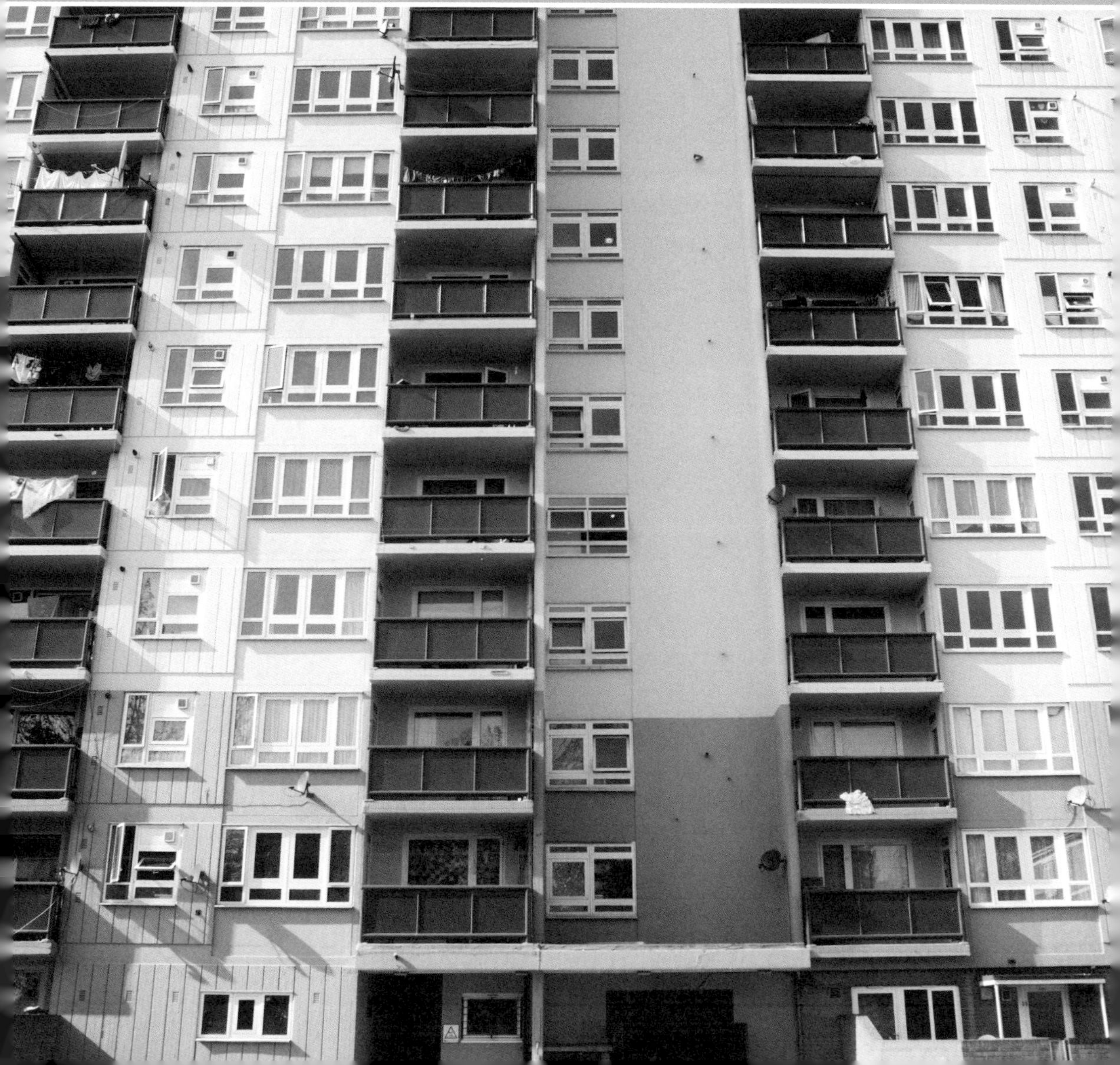

EXPLORATION OF POLEMICS

Once inside the symbolic world the territory can open up and new pathways can be found and speculatively explored, and in doing so the environment within that world can further generate its own meaning. Without the connection with what is already perceived as already meaningful at the point of access by the audience, an inhibition is the likely outcome, a resistance to undertake what, after all, is a deviation from existing established patterns of behaviour, perceptions and thought, thus resulting in a termination of engagement. Similarly once a person is psychologically inside the symbolic world, if the steps towards encompassing new territories of reference are found to be too large or too distant from each other, and there is nothing that can be perceived as relevant, that one can hang on to, again inhibition to go on with the engagement is the result. So on one hand the construction of the symbolic world needs to reflect the existing frame of reference of the audience, and on the other hand, and perhaps as a consequence of this reflection, provide the facility for the audience to load the territory with their own references, to contextualise it to their own circumstances. Both actions are going to be greatly facilitated if the symbolic world is perceived to be built around a 'problem situation' that is already a known polemical issue for the viewer. What is meant by 'problem situation' here is that a number of variables attached to a situation are to a greater or lesser extent unresolved in some way, perhaps even in a state of conflict, or they appear uncertain, or are unpredictable and require from the audience a resolution, a response which removes the personal disparity into a personal certainty. Thus a problem is more than a question, though a question may well be the best route into a problem. Also resolution to a problem may well require imaginative leaps and transformation in thought to conjoin disparate bits of encoding, so as to turn one state into another, to radically change the way the variables within the same context appear not to reconcile; they sit uneasily together, and then they can be considered as a polemic.

QUEST FOR CONTEMPORARY SYMBOLS

I am always looking for contemporary symbols to embody in my work to create an immediate and meaningful connection for the audience with polemics in the world around them, and consequently I entered into a long relationship with the Cha Cha Club, and in particular with Michael and Scarlet who were the principal organizers. This is what I wrote in 1982:

When I first went to the Cha Cha Club I found the rough, tense atmosphere there very difficult to cope with, and it took me several visits before I felt confident enough to start photographing inside the club. The rough tension of the place was very similar to the feeling of tension and aggressiveness I had begun to notice growing on the housing estates where I have been working, where people sensed things are now going wrong for them but had no means to do anything about the situation. This tension in the club was expressed in the way people dressed, all of which was highly individualistic, an outward manifestation of their psychological, sexual and intellectual state. Sometimes it was difficult for me to know if a member was a boy dressed as a girl as a boy, or, for instance, what the persons dressed as athletes were about. In fact there was such a diverse variety of styles that this in itself was a code at one level, and a real explosion of creativity about 'right now' on the other. During the weeks I was acclimatizing myself to the club and then later on when taking photographs there, Scarlet and Michael were also coming to my studio to make several tape-recorded discussions, at first individually and then together, about the inter-relationship of the club with their own lives.

CONFLICT SYMBOL

"Throughout our culture the tower block has come to symbolise the conflicts of modern living. Whether or not a person actually lives in a tower block is not crucial to the power this symbol exerts." — Stephen Willats.

Stephen is an artist who, over a decade ago, developed his interest in portraying the lives of people living in tower blocks. His work has taken him all over the country and even to Europe. The art that he creates is unusual, even eccentric.

ACTIVE PARTICIPATION

His methods involve the active participation of tenants. He succeeds in pursuading people not only to trust him but also to share his enthusiasm and his motivation to create a pictorial expression of their lives. His ability to involve people is impressive.

His projects help to break down barriers that so often exist between people in blocks. They bring together people who may never have seen each other before, let alone have spoken.

This is a positive step towards developing neighbourly feelings and building tenants/community organisations in the blocks and on the estates. It is for these reasons that we feature the work of Stephen Willats here.

Stephen Willats sees tower blocks as projecting an image of institutional conformity which contrasts starkly with the chaotic variety of the lives of the tenants. It is their constant fight for self-expression that forms the basis of Willats' work and inspires the project featured here.

TOWER MOSAIC

Tower Mosaic was a series of exhibitions in the six tower blocks that comprise the Warwick and Brindley Estate in North Paddington (London).

The very fabric of the estate, its physical structure, and the language and

Working with tower-block tenants, artist Stephen Willats portrays their lives

experiences of the residents were central to the idea of Tower Mosaic. In this respect the two tower blocks, Brinklow House and Princethorpe House, selected from the six to house the exhibition, were considered to form part of the work.

Tower Mosaic is an artwork that evolved over time as a result of tenants' participation. Participants in Tower Mosaic were asked to develop pictures of how they see themselves, the network of people surrounding them, the immediate community and the wider society.

The responses of tenants to four problem situations contributed to the building up of a mosaic of images that formed a public statement about living in a tower block.

A small group of residents from Brinklow and Princethorpe were invited to take part in the work's development and focus it on different ways people perceive and understand themselves and their relationship with others.

INDIVIDUAL WORK

Stephen Willats worked individually with six residents to document photographically objects they had acquired in their homes, the ones they considered expressed something about themselves as well as those that specifically denoted a relationship with someone else.

He then tape-recorded a discussion with the residents about those objects. From this material the Tower Mosaic Book was produced.

The Tower Mosaic booklet contained four sheets, each with a problem situation for tenants to consider. Each section asked tenants to make a drawing showing how the objects presented as photographs in the book might influence:

1 How you feel about yourself.

2 Your relationship with someone else.

3 Your relationship with the community immediately surrounding you.

4 Your relationship with a wider society.

VOLUNTEERS

A desk was set up inside the ground-floor foyers of each building for either a morning or afternoon session each day. A group of eight volunteers administered this desk and encouraged everyone coming in and out of the building to join in.

If a person agreed to take part they were given a copy of the Tower Mosaic Book and, using coloured pens and crayons provided, drew their responses there and then.

Inevitably and intentionally participation at the desk became a social event with exchanges between residents who were coming in and out and those who were already taking part.

ANONYMOUS DISPLAY

All the drawings were displayed anonymously on a series of four grids placed in the foyers of the two blocks. They were built up over a 12-day period.

All participants' drawings were considered equally valid and all contributed to the building up of the mosaics and the picture of life in those tower blocks.

Page from The Tower Block national directory.

TWO POLEMICS

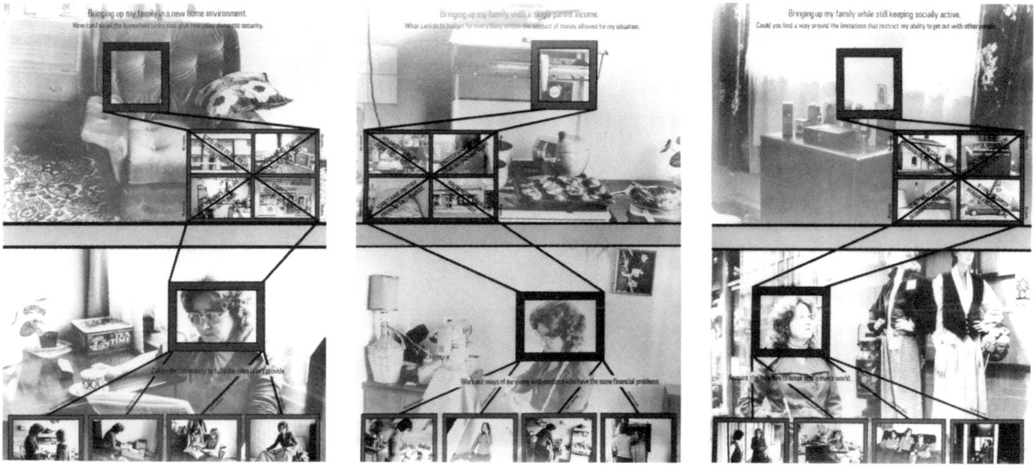

'Single Parent Family', three panel work, 1978.

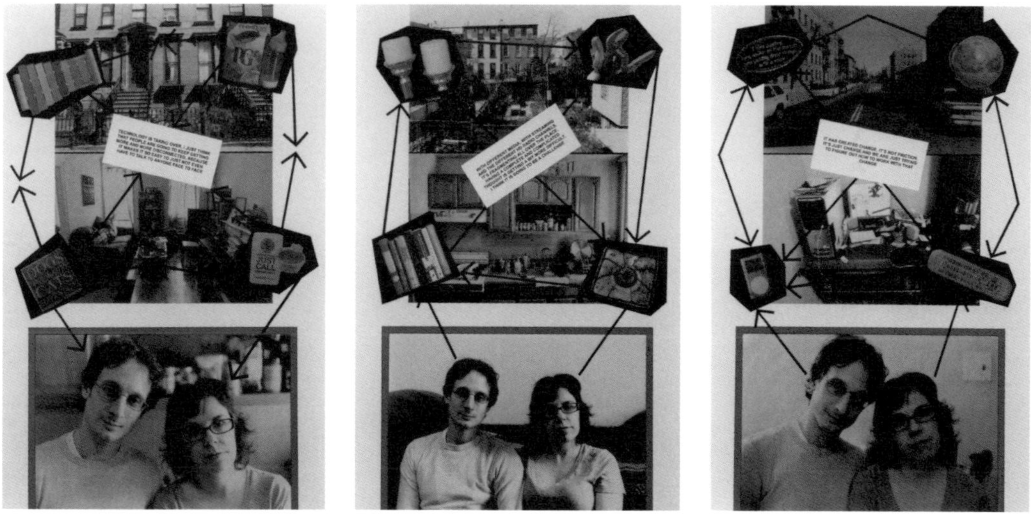

'How The Future Looks From Here', three panel work, 2011.

26
SPECULATION AND EXPERIENCE

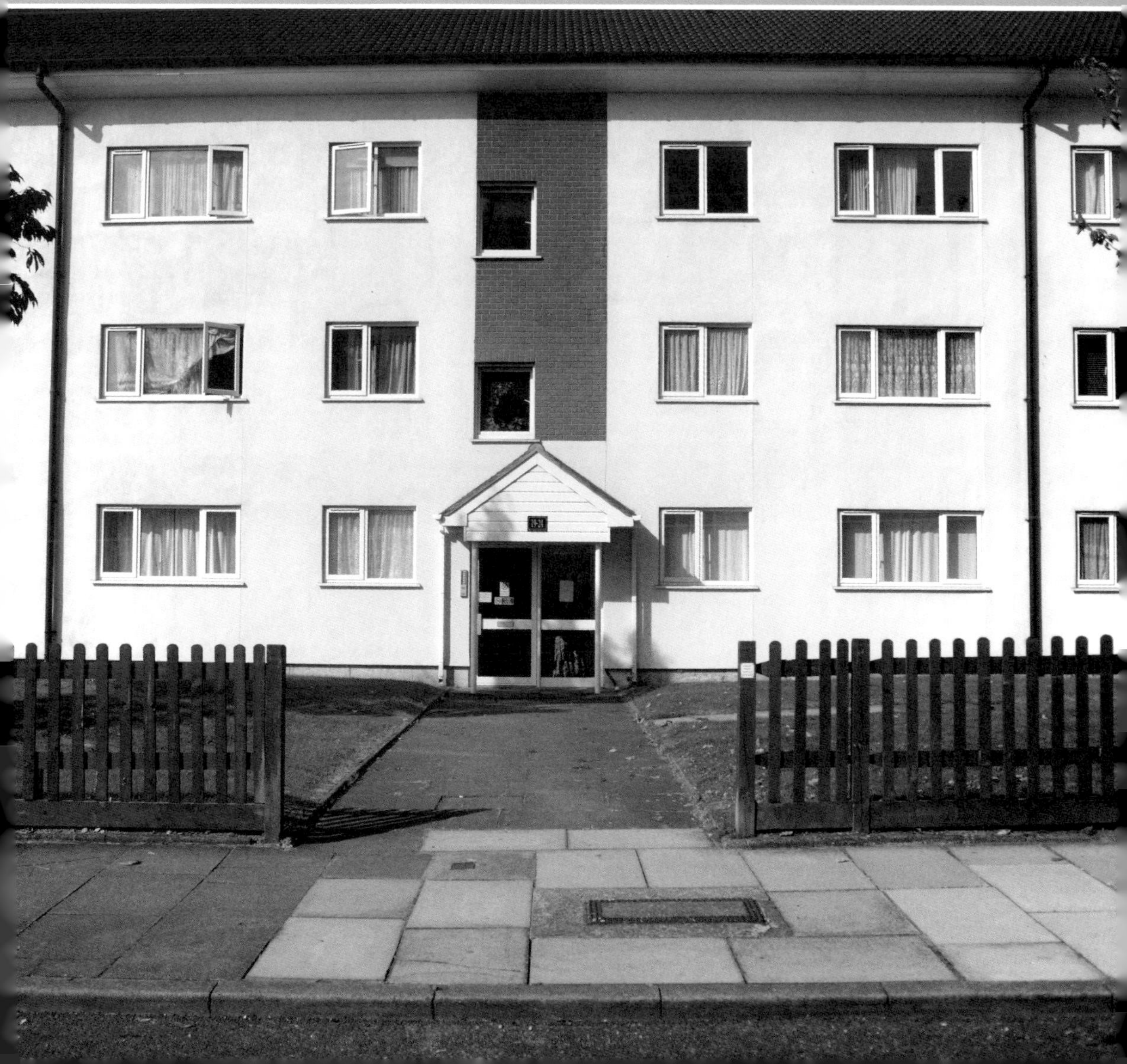

ABSTRACTION AND COMPLEXITY

My point in discussing this work is that the contrast between the abstract model of practice as represented in the diagram, and the complex experience of actually working in the social and physical environment of Milton Keynes' Netherfield Estate could not be more marked. And of course this is the classic polemical dilemma when models created in a divorced abstraction are applied to shaping the real world in which people live. This has to be a flexible process if there is not to be a conflict between intention and implementation, and for this to be eliminated the context itself needs to feedback into the creation of the model to give it intention and form. Interestingly this lack of feedback was exactly the criticism of the planning models such as those that shaped Milton Keynes and which gave rise to the modernist environments of the early 1970s, where in their conception people were perceived as just reduced entities, profiles or even just numbers.

So I think that an important outcome is that while the model in the form of the speculative diagram can provide a direction, even an inspiration, the complexity and reality of the experience being addressed should never be presumed to fit into what is expected if it is going to work. Instead a fluid, dynamic relationship between the conceptual model proposed by the artist, the audience and the context of reception can in itself be taken to form a self-organising system that represents a simulation in a symbolic sense of what is possible for society. For instead of a hierarchically imposed ordering of events in shaping meaning and function in advance, where people are just passive witnesses, an altogether different process is experienced by people where they themselves decide the forms and content of the experience.

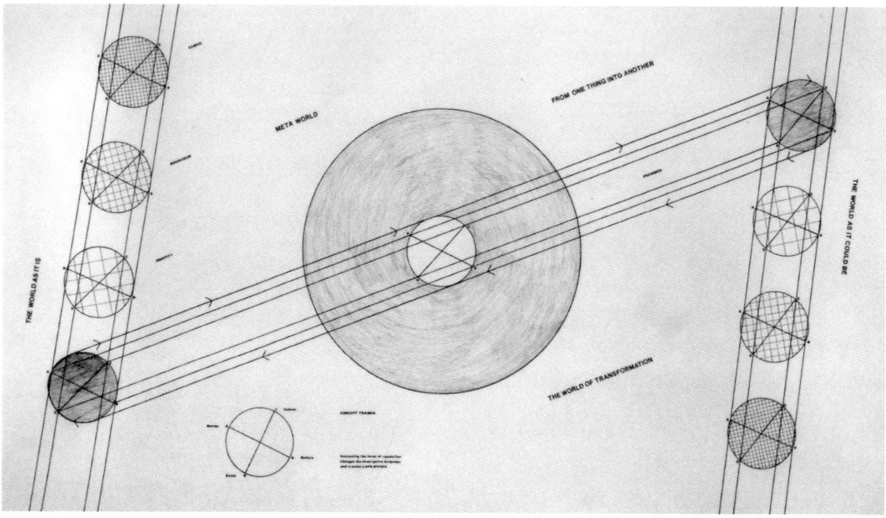

'From One Thing Into Another'.

PARTICIPANTS' RESPONSES TO THE WORK 'VERTICAL LIVING'

The first Problem Display was difficult, because you were not sure what to put, but as it went on you could relate to each Problem Display. If you could look at later Problem Displays and then go back to the first one, rather than having to do the first one first, you could then for it was that much easier because you could understand what it was all about. With the first display on its own it was difficult, but as the programme went on it was more and more easier. You didn't think that, but when you saw some people being honest you thought right, okay we can be honest about it as well.

The displays had an influence on what we wrote down, but I wouldn't say I would be influenced if someone came to me in the street and said 'what would you do for this person if they were living on their own?' you could answer them, but with the Problem Display it was more difficult. It was more difficult to do because it was as if the person was there and you knew them. With the responses we looked at all of them, and we thought "oh that person's got it wrong, they put the wrong thing down, they didn't understand the question". And other people, you think "yea I agree with that, I wish I put that". A lot of the responses did bring out more what other people thought, we probably know these things exist, but being as you don't really see a lot of people, it brought out more of the problems that we didn't think would arise and we could see their point as well about our own problems. We looked at the display and then we filled in the Response Sheet, that's the way we did every single one. And then we went back to the previous Response Board to look at what people had written and then came back home, so up and down more or less every other day to have a look.

I think you got more involved in the project because you knew the people, than if it had for instance been in the local paper, and you didn't know the people. It was better knowing the people in the picture, and knowing that whatever you put it wouldn't harm your relationship. Because a lot of people, you know them by sight, not actually to speak to, but by having a look at the photo's and answering the problem you get a completely different view of them. You get to know them even better. In this respect it was far easier to write what you think anonymously than having to sign your name. You would have to choose your words a bit more carefully and I don't think there would have been so much response.

'CONTAINED LIVING', OXFORD, REPORT BY SOUTH OXFORD NEWS

preachers lane...

Stephen Willats: Living within contained conditions

This exhibition, which ran throughout June, consisted of material collected over the past two years from Paris, West London and Oxford. They focussed on social relationships and problems existing in post-war housing estates or tower blocks. The works, many of which were formulated with the assistance of the residents concerned, started from an intensive study of a particular group. By extension, they seek to expose the social structures within which we all live, and function, as models for possible changes in social behaviour and personal interaction.

The Oxford works were made especially for this exhibition, and resulted from contacts initially made by the Museum. The Friar's Wharf/Preacher's Lane flats were the centre of a three-week neighbourhood project by Steve Willats. The residents were presented with seven different aspects of daily life within the confines of their home environment. Their responses to the problems were then displayed at the Museum. Everyone could then make his own comparisons between his view of daily life within his own home environment, and the way others perceive things.

"Contained Living" provoked various responses, from those directly involved in the Friar's Wharf project and from the exhibition within the Museum, and from the 'general public'. One questions inevitably to what extent the work has affected (if at all) the residents of the estate under scrutiny.

Gi Cheeseman

Below are some of the problems posed and the responses evoked from the residents of Friar's Wharf.

Remembering where we come from:

Q. : What can we do to recreate the same community feeling that terraced housing had in Friar's Wharf?

Reply: 1) By continuing to be as kind as we can to each other, and those who are not should make some effort to do so.

2) To my mind once times have gone nothing is the same again.

Q. : In what way could the confined interiors of our homes be utilised as part of this estate's activity?

Reply: I do not wish my home to be utilised. I wish to be private!

Q. : How can keeping ourselves open to other people's problems change acquaintances into friends?

Reply: By forming a tenants' association... social centre.

.....at moma

The Museum of Modern Art, which is to be found at the back of the new Marks & Spencer shop in Pembroke Street

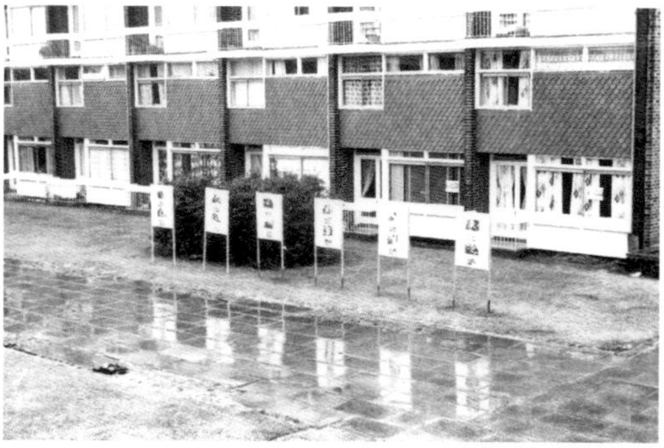

Display Boards from 'Contained Living' on the Friars Wharf Estate, Oxford.

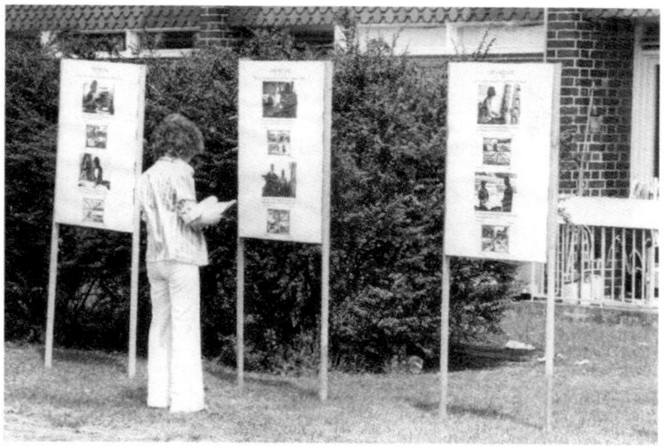

Participant with their Response Sheets developing their conceptualisations to the problem situations shown on the Display Boards located on the Friars Wharf Estate.

HESTON FARM ESTATE, HESTON, WEST LONDON

SW I first visited the Heston Farm Estate in the late '70s, so it was very comparable, the atmosphere there, to that of the Avondale Estate where I worked with Pat Purdy. When I went back in '93 to start working there, you know, I didn't realise what I had let myself in for really, and again, the authorities were sort of very sympathetic and "Yes Mr Willats" you know, they gave me every assistance, "you must be crazy to think about it" so I was working in an incredibly negative climate and it was incredible, very very stressful as a matter of fact.

NK And slightly personally dangerous as well?

SW It was dangerous, there's no doubt, it was dangerous, and when we came to present the work after my being on the estate for a year and a half, we took over the community room on the centre of the estate, we set up our installation and right from the word go, you know, we had a very volatile, extremely volatile situation, but people did start to engage with the work, and as it went on, more and more people engaged with it, to the point when after five days, and it came to the end of the piece 'cos it was only a cycle over five days, quite a short piece, already, more or less the whole estate (there were quite a lot of people living there) had in some way or other been involved in the piece to a point where they didn't want it to stop. And the local authority were really quite amazed, they didn't think anything like this could have happened, and the result was I think, that they felt confident about perhaps doing something else there in fact the output was that they were thinking of another artist going in there to make another work at some point. The reason for rethinking their approach was that on the Heston Farm estate was that what was really important to people was there was a, it was a negative environment, heavily stigmatised and in every direction it was seen as like 'no hope' so the people found themselves felt there was no hope, and when they found that there was something possible, something could happen that was positive, that was working, that they had done themselves, that was enormously important.

27

THE DIAGRAM AS A MODELLING TOOL

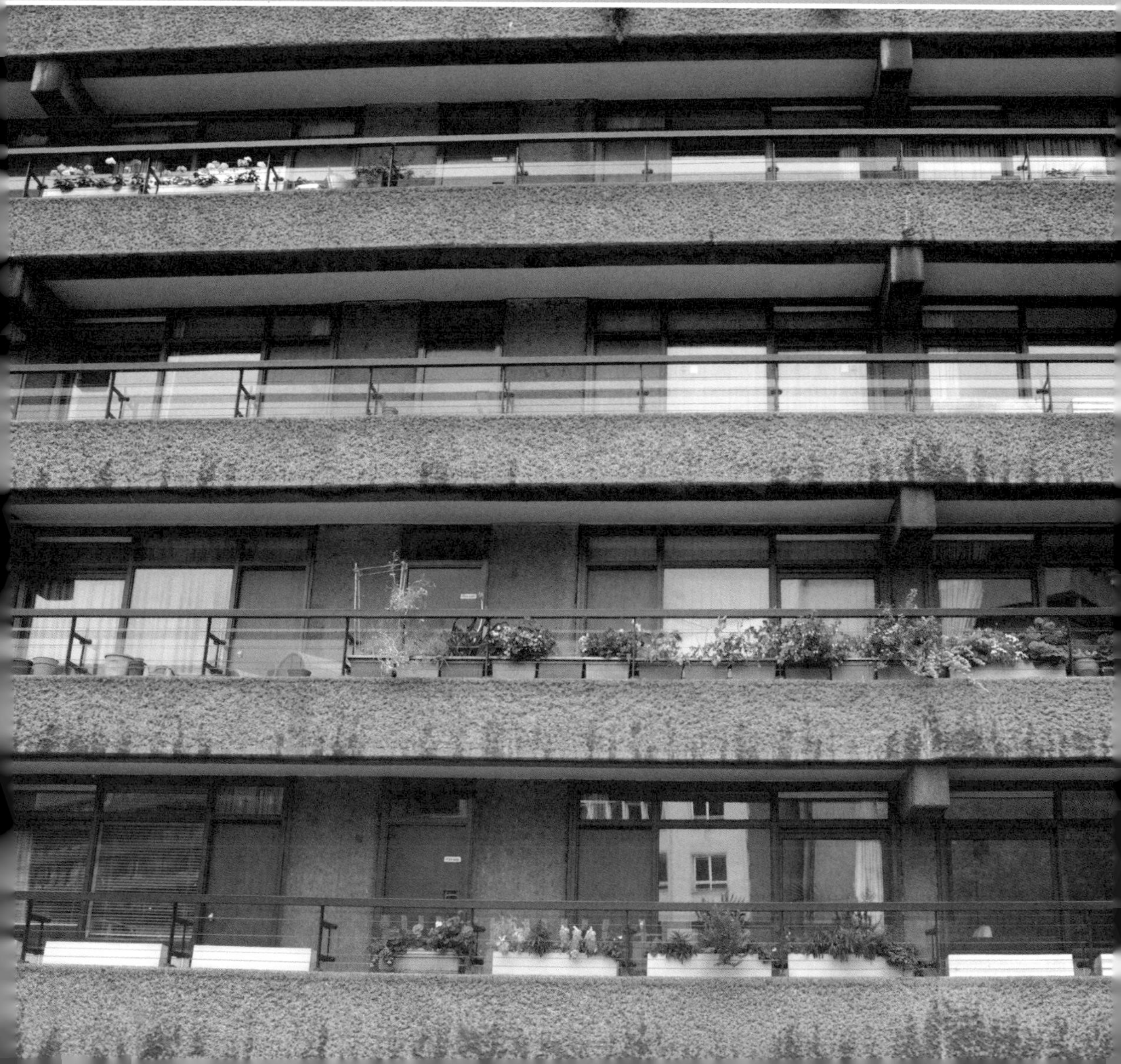

THE ROLE OF THE DIAGRAM

As a speculative modelling tool, the diagram can reduce reality's infinite variables and present a speculative representation of possible relationships and dynamic processes. For a model is not a one-to-one facsimile as is a replica, but a model is created through a paring down of variety to the main component parts, these are then encoded into a symbolic language that can be believed to parallel the variety of the original reality. So, in the selective process of reduction a decision is made as to what to include as essential to the model's symbolic environment, the resulting basic elements can be looked at as an encryption of the original state. Its success as a cognitive tool lies in how successfully the encryption can be taken back to the variety of the original state, how well it can be believed.

The diagram takes the role of the model a stage further by graphically representing flows of information between elements, to show a potentially dynamic state as a simulation of some original system.

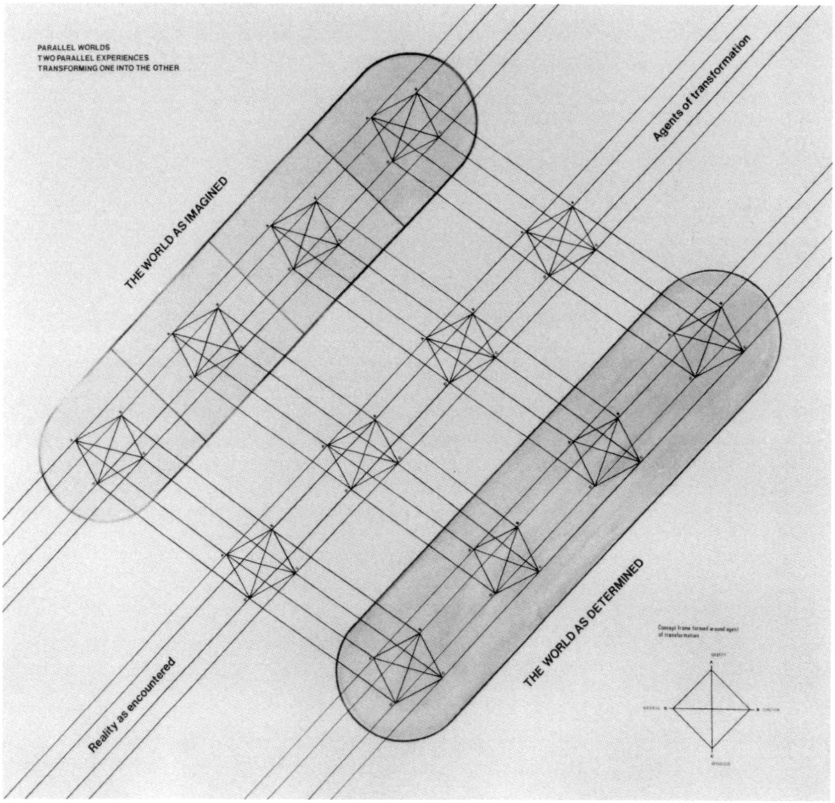

'Parallel Worlds'.

MODEL AS PARAMETER

I found the process of formalising the notion of 'model' important to the development and formation of strategies of communication in my art practice, and to achieving a coherent perception of the environment—socially, culturally, physically—in which it would take place. In speculating about the possibilities of a work of art as a social context; and as an operational set of practical events. In each case the language would be somewhat different, but a model could act as a parameter and inform them all. I defined three inherently diverse types of models: the descriptive model as a representation of how things do occur; the predictive model as a representation of how things will occur; and the prescriptive model as a representation of how things could or should occur. In particular I saw the prescriptive model as a speculative modelling device to represent the notion to someone else of something that did not yet exist, but could exist. Here the potential of the 'prescriptive model' was that it could be taken to a level of abstract resolution, which frees speculation from the complexity of the variety found in the context.

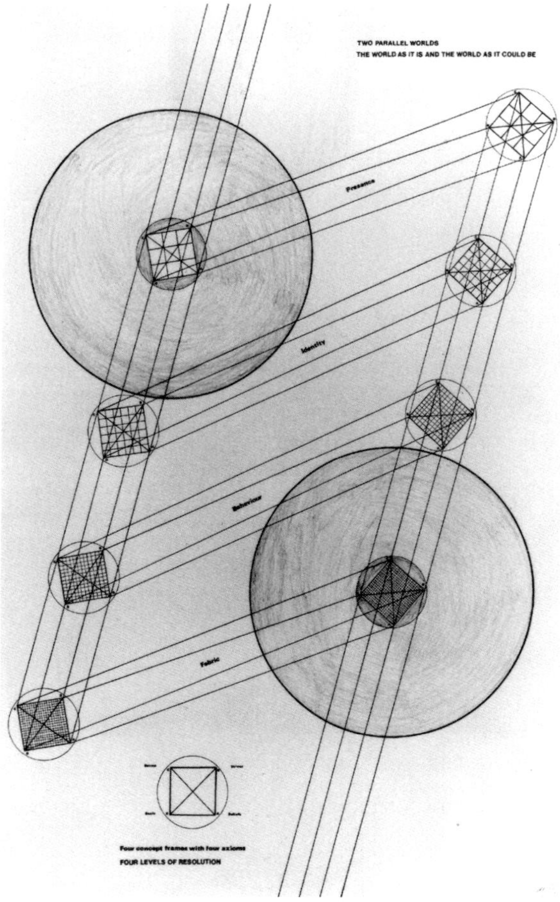

'The World As It Is And The World As It Could Be'.

MODEL IN COMMUNICATION STRATEGIES

The formation of models is essential to someone wanting to transmit a description of something complex to someone else. The simplification of variety inherent in the 'model' is its power as a tool of representation; for capturing the 'essence' of a structure, there is the potential to imagine the whole. So an acknowledged language of representation is required between the transmitter and the receiver to reduce the variety into essential variables that can be seen as an articulate, coherent extraction. We can envisage a kind of process of encryption at the point of transmission, going down the spectrum of variety, and going back up again at another point, which is usually the point of reception. It is this process of rebuilding within the receiver's own frame of reference that makes the model come alive and become available to them. Of course the more predictive the language employed in the model, and the more reliant on previously learnt symbolic meaning, the more redundancy can be built into the reductive process.

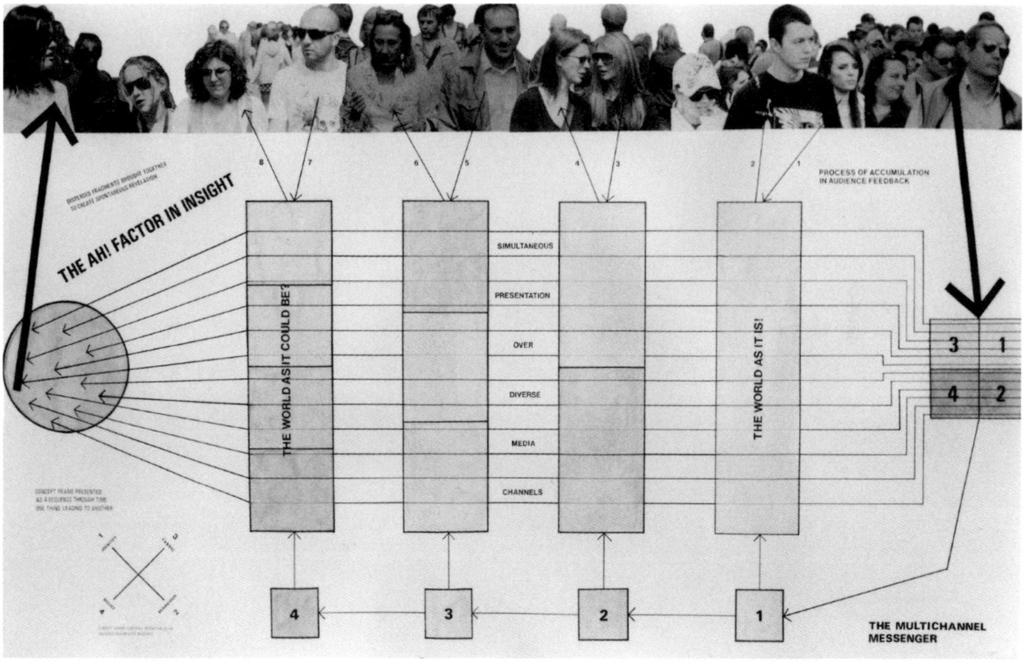

'The Multichannel Messenger'.

THE BLACK BOX

Important to the language of the diagram—especially when presenting concepts about relationships that do not yet exist—is the modelling tool with the name 'Black Box', which was developed in Cybernetics during the early 1960s in order to depict relationships between biological systems and machine systems. At an abstract, conceptual level of resolution, what was deemed important to the description and speculation of possibilities for a system was essentially 'what was observed to happen', not 'how it happened'. So when looking at complex data that perhaps were not totally understood, and by putting a Black Box over it, you could become concerned about just what inputs you would need to be present to give particular outputs etc., leaving the mechanics of how the switch actually worked (another level of resolution), to be dealt with separately later.

A variety of diagrammatic 'Black Box-style' logic symbols were developed to describe input and output switching. These were called 'gates'. For example, the diagrams shown here show the inputs and outputs of AND gates (1 and 2 and 3 and 4 etc.), OR gates (1 or 2 or 3 or 4 etc.), NAND gates (–1 and –2 and –3 and –4 etc.) and NOR gates (–1 or –2 or –3 or –4 etc.). By being positioned on the outside of the Black Box, these give an input/output language that, by being externally observed, implies what was going on inside the Black Box. A very important outcome of Black Box theory was that it enabled speculative and philosophical models to be developed without too much inhibitory concern about realities.

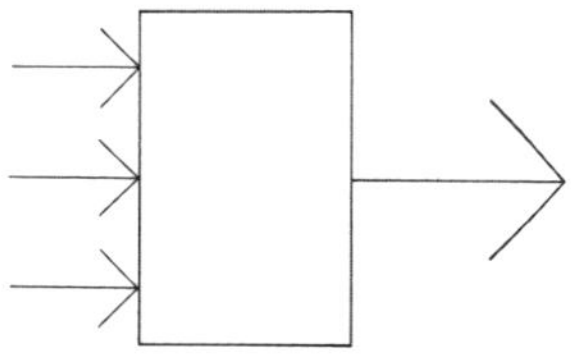

Typical Black Box-style diagram.

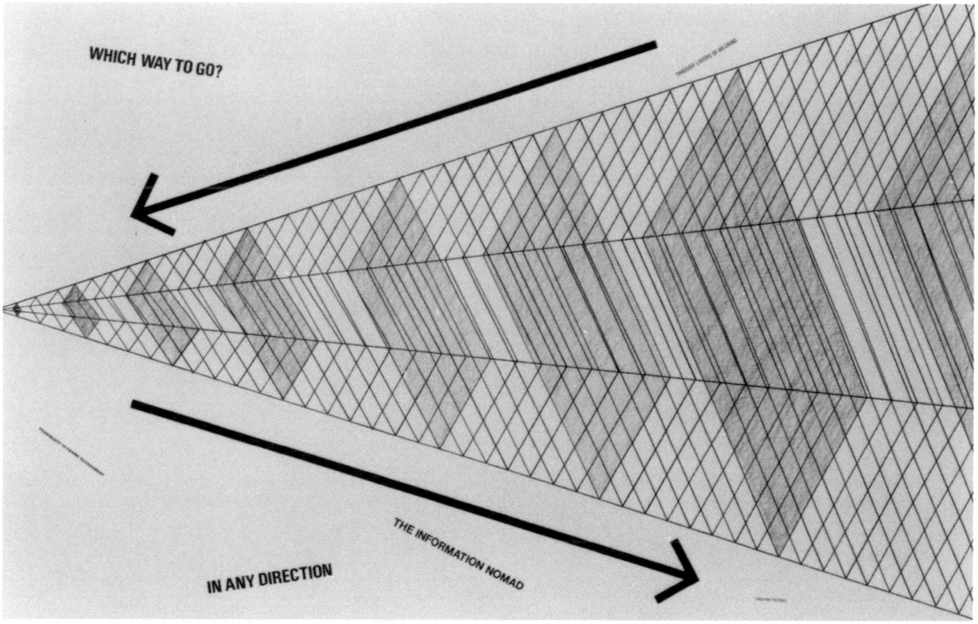

'The Information Nomad'.

28

PERSON TO PERSON PEOPLE TO PEOPLE

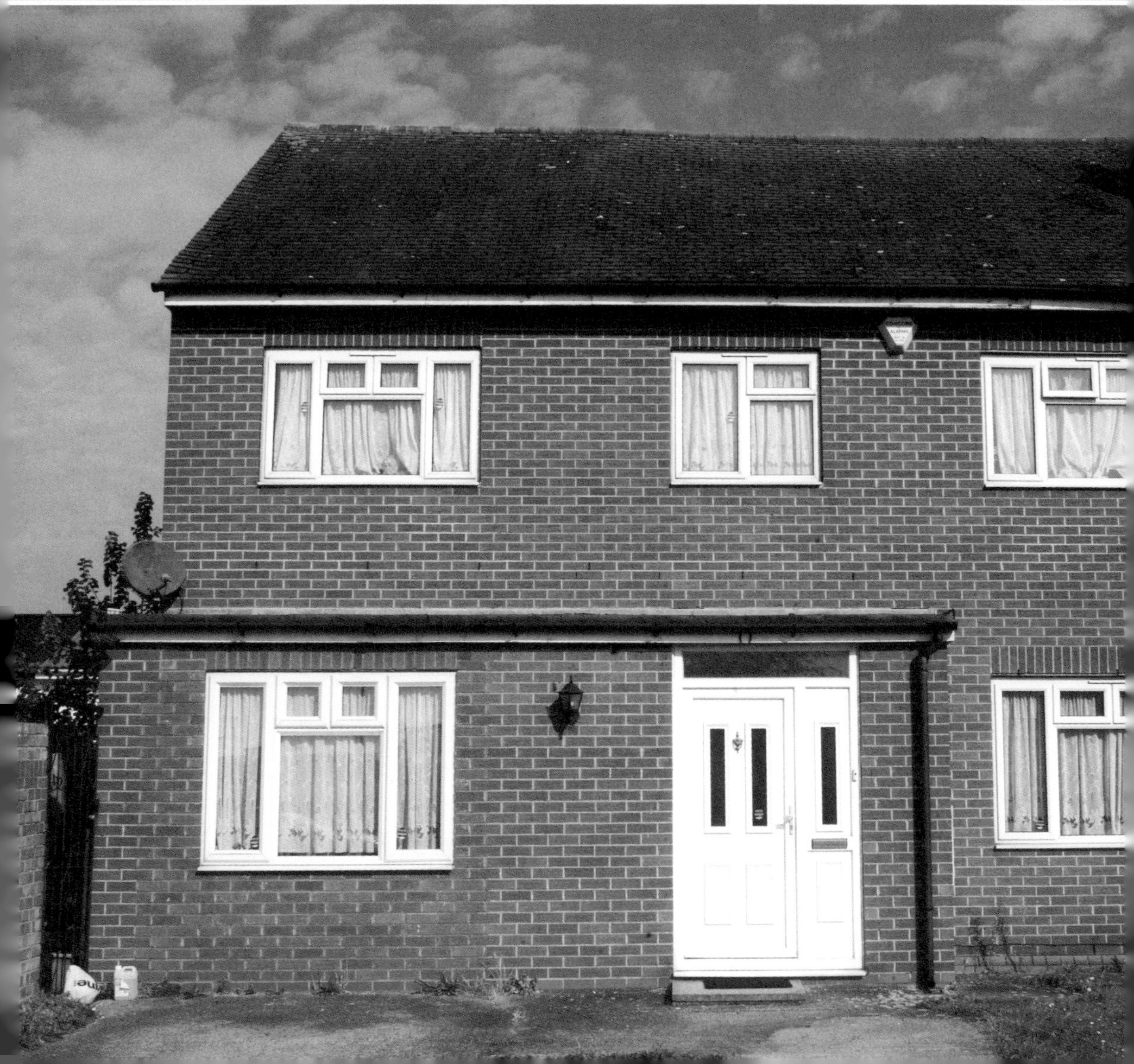

PERSON TO PERSON PEOPLE TO PEOPLE

The rationale behind the work 'Person To Person People To People' was to create a direct connection between the world represented inside the Milton Keynes Gallery spaces and the reality of people's 'actual life' in the environment immediately surrounding the Gallery. Instead of a picture being created from an external observational vantage point, the aim of my way of working is to start from the inside to represent the issues that are important and meaningful to those 'actual lives', of the people themselves, the people who live in that environment.

One part of the work was to be located inside the Milton Keynes Gallery and another part was to be situated on the nearby Netherfield Estate, which would become the context and catalyst for the work. In order for a visitor to the Milton Keynes Gallery to experience a complete viewing of the work, the installation on the estate has to be seen; similarly a visitor from the estate having looked at the installation there, has to go and visit the part located in the Milton Keynes Gallery.

The work centres on the creation and accessing of a self organised parallel world by participating residents of the Netherfield Estate as a counter consciousness to the determinism inherent in the language and form of the encountered reality of that estate; 'the world as it is' to its transformation into an imagined state, 'the world as it could be'.

Residents were invited to join a workshop with the artist and to make a journey around the Netherfield Estate, and to identify and record specific elements in its fabric such as textures, objects, signs etc., that they saw as having the potential to be transformed and seen differently from the given perception or function. All the participants individually took exactly the same route through the estate using both a Super 8 cine camera and a 35 mm photographic camera to make their documentary record, then talking through their thoughts about the various items in a tape recorded discussion with the artist. As the participant walked along the set route, sequences of recorded items began to form a parallel imagined reality from that encountered, which was completely relative and personal to each individual. Later, a process of self editing and articulating the recorded material was facilitated through a two day workshop that took place at the Skills Centre in the shopping parade at the centre of the estate. Computer editing was made available, as well as table space for organising individual documented items into sequences that expressed an imagined journey of association. The resulting edited material forms the basis for the presentation at the Milton Keynes Gallery while the actual cine films made by individual participants are shown in an unedited form simultaneously, as part of a 'film mosaic' situated on a wall within a temporary gallery space housed in the Fathing Enterprise Centre, Fathing Grove, which is located in the main Netherfield shopping parade. There is no analysis made by the artist of these films, they are just presented as they are in an unedited form in a continual loop.

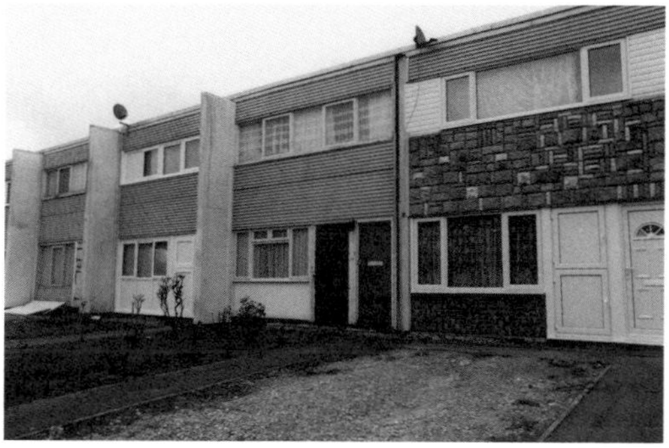

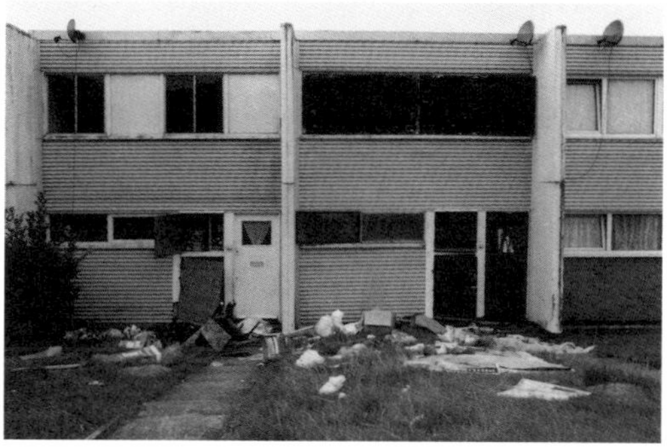

Typical housing on the Netherfield Estate.

TIME LINE OF 'PERSON TO PERSON PEOPLE TO PEOPLE' IN MILTON KEYNES

2005

27 May	First discussion at the Milton Keynes Gallery and an initial reconnaissance around the nearby shopping centre and housing estates.
21 September	Reconnaissance tour of Milton Keynes looking for possible contexts for making a new work.
22 September	Second day of reconnaissance tour.
5 October	Film made of possible locations.

2006

26 January	Meetings with local individuals and officials who could support the work.
15 February	More meetings with local people and institutions who could support the work. Distribution of posters announcing the work.
1 March	Demonstration film made on the Netherfield and Shenley Lodge Estates.
9 March	Presentation and explanation of the work made with slides, films and discussion at an exhibition of local initiatives situated in the Woughton Parish Council Offices.
29 March	Meetings with possible participants. Presentation and explanation of the work made with slides, films and discussion at the Shenley Lodge Meeting Place.
12 April	Presentation and explanation of the work made with slides, films and discussion at the Netherfield Residents Association meeting held in the Woughton Parish Council Offices.
27 April	First workshop held with participants on the Netherfield Estate.
23 May	Second workshop held with participants on the Netherfield Estate.
31 May	Third workshop held with participants on the Netherfield Estate.
19 June	Fourth workshop held with participants on the Netherfield Estate.
3 August	Fifth workshop held with participants on the Netherfield Estate.
11 October	Meeting with organisers of the Skills Centre concerning the Sixth workshop.
24 October	Sixth workshop, held at Skills Centre for the editing of documented material.
25 October	Seventh workshop, held at the Skills Centre for the editing of documented material.
5 December	Visiting the site of the temporary gallery to be located in a unit in the shopping parade, at the Fathing Enterprise Centre, Fathing Grove, Netherfield.

WORKSHOPS ON THE NETHERFIELD ESTATE

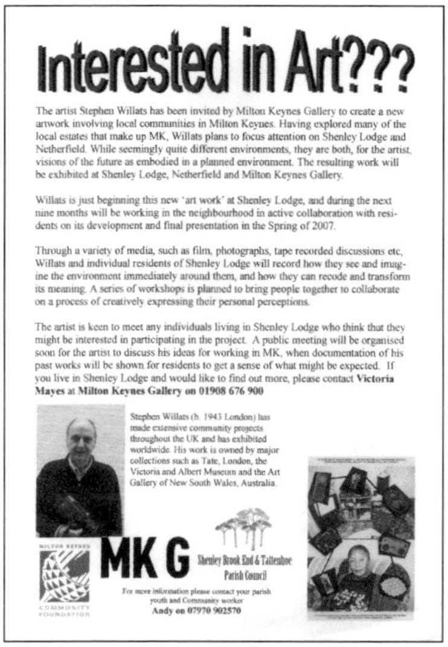

Interested in Art???

The artist Stephen Willats has been invited by Milton Keynes Gallery to create a new artwork involving local communities in Milton Keynes. Having explored many of the local estates that make up MK, Willats plans to focus attention on Shenley Lodge and Netherfield. While seemingly quite different environments, they are both, for the artist, visions of the future as embodied in a planned environment. The resulting work will be exhibited at Shenley Lodge, Netherfield and Milton Keynes Gallery.

Willats is just beginning this new 'art work' at Shenley Lodge, and during the next nine months will be working in the neighbourhood in active collaboration with residents on its development and final presentation in the Spring of 2007.

Through a variety of media, such as film, photographs, tape recorded discussions etc, Willats and individual residents of Shenley Lodge will record how they see and imagine the environment immediately around them, and how they can recode and transform its meaning. A series of workshops is planned to bring people together to collaborate on a process of creatively expressing their personal perceptions.

The artist is keen to meet any individuals living in Shenley Lodge who think that they might be interested in participating in the project. A public meeting will be organised soon for the artist to discuss his ideas for working in MK, when documentation of his past works will be shown for residents to get a sense of what might be expected. If you live in Shenley Lodge and would like to find out more, please contact **Victoria Mayes at Milton Keynes Gallery on 01908 676 900**

Stephen Willats (b. 1943 London) has made extensive community projects throughout the UK and has exhibited worldwide. His work is owned by major collections such as Tate, London, the Victoria and Albert Museum and the Art Gallery of New South Wales, Australia.

MILTON KEYNES COMMUNITY FOUNDATION

MK G

Shenley Brook End & Tattenhoe Parish Council

For more information please contact your parish youth and Community worker
Andy on 07970 902570

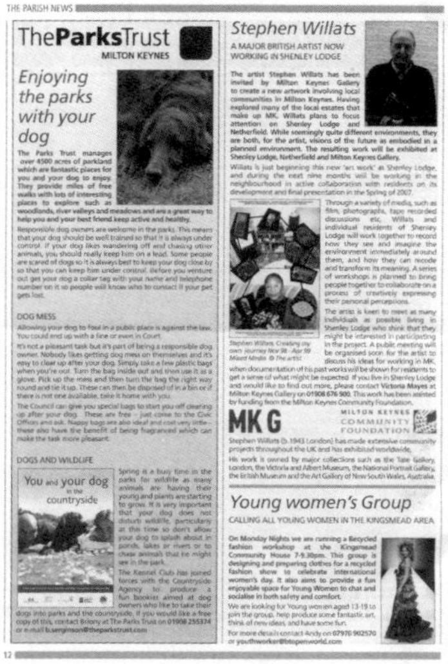

THE PARISH NEWS

The Parks Trust MILTON KEYNES

Enjoying the parks with your dog

The Parks Trust manages over 4500 acres of parkland which are fantastic places for you and your dog to enjoy. They provide miles of free walks with lots of interesting places to explore such as woodlands, river valleys and meadows and are a great way to help you and your best friend keep active and healthy.

Responsible dog owners are welcome in the parks. This means that your dog should be well trained so that it is always under control. If your dog likes wandering off and chasing other animals, you should really keep him on a lead. Some people are scared of dogs so it is always best to keep your dog close by so that you can keep him under control. Before you venture out get your dog a collar tag with your name and telephone number on it so people will know who to contact if your pet gets lost.

DOG MESS

Allowing your dog to foul in a public place is against the law. You could end up with a fine or even in Court.

It's not a pleasant task but it's part of being a responsible dog owner. Nobody likes getting dog mess on themselves and it's easy to clear up after your dog. Simply take a few plastic bags when you're out. Turn the bag inside out and then use it as a glove. Pick up the mess and then turn the bag the right way round and tie it up. These can then be disposed of in a bin or if there is not one available, take it home with you.

The Council can give you special bags to start you off clearing up after your dog. These are free - just come to the Civic Offices and ask. Nappy bags are also ideal and cost very little - these also have the benefit of being fragranced which can make the task more pleasant.

DOGS AND WILDLIFE

You and your dog in the countryside

Spring is a busy time in the parks for wildlife as many animals are having their young and plants are starting to grow. It is very important that your dog does not disturb wildlife, particularly at this time so don't allow your dog to splash about in ponds, lakes or rivers or to chase animals that he might see in the park.

The Kennel Club has joined forces with the Countryside Agency to produce a fun booklet aimed at dog owners who like to take their dogs into parks and the countryside. If you would like a free copy of this, contact Briony at The Parks Trust on 01908 255374 or e-mail b.sergimson@theparkstrust.com

Stephen Willats

A MAJOR BRITISH ARTIST NOW WORKING IN SHENLEY LODGE

The artist Stephen Willats has been invited by Milton Keynes Gallery to create a new artwork involving local communities in Milton Keynes. Having explored many of the local estates that make up MK, Willats plans to focus attention on Shenley Lodge and Netherfield. While seemingly quite different environments, they are both, for the artist, visions of the future as embodied in a planned environment. The resulting work will be exhibited at Shenley Lodge, Netherfield and Milton Keynes Gallery.

Willats is just beginning this new 'art work' at Shenley Lodge, and during the next nine months will be working in the neighbourhood in active collaboration with residents on its development and final presentation in the Spring of 2007.

Stephen Willats, Creating my own journey Nov 98 - Apr 99 Mixed Media © The artist

Through a variety of media, such as film, photographs, tape recorded discussions etc, Willats and individual residents of Shenley Lodge will work together to record how they see and imagine the environment immediately around them, and how they can recode and transform its meaning. A series of workshops is planned to bring people together to collaborate on a process of creatively expressing their personal perceptions.

The artist is keen to meet as many individuals as possible living in Shenley Lodge who think that they might be interested in participating in the project. A public meeting will be organised soon for the artist to discuss his ideas for working in MK, when documentation of his past works will be shown for residents to get a sense of what might be expected. If you live in Shenley Lodge and would like to find out more, please contact **Victoria Mayes** at Milton Keynes Gallery on **01908 676 900**. This work has been assisted by funding from the Milton Keynes Community Foundation.

MK G

MILTON KEYNES COMMUNITY FOUNDATION

Stephen Willats (b. 1943 London) has made extensive community projects throughout the UK and has exhibited worldwide.

His work is owned by major collections such as the Tate Gallery, London, the Victoria and Albert Museum, the National Portrait Gallery, the British Museum and the Art Gallery of New South Wales, Australia.

Young women's Group

CALLING ALL YOUNG WOMEN IN THE KINGSMEAD AREA

On Monday Nights we are running a Recycled fashion workshop at the Kingsmead Community House 7-9.30pm. This group is designing and preparing clothes for a recycled fashion show to celebrate international women's day. It also aims to provide a fun enjoyable space for Young Women to chat and socialise in both safety and comfort.

We are looking for Young women aged 13-19 to join the group, help produce some fantastic art, think of new ideas, and have some fun.

For more details contact Andy on **07970 902570** or **youthworker@btopenworld.com**

12

Leaflets for the first workshop with participants.

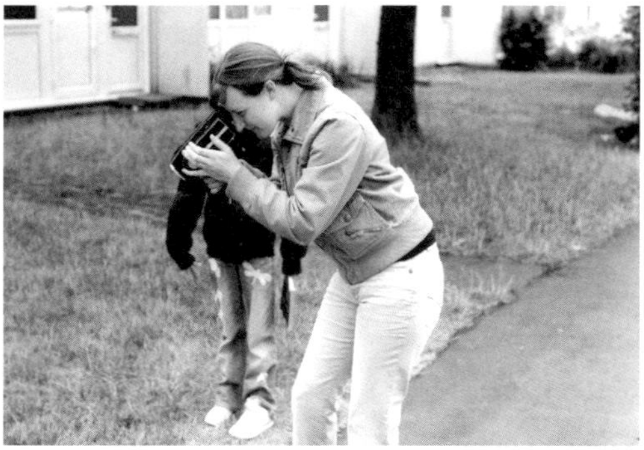

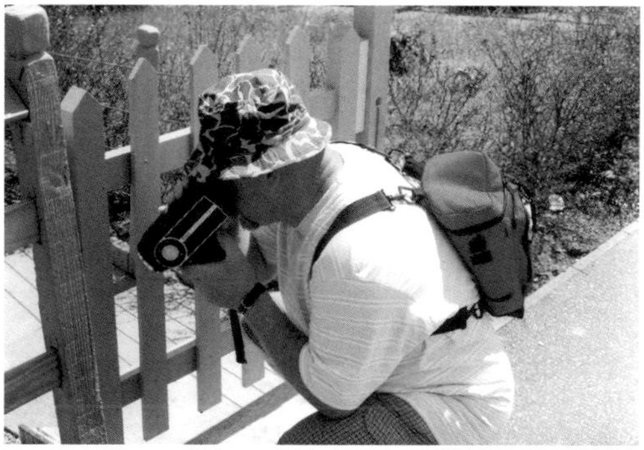

Participants out filming on the Netherfield Estate.

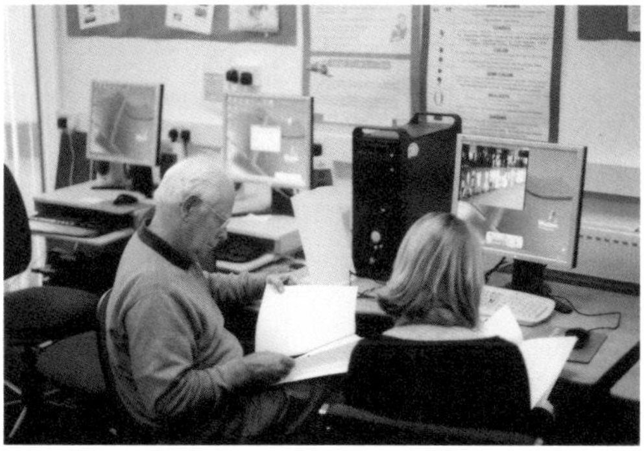

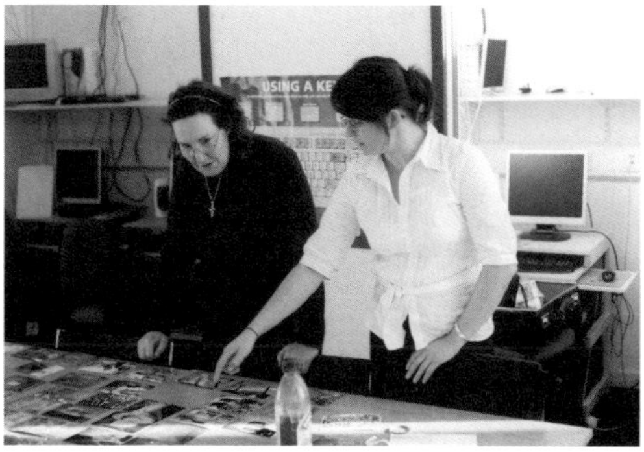

The second collective workshop located in the Skills Centre, Farthing Grove, Netherfield.

PRESENTATION OF INSTALLATION ON THE NETHERFIELD ESTATE

PERSON TO PERSON PEOPLE TO PEOPLE

Farthing Enterprise Centre, 25 & 26 May, 1 & 2 June

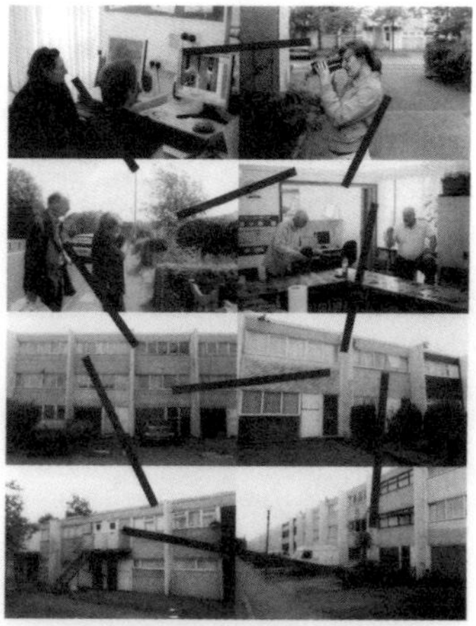

A presentation of films made by a group of residents of Netherfield with artist Stephen Willats will be on show in a special temporary gallery at the Farthing Enterprise Centre. You are invited to come and see this installation and look at the films yourself.

The way you see the world around you can be different from how you have been viewing it. The signs and symbols, the fabric of the environment, can be cues that lead you into a parallel reality, that of your imagination. Starting with their response to the world as it is, the group of Netherfield residents made films of items on the estate that they saw as meaning something beyond their normal association, creating a journey of 'the world as it could be'. Come and see the films, and compare the findings with how you see the fabric of the estate environment.

Milton Keynes Gallery at the Farthing Enterprise Centre
Person to Person, People to People. Stephen Willats
25 & 26 May, 1 & 2 June, 12noon–5pm

Farthing Enterprise Centre, 39 Farthing Grove, Netherfield, Milton Keynes, MK9 4JH

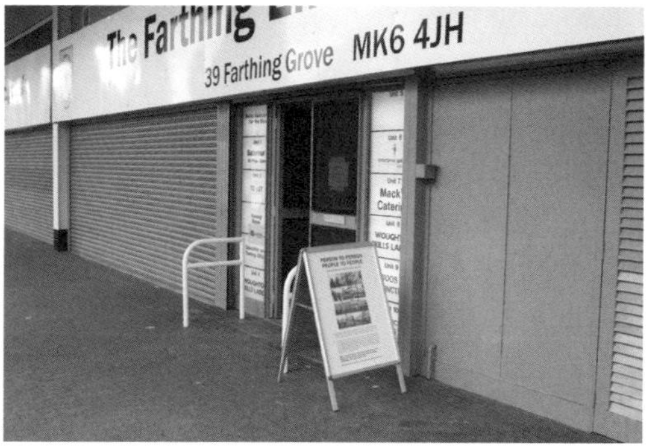

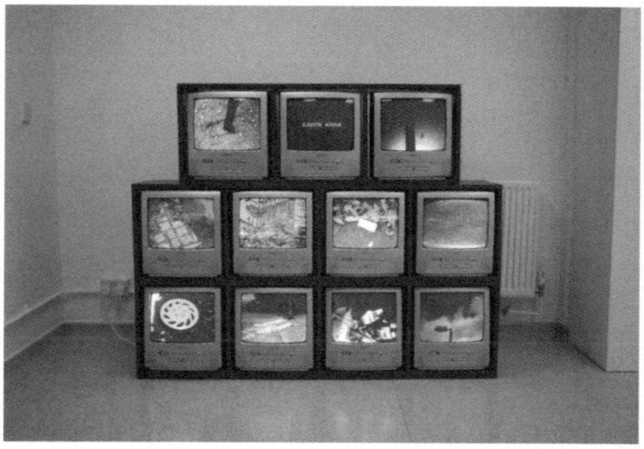

Video installation located in shop space at the Farthing Enterprise Centre, Farthing Grove, Netherfield.

29

A SOCIAL METHOD OF WORK

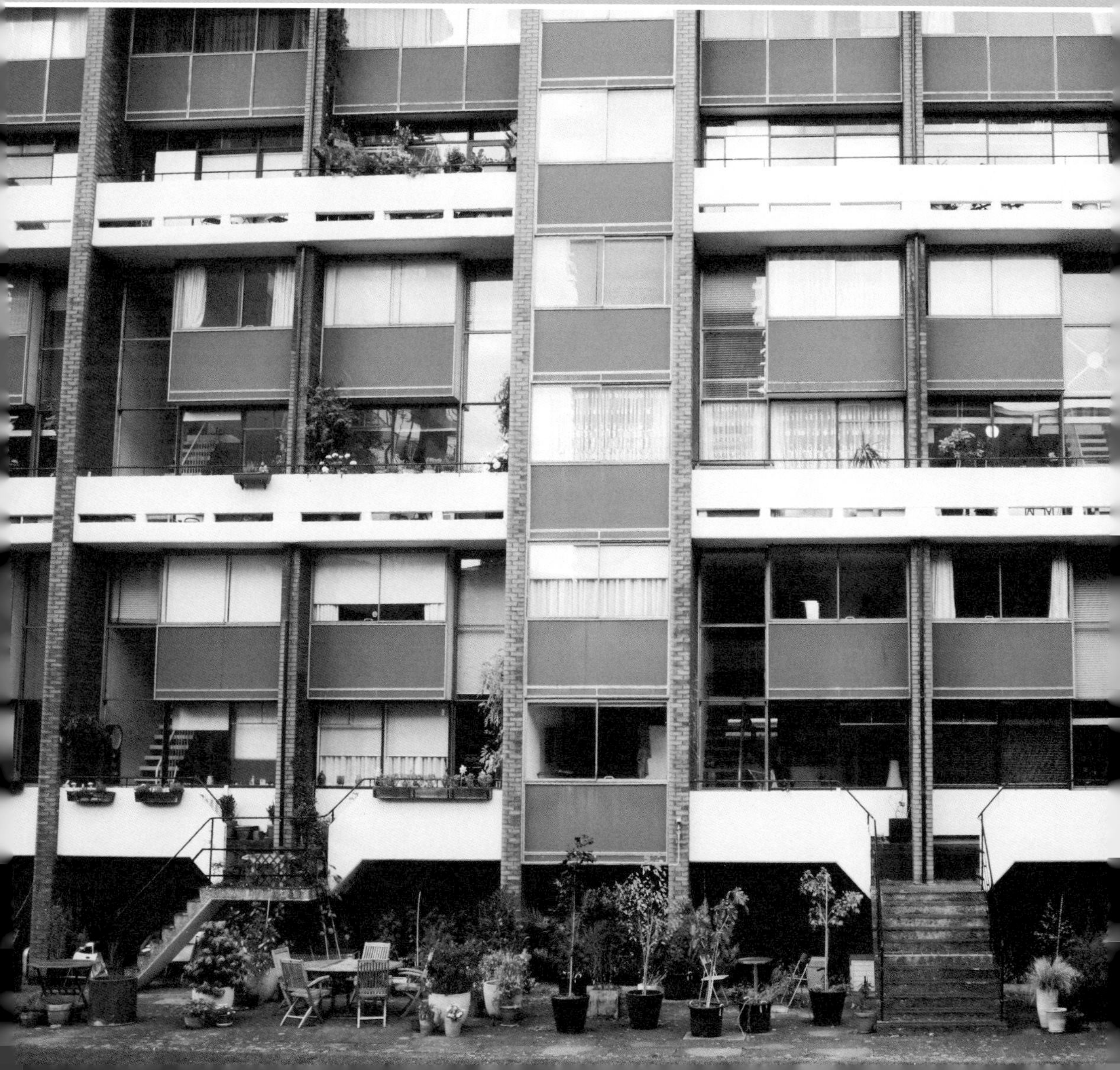

SOCIAL PROCESS

The making of a work involves me in a social process with a person, or persons, who I see as symbolising a particular, enclosed, reality. Initially I will develop a purely theoretical model from which the concept of an individual work derives. I then decide on the type of physical location that I think will embody the model. The next step is to carry out a reconnaissance, to select actual locations and then establish contact with individuals there. For example: when I wanted to make a work centring on the isolation of the individual in our society the type of location I chose was the tower block, which I saw as a physical manifestation of our culture's institutional idealisations and aspirations. The tower block 'Skeffington Court', Hayes, subsequently became the actual location for the work 'Living With Practical Realities'.

While I am exploring the location I have chosen, two parallel orientations are taking place, firstly the conceptual model that I have developed for the work is changing as a result of my becoming familiar with the area, secondly my explanation of the proposed work to people locally increases my contacts. I explain to people my ideas and the kind of person I would like to participate in the making of the work, if they do not become involved themselves they usually suggest someone else they know who I could contact. That my introduction is thus by familiar people is extremely important to the potential participant's confidence in the idea. Several meetings are then arranged when I can discuss with the participant my work in general and the particular work I want to make. From this point the way in which a work is developed radically differs from most contemporary practice, for instead of making it about someone, viewing them as an object, I make it directly with them as a mutually based co-operation.

It is fundamental that there is a binding connection between the theoretical and conceptual model of a work that I make, its realisation and its presentation. The concept of self-organisation is not the only message contained in all my work, but it is constantly manifest in a participant's involvement during its making and the audience's relationship during its reception. The actual reality of the participant, which is encoded by them into the work, is to be used by the audience as a parallel to their own experiences. By making connections between elements presented from the participant's reality, and reference to their own world, a process of re-ordering is made by the audience from a process of ordering made by the participant.

A METHOD OF WORK

Having agreed on a plan of approach with the participant I start documenting the topology of the reality to be represented in the work. I make a number of tape-recorded interviews with the participant which are then transcribed to provide texts that can be used directly in the work to express their attitudes, beliefs etc. With their active guidance I photograph their environment, the objects within it, and the participants themselves engaged in whatever activities they consider reflect their way of life. While I am doing this documentation, which usually takes several months, I also ask participants to collect together objects which they feel are important to them. These objects can be very special and personal or just household rubbish, sometimes just a few things are collected while others may get together sacks of items. I do not just visit the participant, they also need to come to my studio, especially when all the documentation has been accomplished and the work is physically taking shape.

With the help of the participant I always devise a question; I consider the question as a basic stimulus to interaction between people, and in my work it is addressed specifically to the audience. While various elements, such as photographs, handwritten texts, objects etc., confront the audience with the actuality of the participant's world, my question is their access point around which subsequent relations to the work revolve. It is the bridge for the audience between their framework of personal references, and the participant's references that have been encoded into the work. These 'capsules' are tangential to the social norms and values of the dominate culture and, in all probability, are alien to the audience, but they overtly manifest the concepts of self-organisation, self creativity, self-identity and a self-articulated critique of so called 'straight society'.

Each work has its own history, my relationship with a participant being personal and different in each case, even though very much the same procedure is followed when making the work. Sometimes just a few visits are made to my studio and I work mainly at the participant's place, other times a lot of visits are made, it depends on the individual circumstances. However, the work is finally finished only with the approval of the participant, who is free to change what they have done to that point.

DEMOCRATIC JOURNEY

'Democratic Journey' is an expression of basic consensus between different people in the process of creating society and its externalization as culture. The work is enabled and enacted as a simulation by people's direct participation. The transience, fluidity and randomness of people's encounter with the infrastructure of society – the 'reality' governing their daily lives – is manifest in this work as a sequence of interpersonal procedures evolving in time. These take a group of 32 individuals on a journey, both imaginary and actual, in which they build a 'society' between themselves.

The formal structure of the work enables the 32 individuals to become one group of 32 members. There are six stages to this progression, each one of which is built around a participant's response to a question concerning an 'ideal journey'. The questions are open ones: there are no right or wrong replies, no good or bad responses. They are agents for externalizing and articulating people's highly personal, implicit visions of their destiny in time to themselves and to others. Though the idea of the journey is used in the work as a polemical device for people to free their speculative associations, it is also grounded in the actual context in which the work is presented and in which participants are actually present. For the questions are related to images from the immediate environment, the setting that they are in. The environment around them is seen as particularly emotive in relation to the idea of travel and travelling, and provides a context for getting started.

The questions are in six stages. Each one asks participants to form a consensus in their view of the 'ideal journey' by referring to their past responses and their imaginative associations with images taken from the immediate environment. A dice is thrown before the presentation of the second question to generate random pairings of participants. This procedure is repeated before each subsequent question, leading to larger and larger groupings. The sequence of groupings is as follows:

Journey question one: 32 individuals; two: 16 pairs of participants; three: 8 groups of 4 participants; four: 4 groups of 8 participants; five: 2 groups of 16 participants; six: 1 group of 32 participants.

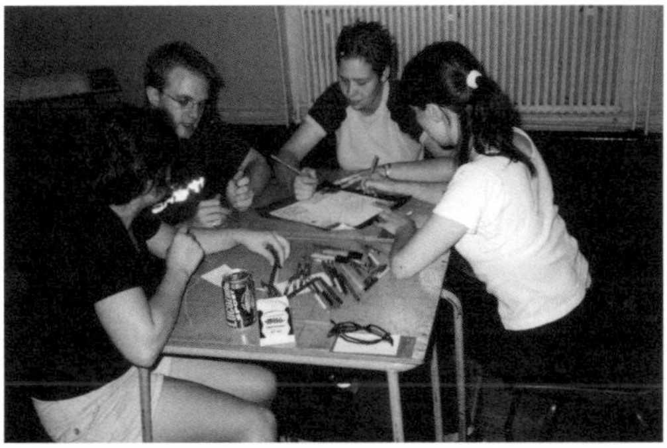

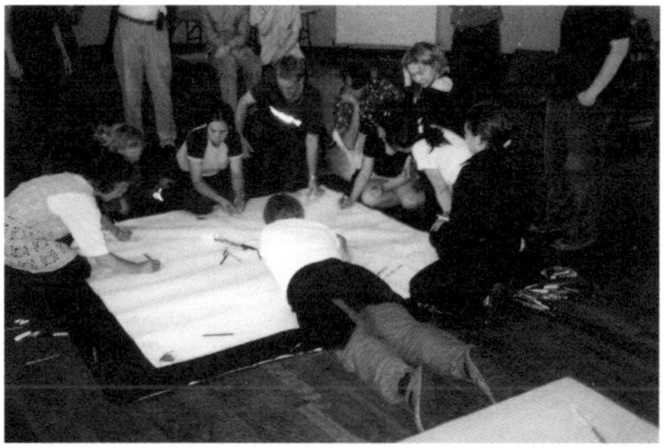

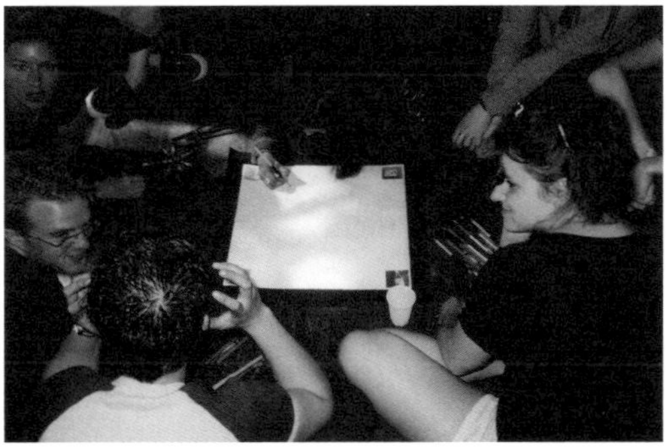

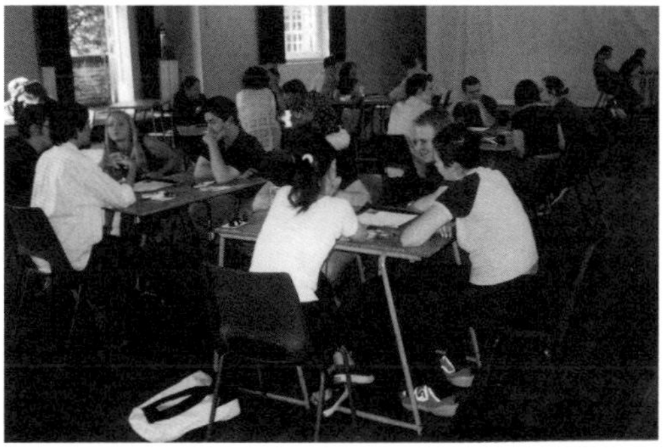

Participants taking part in 'Democratic Journey' in Liverpool at the Bluecoat Galleries.

MULTICHANNEL WORKSHOP, GRAZ

My plan was to set up the basic structure for the workshop to provide a neutral framework to act as a process for perceptual encoding and social exchange, leading to the possibility of agreement, between participants, this later state being considered to reflect a state of society established between them.

In order to symbolically amplify the process of forming society I specified that the workshop should have a time base (three days) over which it could evolve, also the participants were to come from a variety of occupations/backgrounds, and were ideally not to have met each other before. On meeting the group for the first time in Graz, I found a nurse, a theatrical administrator, an accountant, a translator, and an artist were among the participants.

The workshop was to be in three sequentially related parts as three sub-workshops, the first of these involved the group in making a journey together to create a multi-channel encoding of their individual experience of the same event. Previously I had travelled around Graz in a car on a kind of reconnaissance looking for suitable contexts for the journey, a walk to be made by the whole group. A walk where each member would be asked to record a particular bandwidth of information, each person doing so with a different tool for recording reality. I devised an artificial diagrammatic frame that broke perceptual experience down into basic areas, examples being, the material fabric of buildings, the ground walked upon, institutional signs, signs of personal expression, ambient sounds, the atmosphere, objects that denoted behaviour. Each member of the group elected to record just one area from the diagrammatic frame, using just one particular means, selecting it from a range of possibilities that included a video camera, instant snappy cameras, Super 8 Film cameras, drawing pad, notepad, tape recorder, etc.

As a result of my reconnaissance a large slab-like modernist housing block between Starhemberggasse and Laudongasse in the inner suburbs of Graz, which I saw as a symbol of the projections of an institutional society, became the context for a journey to be made by the encoding group. The groups set off together, each person recording the particular bandwidth of information they had elected to document, but what and how they recorded the material they came across was just left to each individual.

The material individuals recorded from the walk was then processed in the next stage of the workshop and reworked by each participant into another journey, their own private journey made as a progressive sequence over sixteen stages. Stages in the journey were represented by a square response sheet, each being a page in specially made spiral bound books given to all participants. Response sheets were open frame, a white square with black border, the space being left completely blank, without lines or cues, for the participant to express in whatever way they wished, their own private journey taking the reprocessed information recorded in the walk as the material from which their imagined private journey was created.

How they did this, what strategies they used was up to them, for instance, one participant projected her Super 8 film, frame by frame and made pencil drawings from selected stills, another made a montaged story of texts and photographs.

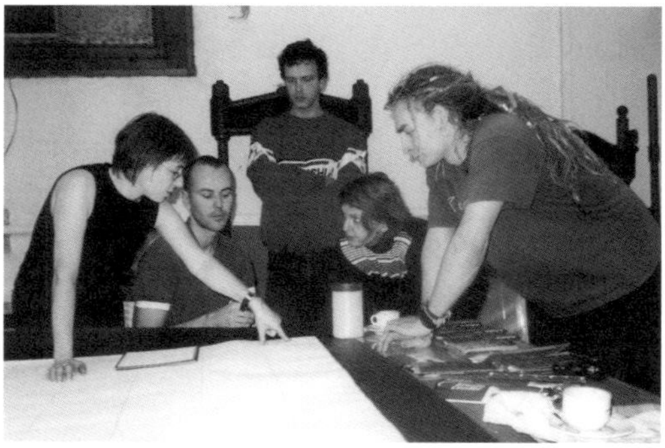

Participants workshop at the Kunstverien Graz.

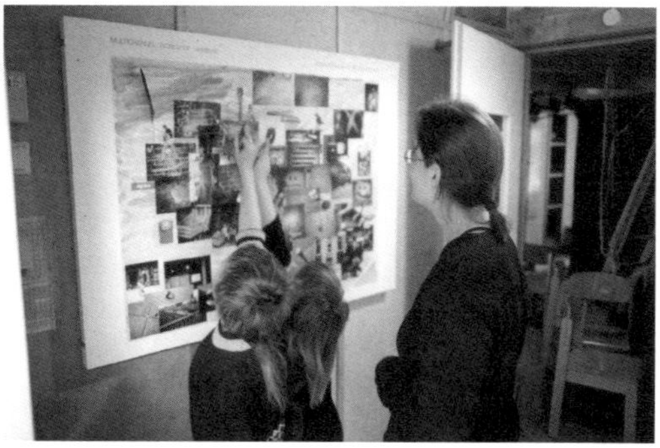

Display presented in local community centre in Graz.

30
MEETING OF MINDS

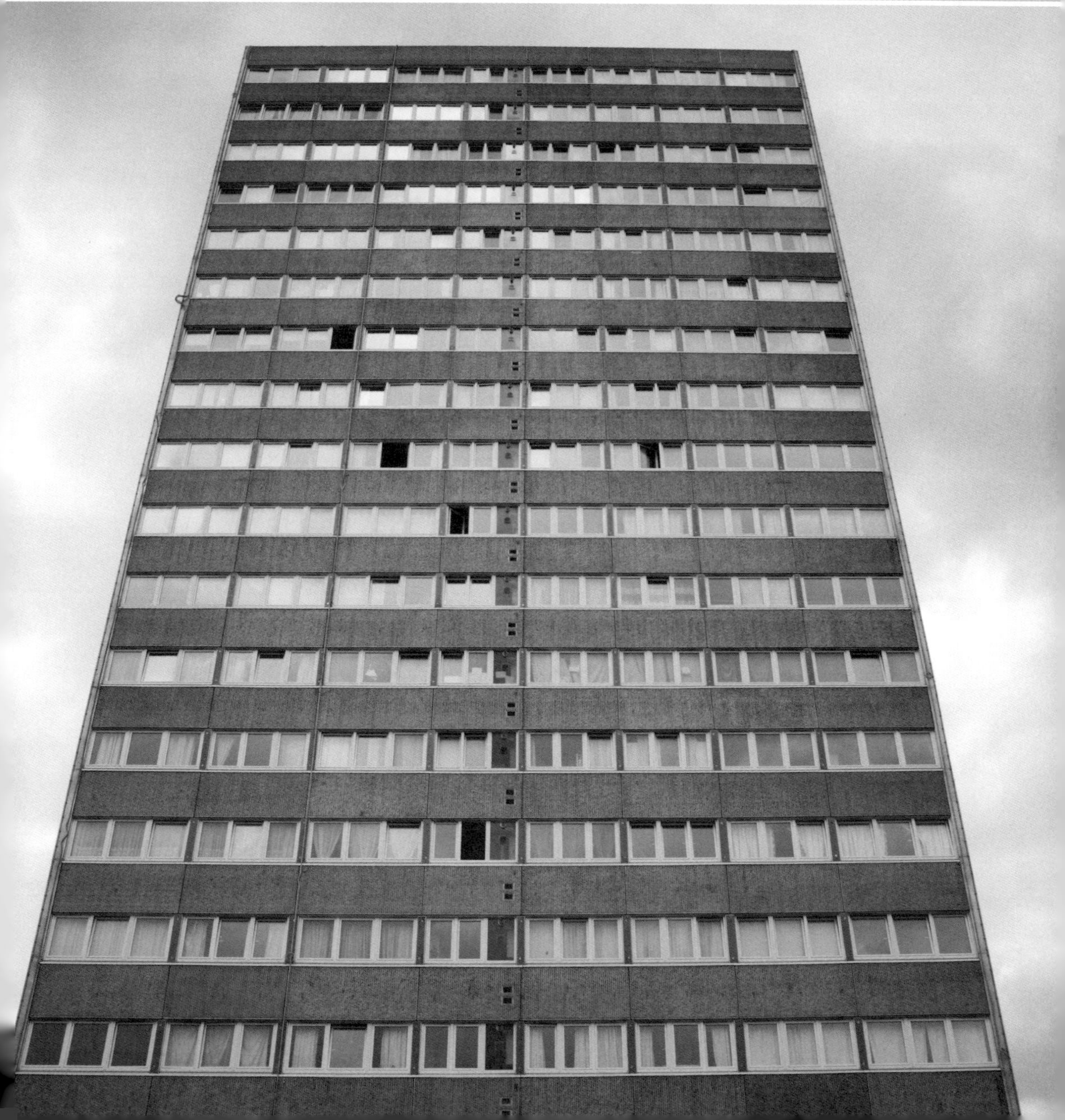

INITIAL PROCEDURES

Rarely are a person's beliefs and values transformed by a single event, usually it is achieved by a gradual process of assimilation through time, and in the development of 'Meeting Of Minds' this observation was fundamental to the rationale that shaped it from the very beginning. The work was envisaged as an expression of a model of social relations based on an interpersonal network of mutual exchange and self organising community. The work would take people on a symbolic and conceptual journey that started from the process of building a descriptive picture of the world immediately surrounding them, to then transforming that same reality through re-looking and recoding the language of those surroundings into an imagined state of reality. Fundamental to this imagined state was the expression of agreement between two people who undertook all aspects of the journey together.

'Meeting Of Minds' originated from an invitation from FACT, a Liverpool based arts organisation who were acting on behalf of tenants' groups at Croxteth Drive, adjacent to Sefton Park, situated on the inner ring of the city's suburbs. The remoteness of existing art institutions to the estate meant that it was fundamental to the model of practice to be developed that it took place directly within the surroundings of the estate, contextualising its physicality, language, issues and polemics. Therefore the next decision followed on from this, that the model of practice used their language, the languages embedded in the environment around them, and focused on issues the residents saw as important to living at Croxteth Drive, Sefton Park, so as to enable people to freely load the work with their own references. Thus the model of practice was to have four distinct parts that were all individually time dependent, and when implemented contributed to an overall evolving social process with the community.

THE FIRST WORKSHOP

In order to maximise the effect of coming together, residents from different blocks, who were not familiar with each other, became participants. The procedure for each workshop session was essentially the same, the two participants would meet with me, at the foyer of York House, and each be given a Super 8 film camera, loaded with a 50ft roll of cine film. They were then asked to make a walk together along a designated route, that started where they were at the base of York House and went across Croxteth Drive, then into the adjacent Sefton Park, following a labyrinth of pathways past various monuments and amenities to the recently restored Palm House at its centre.

So starting at the base of York House, the two participants searched around for discrete items such as an object, sign, pattern, texture etc. that one of them could identify as having the possibility of meaning something else in their own imagination, other than the given normal meaning. Having identified an item a participant would film it trying to encapsulate its new imagined meaning, and then the other participant would try and think what the first participant was getting at and then film it themselves. So an item having been identified was recorded twice on film, thus facilitating exchange between the participants and then helping the expression of relativity and the finding of agreement, the participants taking it in turns to locate new items on the route of the journey. Once the Palm House had been reached, which often took one hour or more, participants were given a snappy instant style photographic camera, and then on their return walk, made along a slightly different route, were asked to photographically record items in the same manner as filmed on the journey out.

Immediately after the walk a tape-recorded discussion was made with participants in the community room situated in Brompton House, where they each talked about the associative meanings they had attached to the visually recorded items. These tape recordings were transcribed so that texts could be used from them later in the work. The workshop took on a regular pattern so that people could expect it to take place, and lasted two days every two weeks, there being sometimes two sessions in a day, for once residents had seen or heard what the initial group of participants had done, others wanted to join in the workshop and become participants.

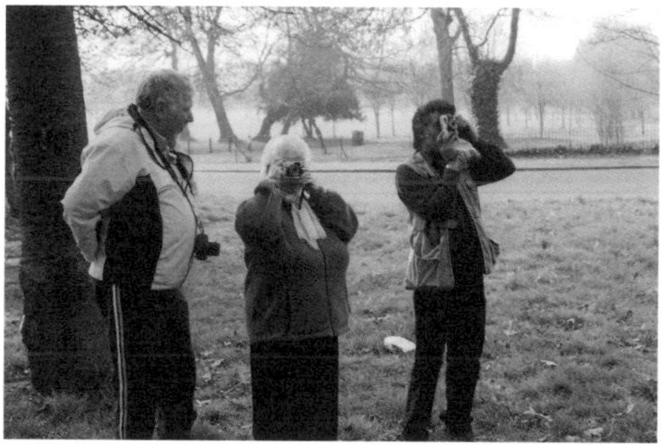

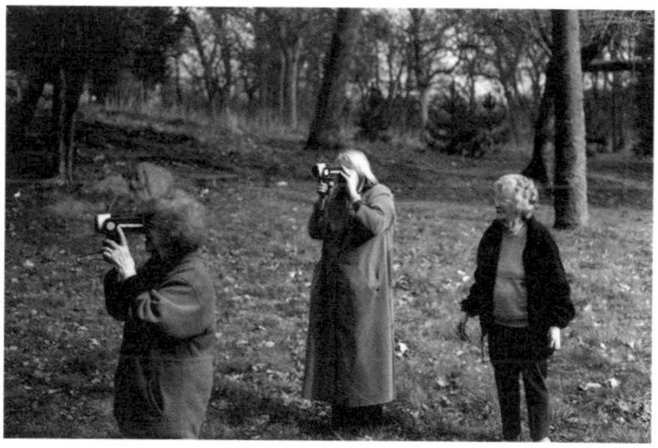

Participants workshop in Sefton Park with 35mm film cameras and Super 8 cameras.

THE SECOND WORKSHOP

The next stage in the timeline of 'Meeting Of Minds' was a workshop that would facilitate transformation, the reordering, recoding of the material documented during the journey made in the first workshop, forming it into an imagined journey based on agreements between two participants. When making this new symbolic journey, the associations attached to the encodings documented when making the first walk were central to the process of exchange and agreement between pairs of participants. Rooms at a local cricket club were hired for the workshop which was to take place over a two day period.

It was considered important that all manner of media, and organisational facility and expertise, should be on hand to help participants come together and seek to find common, or agreed, meanings in the material chosen to represent their new journey. So every participant pairing had their own table to work on, and were given pens, pencils, coloured crayons etc. as graphic tools. They were also given a display board that had on it a simple grid to provide a structure for the laying out of material to represent the imagined journey. In addition computer processing facilities, film editing and printing equipment was provided, as well as video players for relooking at VHS copies of the original participant films, film projectors, tape recorders, typewriters.

In addition a small group of 'experts' from FACT who were dexterous with the equipment and who would enable participants to get the most out of it in the time available were on hand. The 'experts' from FACT acted to amplify their possibilities for participants.

The two day workshop started at 11am and finished at 6pm, so for participants it was to be a very intensive experience with another person who they had met in the first workshop, and with the group of other participants. Taking the photographs, films, still from films and as well as the transcribed texts, the participants discussed and decided what they agreed between themselves could be used, or needed to be edited, adapted, or transformed, to express the journey they wished to make. During the course of the two days, other residents and friends came to the Cricket Club to see how participants were getting on, and to talk with them, even advise them, and this also contributed to the collaborations, lessening participants' inhibition and helping them express themselves.

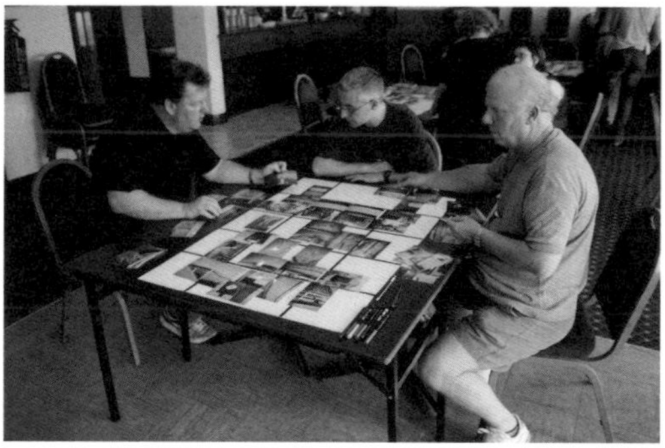

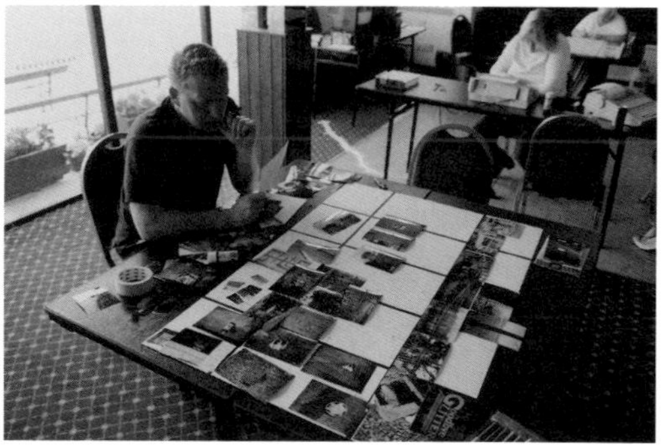

Over two days participants collaborated in pairs in a workshop situated at the Cricket Club, Sefton Park.

PRESENTATION OF THE INSTALLATION

Several weeks later the finished display boards were mounted on freestanding stands, and were presented in the foyers of the tower blocks at Croxteth Drive as the focal point for 'Meeting Of Minds'. A display board was positioned at either side of the foyers, with two video monitors next to each of them, so that the uncut unedited documentary films by participants made in the first workshop could be shown in relation to the imagined journey presented on the boards. The installation was made so as not to be too intrusive or threatening to residents coming in and out of the tower blocks or to be constructed in a way that was too far removed from what residents could have achieved themselves. In this respect it was important to have an agent, a means of getting them involved in internalising the content and ideas present. So during the hours the installation was open, there was always an administrator present to discuss the work with visitors and a printed guide to the work could be collected.

The presence of an administrator and the housing of electrical monitoring equipment in the public space of the foyer meant that the installation had to have set opening times, for three days a week over one month. Both the primary and secondary audiences on visiting the installation in one block were encouraged to go to the other tower blocks to see the other installations and, importantly, then to make the same walk in Sefton Park that participants had made. This latter activity had quite a profound effect on those that made the walk, people reporting that they revisited, relooked and discovered new things in what was, especially to residents, an already very familiar world.

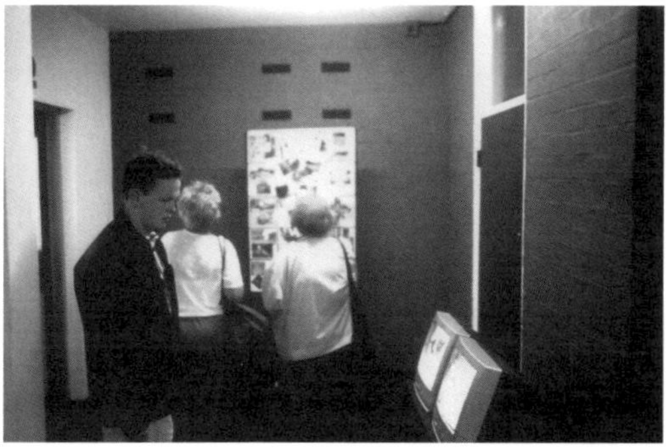

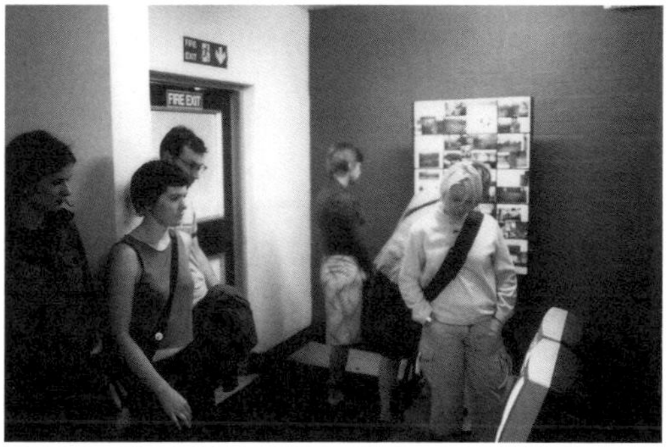

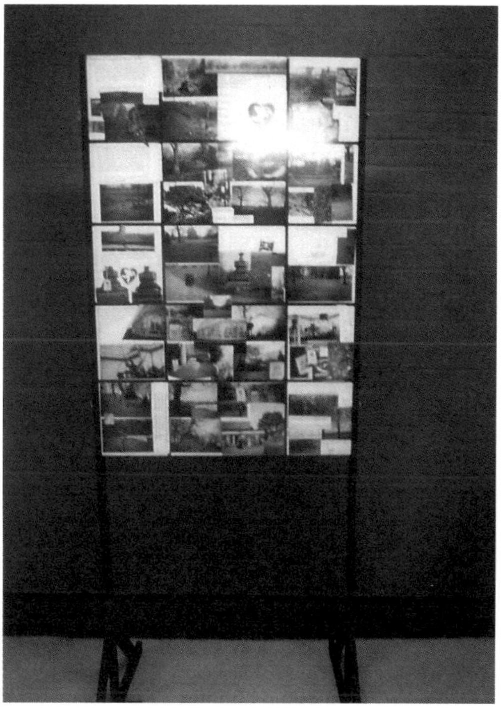

Installation with Display Boards and DVD films presented in the foyers of the tower blocks that made up the Croxteth Drive Estate, Sefton Park.

31

FROM MARGINAL DIVERSITY

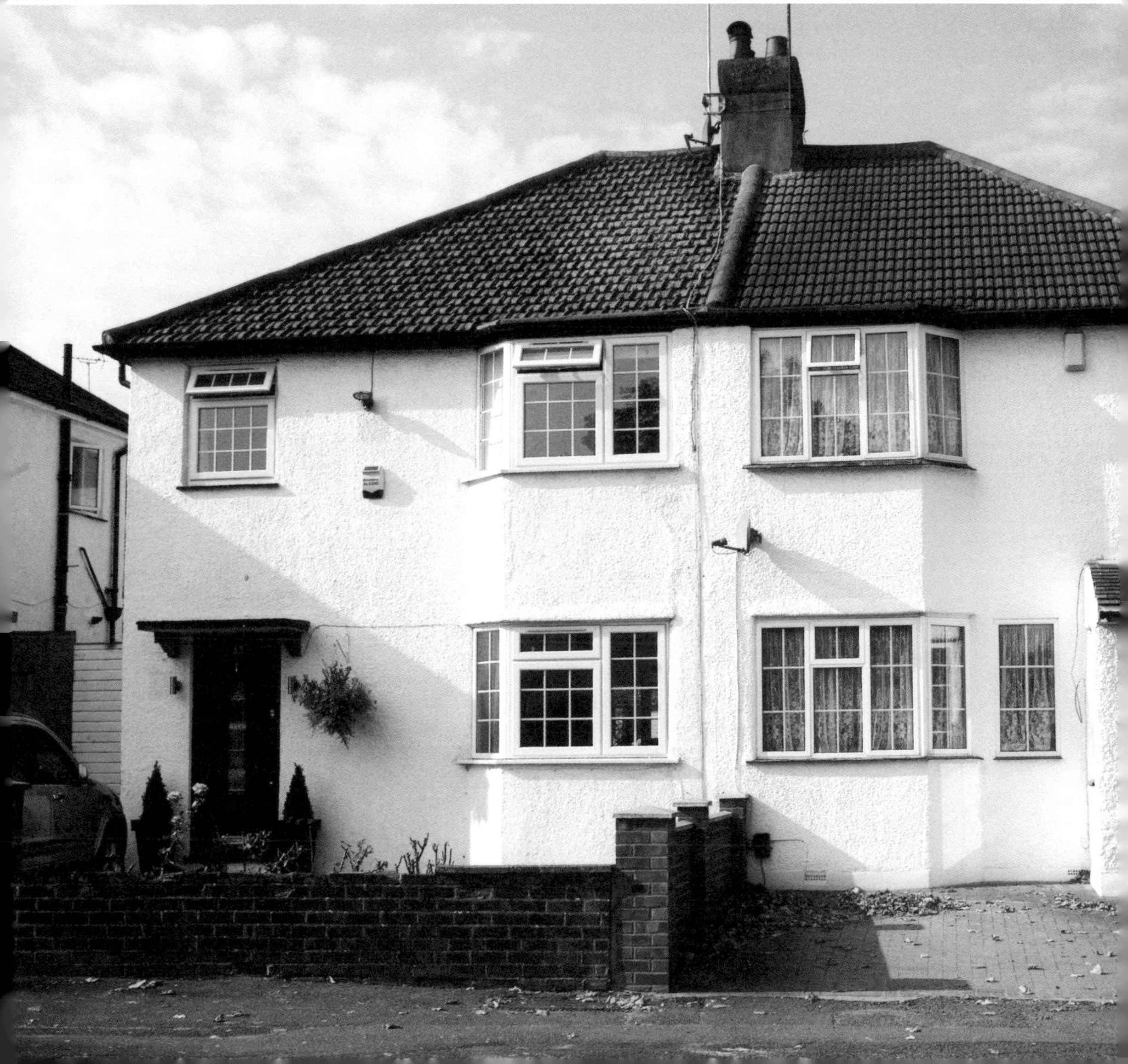

THE CAPSULE

The process by which the group defines their 'capsule' I found relevant to the presentation in my artwork of a parallel world. For such a 'capsule' is made by a group to exclude the determinism of the world around it, this necessitating a strong exhibition of tangential codes not only to the exclusion of others outside the group but for the attraction of other like persons as members. It was my work in the 'wastelands' in the early 1970s that led directly to my becoming interested in the various manifestations of night culture that exploded in the early 1980s. For I saw this night culture as a container of many 'social capsules' created purposefully by different groups in order to express themselves outside the norms of the dominant culture.

Freedom of the Night

The Night has long held a special significance as a cover, a refuge from the boring routines of the determinism of the day. It is, therefore, not surprising that many groups of young people, alienated by the depressing, constructing reality of society, found their personal freedom in the darkness of the night. A generation, reacting to the stereotyped values of a mass clone-like culture and the predetermined physicality of the 'new reality' environment on the municipal housing developments they had been brought up on, found that the cover of the night provided a territory in which they could forget the day, the everyday, and could establish their own 'social capsule'. Simply the proliferation of the private, individual club in the period of the early 1980s was a profound cultural phenomena in that it overtly stated the values of a 'counter consciousness' which for a short while became visible in the fabric of society.

These private clubs had been set up on the inspiration of a few individuals who themselves belonged to the particular group that made up its membership (aged 18–30) and they stated overtly the values and codes of that group. It was in the nature of these private clubs that they were very transitory, new ones opening as fast as others closed though the general principle seemed to be to rent an existing club on its quiet night, and then to change the name just for the night to fit the self-image of the group going there. I saw these transitory clubs as an expression of self-organisation, a 'social capsule' being created by a community to state their personal and group alienation from ordinary society. For within the club environment the group felt free to express codes tangential to those of normal society, to find a personal freedom that was socially, psychologically, sexually and intellectually a flight from the social ramifications embodied in the symbolism of the 'new reality'. For it seemed that most of the people that went to the 'private clubs' were unemployed and actually living in the 'new reality' housing estates. The private clubs I saw as a positive stage on from life in the 'new reality', in that members had left behind for that night the depressing environments in which they lived.

CONSTANTLY EVOLVING CULTURE

I feel that Punk culture's incredibly important to everyone because of its aspects of self-organisation. It was about DIY, making your own kind of music, your own records, your own magazines, and at the start this was a reaction against the new reality environment, the sort of institutional environment that was building up in the '60s which was paternalistic, about a kind or reality in which the authorities ruled. This imposed on the inhabitants of the new reality a kind of moralistic tolerance, which was really a passivity that was expected. They had to behave in a certain way within this environment, hold certain attitudes, and so on. Punk was also a reaction against professionalism, for professionalism is an inhibiter of expression because it requires special knowledge, special equipment and special procedures. Punk was a reaction against all this. In a way the importance of the fact that the spirit of punk is still there, still going on, is the lesson that you learn from it, for it is always going to be relevant. So, I don't think that, shall we say, a work that I made five years ago will be less important because things have changed. I think, however, that things are always evolving; for instance, I noticed when I was working in housing estates in the late 1970s that people actually changed, the cultural climate changed. They did actually become more aggressive and more anxious and weren't so open. Things are obviously continually changing and here I think it's important that the artist is always engaged directly with the evolving culture: that s/he is all the time articulating the forefront of cultural activity and seeking to intervene in the cultural process, to inject into it the different perceptions of a counter consciousness.

PERCEPTIONS FROM INSIDE THE CAPSULE

You can tell by looking at them, you can, you can tell if they're dressed up to the tits, but they look naff, even if they look brilliant visually you can tell what they're like by the way they stand, by the way they carry themselves, by their attitude, the group they're in, if they're a laugh or not. It's just so boring all the time it's like, oh go on, oh please let me in, why aren't you going to let me in, I just tell them I don't have to give you a reason and stop blocking the queue.

What I'd like most would be for everybody to be able to talk to absolutely everybody else without having to sort of worry about, oh I don't know them, because that's what it used to be like. I mean, everybody spoke to everyone. I mean, I made so many new friends, proper friends, not just people that are trying to use you, proper friends, through doing the Club because you could just go up to anyone and talk to them and if people have got the right attitude you can go around and have a good laugh.

We had like a six foot three girl on the security, this Amazon girl with black hair down to her waist, she was security, then when she wasn't on we had a drag queen a six foot four drag queen, you know, nine inch heels, we didn't have any proper security at all, never seemed to need it.

I have become so used to mixing with gay people all the time, or being with people that are completely open minded you forget all about the narrow minded people that really exist and that's the whole thing that I got into, you just forget about the whole straight world.

It's the only club that is run by people they know, the drink's cheap, it's sleazy, it's not pretentious and it's just a place, well basically it's a place just to get pissed and dance and have a good time. If you say, you know, you actually have to dress up well you don't, you can go along in a pair of jeans and a ripped shirt, it's the attitude of people that we let them in by, not the way they dress you know, it's their attitude that's the important thing.

It was only really tacky but it was actually doing something, so many of my friends moan about how boring London is, they never actually do anything about it, that's what gets me—they go on, oh it's so boring, there's nowhere to go, there's nothing to do but anyone that starts doing things would just rip them to shreds and say, you know, that's pathetic or something.

THE CHA CHA CLUB

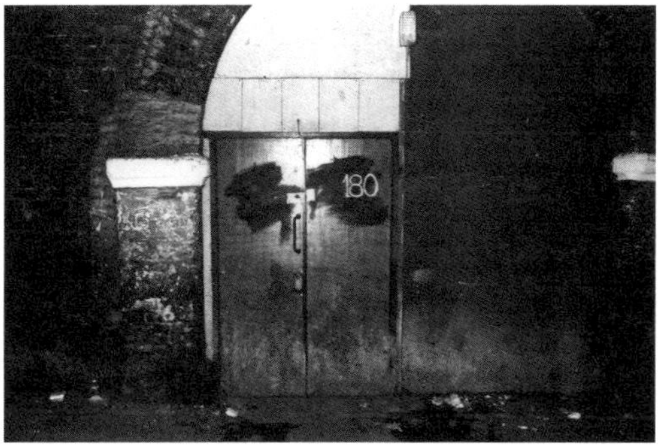

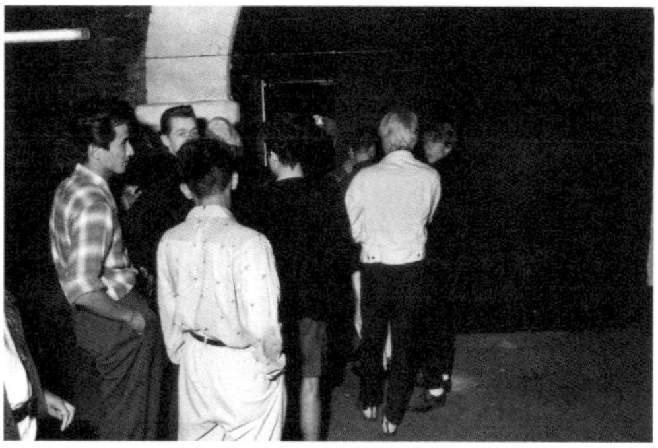

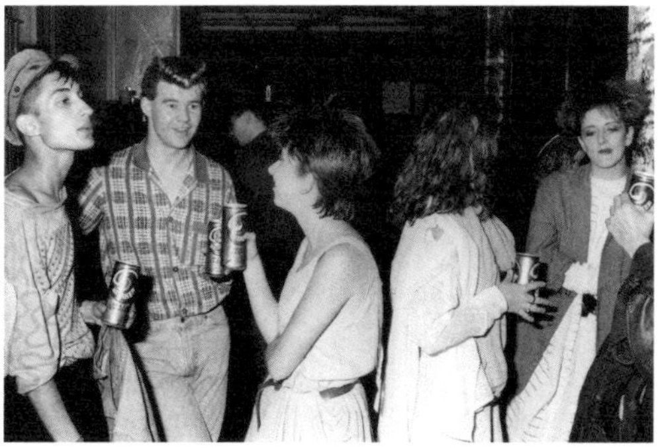

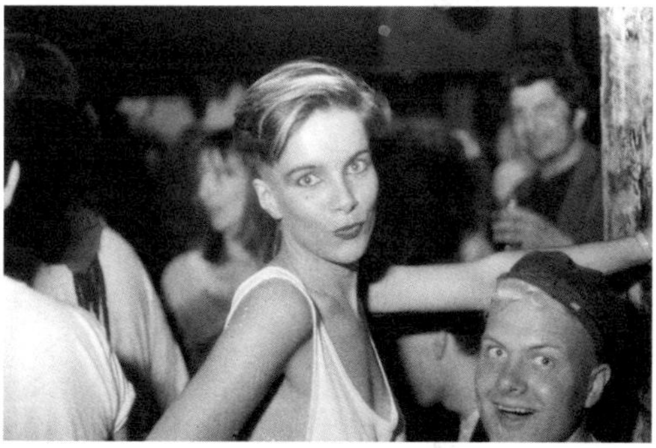

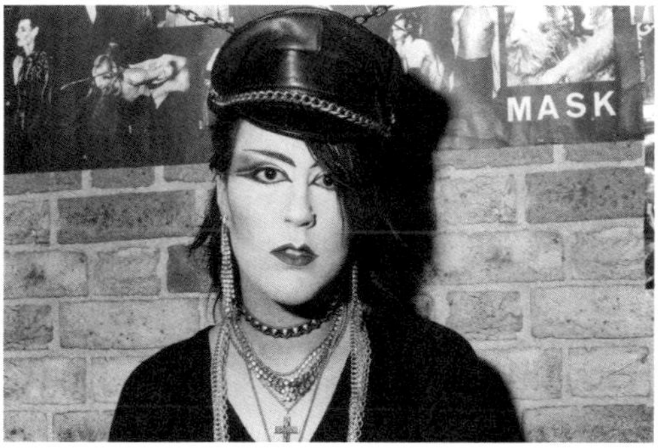

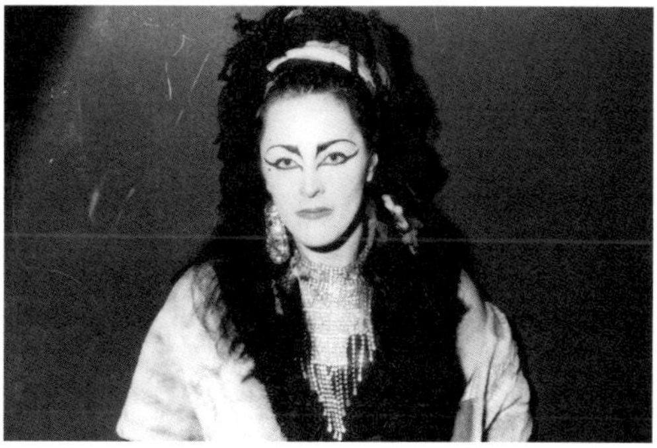

32
TRANSFORMATION AND OPEN NETWORKS

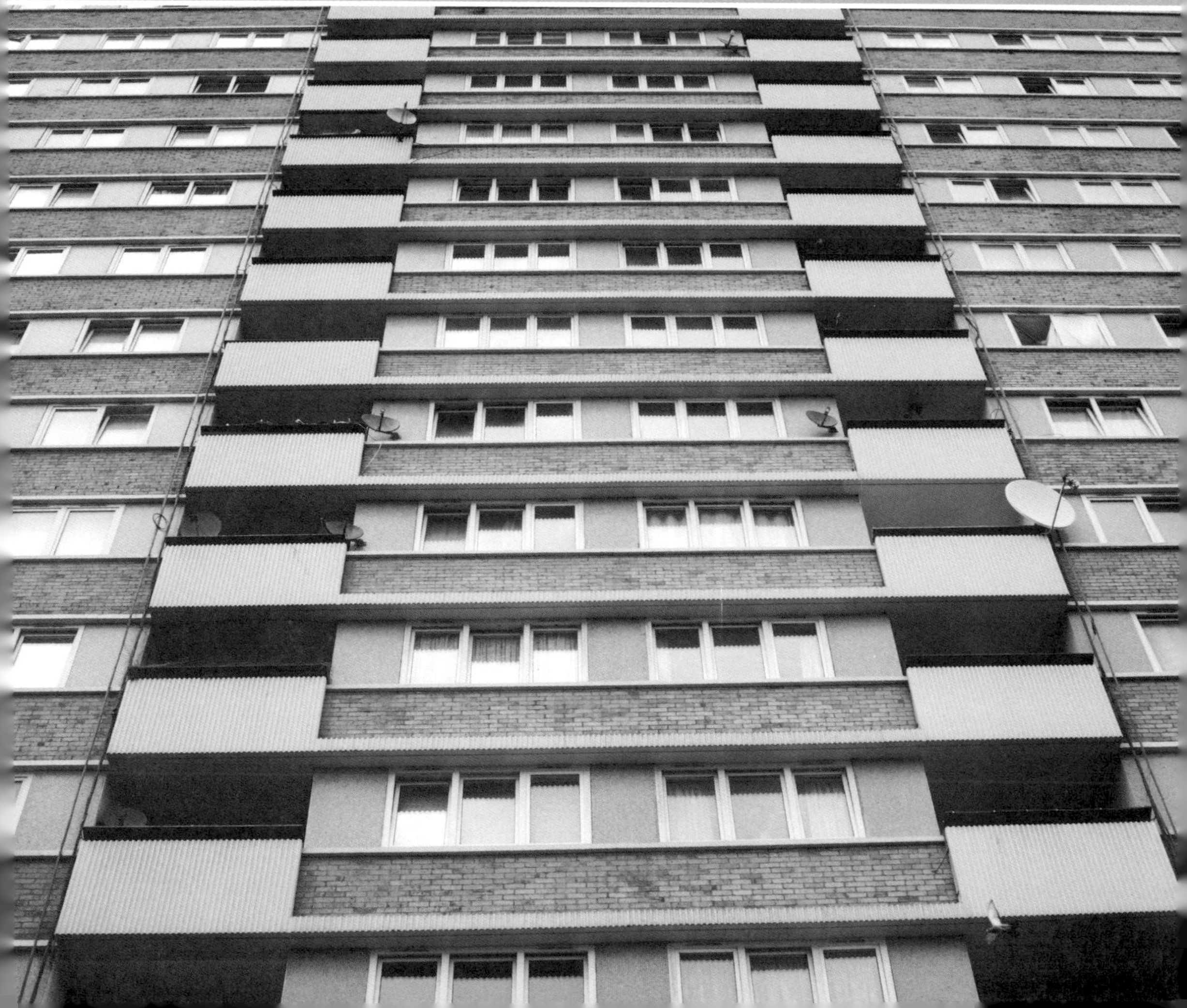

TRANSFORMING THE MEANING OF SURROUNDING SPACE

I saw that residents' acts of vandalism, directed against the building that they lived in, the graffiti they made on its walls, the objects that they discard and perhaps throw out of the tower block itself, all state a consciousness of a people in opposition to the hard, grey, uniform, concrete block that contained their home, and which constantly and unmovingly radiated the message of a higher authority which is ultimately that of society itself. Now, the fundamental creative act is the act of transformation, and I considered the debris of residents' activities, both casually discarded and consciously placed within the immediate territory of Harvey House, as agents for people to conceptually transform that environment into another consciousness, that of community. For all these traces of activity act as signs to other people, giving notice that, the concrete object, the tower block does have a social identity, moreover one that has been created by residents to subvert the imposed consciousness embodied in the building's very physicality.

My map of these discarded residues of residents' activities makes a further transformation through my photographically encoding what I found during a slow walk around the base of Harvey House over the period of one day. But I started making the map by simply going to the roof of Harvey House and leaning over the side so as to photograph the ground on each side of the block. I then searched the area on the ground covered by my roof-top photographs, and recorded with my camera the different objects and marks that I encountered in my wanderings. These photographed objects were then later assembled into a map that showed where they had been found. I see my map is one of social alienation and of struggle to express identity, the need to create a personal landscape within an anonymous contemporary society.

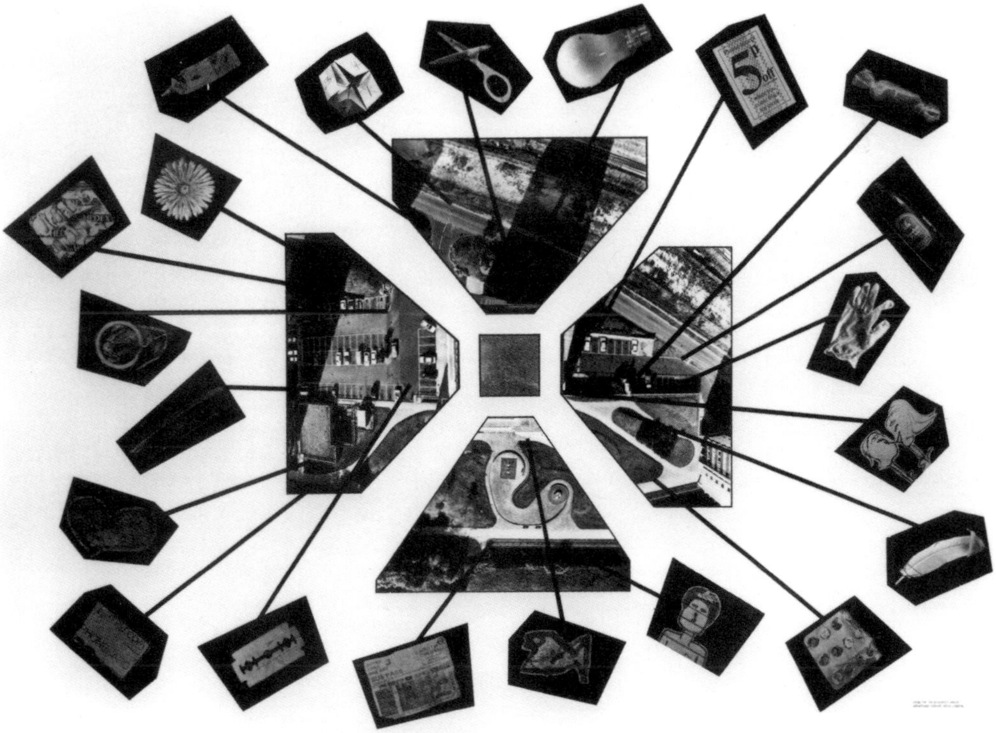

'From The Top Of Harvey House'.

IN AND OUT THE UNDERWORLD

I see that my passage through the City, along any street, is a multi-channel time transient experience, an encounter with a random bombardment of information hitting all senses. And yet there seems an order to this experience, for in real time I am filtering out what I will attend to from this bombardment, what I am going to prioritise, mostly just implicitly, I create the reality I want to see according to my beliefs and my intentions. So while I may be actively attending to this or that, the rest of the information has not gone away, it is still being received, providing a psychological constant, a peripheral realm of references that give support, give me a feeling of stability, until new events intervene. This is the environmental wrap around, during my progression down the street, being comprised of a culturally encoded fabric of references that give a context, an environment. So this encoded environment gives me a constant background message of certainty that reflects the ideology, beliefs, of the society determining the culture, that originated those encodings. Thus the ideology embodied even in the very physicality of the environmental wrap around is ever present in the concrete reality that is Ebertplatz Köln. Ebertplatz exists as an island surrounded by the jungle of the City, that during my passage from one side to the next has an intended institutional determinism, the dream of the planner of this place. But the intended vision for Ebertplatz, like many Modernist ideals from the 1970s, has been subverted, appropriated by people seeking a refuge in the modern City, wanting somewhere to hide, and consequently it contains the possibility of encountering other values than those envisaged in the plan. Layered onto the concrete are the signs and messages of a counter consciousness of values made by those seeking refuge from the presumed order and monumentality of this island environment. Despite these expressions it is the potential of society, of an encounter with someone else, that is the dynamic of this actual public space. For while I am in passage from one side to the other I enter into the tunnel of transition, from one reality into another, from the conscious to the unconscious, and while in the later state there then is always that social possibility of who I might expect to meet, and who I might meet unexpectedly. Encounters in the underworld of the Ebertplatz are coded within its realm of meaning, and when eventually I pass beyond its domain, going out through an exit channel, I move from the potential of counter consciousness to the normality in the surrounding City.

'In And Out Of The Underworld' takes you on a journey through the concrete island of Ebertplatz, presenting you with time-sequenced fragments of encoded information that have been generated by past events and behaviours that have occurred in this place. Your own personal encounter with the reality of this island is put into a relation with the traces of other people's experiences as presented within the 'Symbolic World' of the work. The Symbolic World is the territory of the work in Ebertplatz and is formed from encoded references created by a group of individuals, who live or work in the vicinity of Ebertplatz, who took part in a special documentary event on the 16th April, using a variety of media to create and record multiple channels of experience. 'In And Out Of The Underworld' presents you with a group of people who are constantly changing their individual identity and their relationship with other individuals. The group is encountered entering Ebertplatz in pairs, two people being seen as the basic unit of any network or any society.

On entering the territory the pairs descend into the depths of the underworld, where in the middle of Ebertplatz they enter a 'black box' zone where they meet two other people, and for a moment inside the 'black box' the pairs are free to form a spontaneous transient grouping of interaction and exchange. While observing another person, especially fleetingly, we construct a representation of who they might be, who we think they are, and we react accordingly, intuitively. The group here is in a constantly changing state, and the act of meeting takes on many different forms and expressions, it being left to the viewer to project into the 'black box' their own imagined understanding of what's happening, there being no correct or preferred response.

The journey through the underworld is continued, and on exiting out the other side the individuals coming in are now with someone else, perhaps they even have a completely different persona and identity. The constantly changing nature of the flow of people moving through the passage of the Ebertplatz underworld, the random encounters made, mirrors the informed, transient experiencing of people in our daily lives, and our processes of instant imposition of a recognisable certainty that is then instantly forgotten. The 'Symbolic World' is distributed around the immediate area in which the documentary event took place, so that individual fragments of information are experienced discretely, and are then to be related and pieced together by yourself.

The work was created from an event involving three groups of people, administrators, documenters and actors, that took place in and around Ebertplatz on Saturday the 18th April 2009. A variety of media was used in the making of the work, including Super 8mm Kodak Cine film, and audio cassette tape recording.

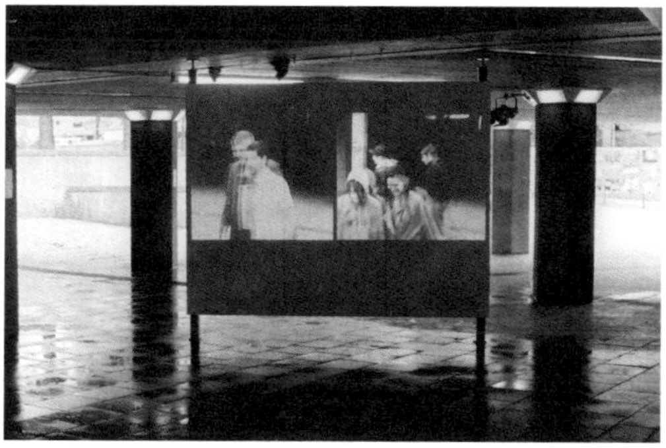

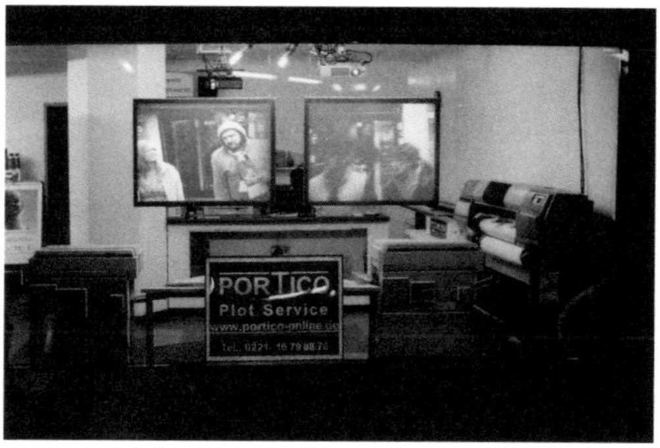

Installation in the Ebertplatz, Köln, Germany.

TRANSFORMING IDENTITIES

When I came to work with 'Inside The Night' I was interested in confronting the audience with what wasn't normal and a context they couldn't access, or were very unlikely to be able to access—it was aggressive, alienated from the normal and probably alienated from themselves. Through this confrontation I wanted them to re-examine aspects of themselves and of their own reality. Centring the work on the culture within the night, although not giving access to these clubs, did refer to an aesthetic, a sensibility that was in the street—it was familiar though distant. The Doppelganger and the strategy of the Doppelganger is a combination of two things really, one the normal self, and normality in society, taking what is familiar on one side of the piece and then what is not familiar on the other side of the piece; from the familiar you go to what is not familiar—the familiar provides access to the other. Exposure to a single presentation is rarely able to rapidly change somebody's attitudes. What is important is to have a sequence of presentations through time so that gradually a person is able to build up another model of reality, another change of attitude, another set of attitudes. This is what I have tried to do with this work.

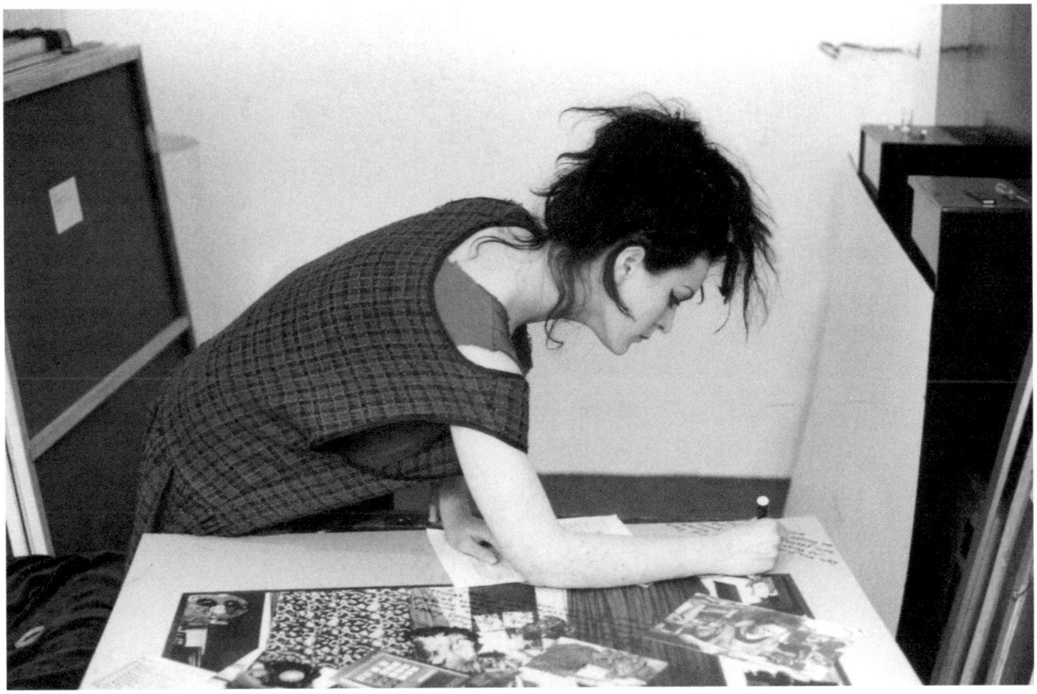

Participant working in the artist's studio to create a 'Symbolic World'.

THE STRUGGLE TO ESTABLISH THE SELF

There is always the eternal struggle between the self having to deal with society, having to socialise, having to exist, having to co-exist with a deterministic, authoritative society—a world which one does not determine oneself but nevertheless one has to live within—and then the inner self, the real self say, of privately accepted values and beliefs. Those beliefs that state one's own creativity, one's own personal kind of identity. You get two communities—you get from the second, a community of like-minded persons which you associate with in terms of natural kinds of affinities and so on, and then you have the community which is imposed upon you by the society, like at work, having to work or just having to comply.

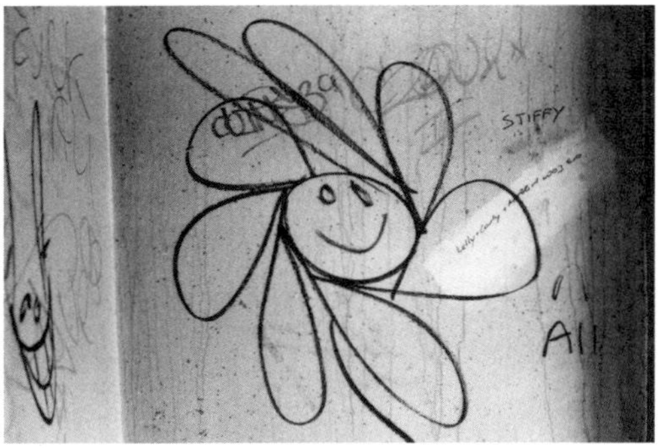

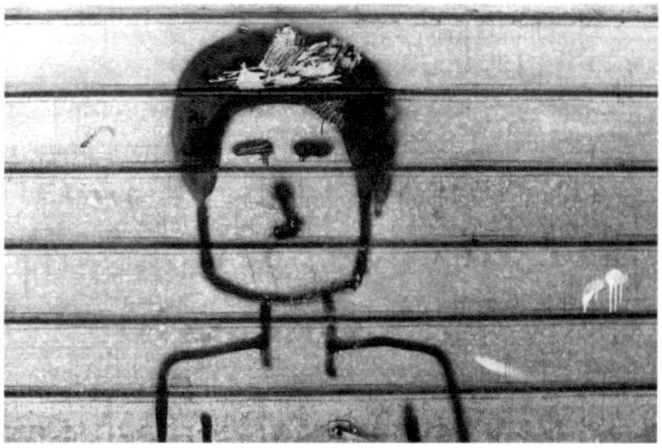

Signs of existence and identity.

With support from The Henry Moore Foundation

ISBN 978–0–9569024–2–9
Copy editing by John Bevis
Designed by Colin Sackett
Printed and bound in China

RGAP
(Research Group for Artists Publications)
Yorkshire Artspace
21 Brown Street, Sheffield S1 2BS
www.rgap.co.uk

Distributed by
Cornerhouse Publications
70 Oxford Street, Manchester M1 5NH
www.cornerhouse.org